TRADE AND NATION

THE MIDDLE RANGE

THE MIDDLE RANGE

Edited by Peter S. Bearman and Shamus R. Khan

The Middle Range, coined and represented by Columbia sociologist Robert Merton, is a style of work that treats theory and observation as a single endeavor. This approach has yielded the most significant advances in the social sciences over the last half century; it is a defining feature of Columbia's department. This book series seeks to capitalize on the impact of approaches of the middle range and to solidify the association between Columbia University and its Press.

The Conversational Firm: Rethinking Bureaucracy in the Age of Social Media, Catherine J. Turco

Working for Respect: Community and Conflict at Walmart, Adam Reich and Peter Bearman

Judge Thy Neighbor: Denunciations in the Spanish Inquisition, Romanov Russia, and Nazi Germany, Patrick Bergemann

Concepts and Categories: Foundations for Sociological and Cultural Analysis, Michael T. Hannan, Gaël Le Mens, Greta Hsu, Balázs Kovács, Giacomo Negro, László Pólos, Elizabeth Pontikes, and Amanda J. Sharkey

The Corsairs of Saint-Malo: Network Organization of a Merchant Elite Under the Ancien Régime, Henning Hillmann

Trade and Nation

HOW COMPANIES AND POLITICS RESHAPED
ECONOMIC THOUGHT

Emily Erikson

Columbia University Press
New York

COLUMBIA
UNIVERSITY
PRESS

Columbia University Press gratefully acknowledges the generous support for this
book provided by Publisher's Circle member Harriet Zuckerman.

Columbia University Press
Publishers Since 1893
New York   Chichester, West Sussex
cup.columbia.edu
Copyright © 2021 Emily Erikson

Names: Erikson, Emily, author.
Title: Trade and nation : how companies and politics reshaped
economic thought / Emily Erikson.
Description: New York : Columbia University Press, 2021. |
Series: The middle range | Includes bibliographical references and index. |
Identifiers: LCCN 2020056181 (print) | LCCN 2020056182 (ebook) |
ISBN 9780231184342 (hardback) | ISBN 9780231184359 (trade paperback) |
ISBN 9780231545440 (ebook)
Subjects: LCSH: Great Britain—Commerce—History—17th century. |
Free trade—Great Britain—History—17th century. |
Merchants—Great Britain—History—17th century. |
Great Britain—Economic policy.
Classification: LCC HF3505 .E75 2021 (print) | LCC HF3505 (ebook) |
DDC 381.0942—dc23
LC record available at https://lccn.loc.gov/2020056181
LC ebook record available at https://lccn.loc.gov/2020056182

Cover design: Julia Kushnirsky
Cover image: Jan Gossaert, *Portrait of a Merchant*, c. 1530.
Ailsa Mellon Bruce Fund. Courtesy of the National Gallery
of Art, Washington, D.C.

CONTENTS

ACKNOWLEDGMENTS

In the listing of primary sources, a serious attempt has been made to retain period capitalization and spelling. This attempt produces inconsistencies. A reader might notice, for example, that Denzil Holles's name is spelled Hollis in the title of one of his publications. That kind of thing was not uncommon in the seventeenth century. It is also difficult to separate typographical flourishes commonly used on frontispieces in the early modern era from capitalization practices, ESPECIALLY WHEN PRINTERS USED ALL CAPS FOR PORTIONS OF VERY LONG SUBTITLES. I did not adopt this style and ultimately relied on the title as presented in the Making of the Modern World database or, in a smaller number of cases, another catalog. When I began the research project and collected my data, the Making of the Modern World database had a different graphical user interface. The new interface is a contemporary update and looks nicer, but it has been harder for me to work with, and I cannot call up some of the titles accessed previously. There are also some differences in who is listed as author that have left me unsatisfied. Many of these differences are related to legitimate controversies over authorship, which is complicated in this period in which pseudonyms were commonplace. In these cases, I have tried to follow the most recent research and consensus. I did not, however, dive into analyzing texts for authorship and make no claims that I am adding any new information to these debates or legitimacy to one side or another.

I list original works under primary sources. Some of these are Dutch works. I use the Dutch title when referring to the primary document; however, I do not read medieval Dutch nor Latin. I read these texts in English translations, which are listed in the secondary sources when appropriate. Unless otherwise indicated, all figures and tables were produced by the author.

Many people helped me over the years it took to produce this book. Of the many thanks I want to distribute, the first I owe to my family, who make all of this worthwhile. Joe helped me innumerable times with coding problems and actually collected some of the Dutch publication data. Gabriella's naturally supportive personality and pride in my accomplishments lifted my spirits many times, just as simply being around her does.

Heather Haveman deserves special credit for extensive comments on an early draft. Peter Bearman was encouraging early on, as were Woody Powell, Jennifer Lena, Nitsan Chorev, Richard Breen, Mark Mizruchi, Elizabeth Bruch, Damon Centola, and many other people that I will not be able recall properly. I owe a particular debt of gratitude to Joe Parent, who read through the entire manuscript at a late stage and offered numerous comments and complaints that were both a pleasure to read and a huge help. He is responsible for one pun that entered into the manuscript; I won't say which one, but will say that he is a big Diana Ross fan. William Goetzmann, who is a wonderful colleague, also read through the entire draft and gave me extremely helpful comments and some peace of mind. Other people who read chapters and commented include Daniel Hirschman, Cristobal Young, Joscha Legewie, Mattias Smångs, and Patrick Bergemann. Henning Hillmann allowed me to use the data he collected on company investment for chapter 4. Mark Hamilton and I coauthored the paper on which chapter 5 is based, so he contributed a great deal to this chapter. He is a terrific person and a pleasure to work with. Parts of that article, published in the *American Journal of Sociology*, are present in chapter 5 and appear in other places in the book. A version of chapter 6 has appeared in the *Socio-Economic Review*. The Yale Library is a treasure, and I received help from Michael Printy, Gwyneth Crowley, Peter Leonard, Michelle Hudson, and Christine Riggle. Douglas Douhaime needs to be singled out for being a miracle worker. I also received help from librarians overseas. Thank you, Ida Nijenhuis and Marinus Bierens!

I had a huge amount of research assistance. Thank you to Garth Holden, Elexis Ellis, David Ko, Eric Feltham, Brian Kitano, Tina Wang, Jason Arroyo, and Kimberly Cruz! I look forward to seeing your books in print eventually. I first developed the idea that began this book at a conference held by Julian Go and George Lawson, two lovely people to whom I am intellectually and personally indebted. I am extremely grateful for the advice I got at a prepublication conference attended by many illustrious figures, including Naomi Lamoreaux, Steven Pincus, Phil Withington, Julia Adams, Phil Gorski, Mattias Smångs, Kate Stovel, Tim Rutzou, and my amazing editor, Eric Schwartz. There are so many others to whom I am indebted. Let me close by dedicating the book to Harrison White, for surely I would have never taken this path or had these ideas without his influence and support.

TRADE AND NATION

INTRODUCTION

The ideas of economists and political philosophers, both when they are right and when they are wrong, are more powerful than is commonly understood. Indeed, the world is ruled by little else.

—JOHN MAYNARD KEYNES, *THE GENERAL THEORY OF EMPLOYMENT, INTEREST AND MONEY* (1936)

This is a story about the creation of a new way of thinking about the world. It revolves around the relationship between two spheres of life: the political and the commercial. As is fitting for a story about the creation of something new, it is less a clashing of titans and more a courtship.

The seventeenth century witnessed the emergence of the nation-state and the rise of a newly powerful commercial class. These developments were mainly confined to Europe. In England, something even more uncommon happened. In an attempt to influence state economic policy, commercial actors began to write and publish large amounts of work on issues related to trade and finance. In doing so, the commercial world inadvertently shifted the trajectory of economic thought by developing a new kind of literature about economic matters. This new literature, which ultimately served as the foundation of classical economics, was the product of the courtship that played out between the state and commercial actors.

Economics is a new discipline. In the medieval world, there were universities but not economics departments. Indeed, there is no evidence that a concept of "the economy" as a distinct and self-regulating system existed yet.[1] In Europe, the scholars who addressed what we now think of as

1. Joyce Oldham Appleby, *Economic Thought and Ideology in Seventeenth-Century England* (Los Angeles: Figueroa Press, 1978).

economic matters considered economics from the perspective of a Judeo-Christian moral framework. They chastised usurers and expounded upon the principles of fair exchange and just price. They were concerned about greed and corruption. They were worried the rich and powerful might take advantage of the poor. And behind all these concerns lay the moral imperative of salvation. Money was considered a necessary evil, and medieval scholars most often were devising ways to circumscribe its corrupting effects on humanity.

In the seventeenth century, people began to frame and conceptualize economic matters differently. In what is known as the mercantilist era, the old concerns for equity, justice, and salvation that used to drive scholarly activity in the area were replaced by a new moral framework grounded in the wealth and prosperity of the nation. Growth replaced fair exchange as the standard by which economic activity was judged. This book describes the change that took place in the economic literature and then attempts to explain why that change occurred.

The century was tumultuous. Actors and institutions evolved and transformed in many ways during the two centuries covered in this book. In England, there was a civil war as well as a revolution. The rise of representative governance took place; new religions took root and flourished; colonial ventures were initiated; an incipient quest for empire began; bureaucracy and administration grew; state power was centralized; and the civil sphere expanded to incorporate new political participants and new modes of political participation.

All of these changes formed important institutional backdrops to the emergence of the new literature on economics. The main actors, however, were merchants and state elites. As the century wore on, financiers, entrepreneurs, and manufacturers—others of the commercially active class—joined in the fray, but from the beginning merchants were a dominant voice. The merchant class in England was fractured. There were divisions between the more politically connected merchants of London and the outport merchants of the countryside. There were feuds between guilds, and there was a well-documented division between the old, commercially minded merchants and the new, colonially minded merchants.[2] One newer source of discord was

2. Robert Brenner, *Merchants and Revolution: Commercial Change, Political Conflict, and London's Overseas Traders, 1550–1653* (London: Verso, 2003).

the English state's adoption of the practice of offering commercial charters. These charters were granted by the state. The Crown issued charters in the first half of the century; after the civil war, charters came briefly from Oliver Cromwell; later, both the Crown and Parliament were able to issue them.[3] Charters began to be used to create companies with exclusive privileges in different areas of trade. The rise of chartered companies was controversial. The company/noncompany divide mapped closely with other areas of contestation within the commercial world and proved to be a significant stimulus, on issues both new and old, in debate among merchants.

Contesting the charters required making appeals to political actors. The charters were an attempt by the state to woo commercial actors, to guide them into actions and practices favorable to the state. When merchants published their arguments about the effect of charters on trade, they were pursuing state actors in an attempt to influence policy. And while the charters were a particularly important point of contention, other elements of the state were also involved in setting trade and commercial policies of interest to merchants and other commercial elites. Merchants addressed tracts to the Crown, the Privy Council, various councils and committees of trade, and Parliament.

These mutual attempts at control—or, more favorably put, negotiation and cooperation—arose because of a context in which those who held power in the political and commercial spheres of influence were not already closely coordinated. Merchants in England were not well represented in the state. The limited nature of their direct influence led them to take their debates public. In other words, it was the distance between the commercial and political spheres that encouraged public debate. By publishing tracts, merchants hoped to indirectly influence state actors to enact policies favorable to their commercial interests. They used national wealth and prosperity as the moral framework for the arguments they constructed because that framework was most likely to persuade the state actors they hoped to influence. The consequence was the creation of a new kind of economic discourse—one that would shape the trajectory of economics for centuries to come.

This argument does not have a single input/output structure, the type of which rarely captures the complexity, interdependence, and feedback of

3. Margaret Patterson and David Reiffen, "The Effect of the Bubble Act on the Market for Joint Stock Shares," *Journal of Economic History* 50, no. 1 (March 1990): 163–71.

lived history. While it may be cliché to say that history is a rich tapestry, the metaphor captures the idea of intertwining processes of considerable duration. In this case, the overarching process is the courtship, dance, or mutual attempts at control between the political and commercial worlds. This courtship is not a uniquely English phenomenon (nor is it uniquely European). The elements of the process that were unique to England, and therefore take on greater significance in the argument, are, first, the chartering process, which magnified old fractures within the merchant class while also creating new ones, and, second, the marginal status of merchants in the political sphere. The chartering and related contention created both reason and substance for debate. The slow development of representative government in England made the public sphere a site of influence. The marginality of merchants drove them to take advantage of the new space of civic engagement in their quest to air grievances, voice concerns, and lobby for hugely profitable privileges and concessions.

Once the merchants were engaged in this new civic space, another process magnified the impact of their contributions. The public sphere imposed its own discipline. Authors suspected of merely cloaking their own self-interest in the language of the common good sought to make their argument more compelling by introducing their knowledge of trade and commerce. Over time, many turned to data, logic, and even the scientific method. Self-interested or not, the authors ended up producing valuable information about commercial and financial processes and theoretical models that advanced economic knowledge. Ultimately, their debates and arguments provided an empirical and theoretical foundation for Adam Smith's great work, *The Wealth of Nations*, and contributed significantly to our knowledge of the world.

A SUDDEN SHIFT

Because of his uniquely significant role in the development of modern economic thought, Adam Smith is an important marker of the influence of the works under consideration though he falls outside the period of analysis. The major shift in economic thought that made his work possible occurred in the seventeenth century, more than a century before the publication of *The Wealth of Nations*. I focus on the years between 1580 and 1720, but stray occasionally outside of these bounds. Beginning in 1580 allows for some investigation of what economic thought was like in England prior to the shift and makes it possible to understand what changed. It also predates the wave of incorporation that served as one of the central mechanisms regulating the relationship between the state and merchants. This important stimulus was legally redefined in 1720 with the passage of the Bubble Act, which limited incorporation possibilities.[4] The year 1720 also lies after the main contours of economic thought had already been changed.

In the years between 1580 and 1720, after centuries of incremental additions to economic thought, the number of published works on economic matters went from a drip to a flood. In the 1580s, three or four economic pamphlets might have been published in an exceptionally productive year. By the 1690s, one hundred to two hundred works were being produced annually. The transformation was not just quantitative. The landslide of works contained a fundamentally different perspective on the problems of economics and commercial exchange.

Predating the seventeenth century, there were two major traditions in early economic thought of the medieval period. Xenophon's *Oeconomicus*, dating from the early fourth century BCE, was the wellspring of the first: care of the household. Husbandry, which belonged to this category, was a popular topic. These books consisted of lists of ideas and tips for increasing individual wealth through improved farming and livestock techniques. While useful, such a body of knowledge is quite distinct from the discipline of economics we are familiar with today.

Closer in substance was the second major tradition, which was kept alive in the church and developed by the scholastics. The scholastic discourse revolved around the determination of a just price and the rules of fair exchange. Many of the relevant works were simply denunciations of usury and exhortations against the corrupting influence of money and commercial exchange, but more sophisticated treatments were also produced. The question of a just price generated sophisticated theoretical work because theories of value were constructed in order to evaluate price levels of goods. One had to understand the source of value in order to establish whether a price was fair. In particular, in order to understand when usury was unfair, one had to understand the source of the value of money itself. Scholastics advanced metalist theories of value, arguing that the value of money derived from the physical properties of gold and silver, and quantity theories of money, linking the value of money to the availability and supply of bullion. Many of the most sophisticated work on these topics

---

4. Ron Harris, "The Bubble Act: Its Passage and Its Effects on Business Organization," *Journal of Economic History* 54, no. 3 (1994): 610–27.

were produced in sixteenth-century Spain in the school of Salamanca.[5] We now associate scholasticism with rigid, dogmatic traditionalism. These works were heavily text-based, weighted down by their reliance on Aristotle and Scripture for evidentiary support. A central, foundational concern of these works was the moral conduct of Christians and the threat of the worldly temptations posed by money and commerce to the salvation of the human soul.

The English works of the seventeenth century broke with the scholastic tradition. Few were written by men or women of the church. The works were empirical rather than textual. Frequently written by merchants, the books presented trade data rather than biblical passages to support their arguments. William Petty and his political arithmetic introduced statistics into the literature. Worldly matters replaced moral concerns, and the pursuit of power and plenty became valued as a good in itself. The English authors cared little about the idea of a just price or fair exchange. Treatises on the balance of trade replaced sermons railing against predatory lending practices. Their goal was not to achieve equitable exchange or alleviate the plight of the poor. They put the needs of the Crown, the state, and the commonwealth at the center of their arguments.

It was a sea change in economic thinking with long-lasting consequences for its trajectory.[6] Central questions were established, and the problem space was redefined from one of equity to one of national development.

5. José Larraz, *La época del mercantilismo en Castilla (1500–1700)* (Madrid: Ediciones Atlas, 1945); and Marjorie Grice-Hutchinson, *The School of Salamanca: Readings in Spanish Monetary Theory, 1544–1605* (Oxford: Clarendon Press, 1952).

6. Terence Hutchison, for example, wrote that the work of the era established "most of what were to become, and have so long remained, the central perennial issues and questions of political economy, together with most of the persisting, conflicting viewpoints regarding these issues and questions, of method, theory and policy." Terence Wilmot Hutchison, *Before Adam Smith: The Emergence of Political Economy, 1662–1776* (Oxford: B. Blackwell, 1988), 11. Karl Přibram wrote it was a "new approach to economic analysis." Karl Přibram, *A History of Economic Reasoning* (Baltimore, MD: Johns Hopkins University Press, 1983), 37. Paul Slack describes it as "the deliberate creation of political economy." Paul Slack, *The Invention of Improvement: Information and Material Progress in Seventeenth-Century England* (Oxford: Oxford University Press, 2015), 3. The authors were "first in the field." Joseph A. Schumpeter, *Economic Doctrine and Method: An Historical Sketch* (New York: Oxford University Press, 1954), 40. Joyce Appleby, Lars Magnusson, E. A. J. Johnson, Paul McNulty, and Andrea Finkelstein have all contributed important volumes documenting the importance of this moment in thought and its continuing influence in shaping economic discourse. Joyce Appleby, *Economic Thought and Ideology*; Andrea Lynne Finkelstein, *Harmony and the Balance: An Intellectual History of Seventeenth-Century English Economic Thought* (Ann Arbor: University of Michigan Press, 2009); E. A. J. Johnson, *Predecessors of Adam Smith: The Growth of British Economic Thought* (New York: Prentice-Hall, 1937); Lars Magnusson, *Mercantilism: The Shaping of an Economic Language* (London: Routledge, 1994); Lars Magnusson, ed., *Mercantilist Economics* (New York: Springer, 2012); and Paul J. McNulty, *The Origins and Development of Labor Economics: A Chapter in the History of Social Thought* (Cambridge, MA: MIT Press, 1980).

The works were to have a substantial impact on Adam Smith. In *The Wealth of Nations*, Smith introduced the phrase the "mercantile system," in order to attack nationalistic economic policies. In order to do so, he mobilized mercantilist economic insights. While Smith critiqued government policy, he built upon the conceptual and theoretical work of his precursors, drawing heavily from the insights, approaches, and abstractions developed by the mercantilists.[7] He quoted at length Thomas Mun's work, in particular, describing it as "a considerable step in the progress to sounder opinions."[8]

While Smith is often credited as originator of modern economic thought, the first coherent defenses of free trade were written nearly a century earlier. The earliest analyses based on principles evoking the idea we have come to know as comparative advantage were constructed in the seventeenth century.[9] Smith drew liberally from their work. The influence of these works stretch in an unbroken line through the work of Adam Smith, a key inflection point, to contemporary economic theory.[10] The theories

7. Gary M. Anderson and Robert D. Tollison, "Sir James Steuart as the Apotheosis of Mercantilism and His Relation to Adam Smith," *Southern Economic Journal* 51, no. 2 (October 1984): 456–68, https://doi.org/10.2307/1057824; Mark Blaug, *Economic Theory in Retrospect* (Cambridge: Cambridge University Press, 1962), 31; Raymond de Roover, "Monopoly Theory Prior to Adam Smith: A Revision," *Quarterly Journal of Economics* 65, no. 4 (November 1951): 492–524, https://doi.org/10.2307/1882577; William D. Grampp, "The Liberal Elements in English Mercantilism," *Quarterly Journal of Economics* 66, no. 4 (November 1952), 499, https://doi.org/10.2307/1882100; Alexander Gray, *The Development of Economic Doctrine: An Introductory Survey* (London: Longmans, Green, 1933), https://mises.org/library/development-economic-doctrine-introductory-survey; Hutchison, *Before Adam Smith*; John A. La Nauze, "The Substance of Adam Smith's Attack on Mercantilism," in *Adam Smith: Critical Assessments*, ed. John Cunningham Wood, vol. 4, *Specialised Topics*, 55–57 (London: Routledge, 2004); Magnusson, *Mercantilism*, 2; Salim Rashid, *The Myth of Adam Smith* (Cheltenham, UK: Edward Elgar, 1998); Salim Rashid, "Smith, Steuart, and Mercantilism: Comment," *Southern Economic Journal* 52, no. 3 (January 1986): 843–52, https://doi.org/10.2307/1059280; and Schumpeter, *Economic Doctrine and Method*, 184.
8. Adam Smith, *The Wealth of Nations* (New York: Bantam Classics, 2003; first published 1776), xxi.
9. Joseph A. Schumpeter, *History of Economic Analysis: With a New Introduction*, rev. ed. (New York: Oxford University Press, 1954), 41, 365–74; and Douglas Irwin, *Against the Tide: An Intellectual History of Free Trade* (Princeton, NJ: Princeton University Press, 1996), 54–55.
10. Appleby, *Economic Thought and Ideology*; Finkelstein, *Harmony and the Balance*; John Maynard Keynes, *The General Theory of Employment, Interest and Money* (1936; repr., New Delhi: Atlantic, 2008); Magnusson, *Mercantilism*; Wilhelm Roscher, *Principles of Political Economy: With Additional Chapters Furnished by the Author [. . .] on Paper Money, International Trade, and the Protective System*, trans. John J. Lalor (New York: Henry Holt, 1878); Gustav von Schmoller, *The Mercantile System and Its Historical Significance: Illustrated Chiefly from Prussian History; Being a Chapter from the Studien ueber die wirthschaftliche politik Friedrichs des Grossen*, ed. and trans. William James Ashley (New York: Macmillan, 1897), Making of the Modern World; Schumpeter, *Economic Doctrine and Method*; and Philip J. Stern and Carl Wennerlind, *Mercantilism Reimagined: Political Economy in Early Modern Britain and Its Empire* (New York: Oxford University Press, 2013).

developed in the English texts of the seventeenth century expanded collective knowledge and spurred on later development.

A SINGULAR DEVELOPMENT

One of the remarkable features of this literature was that almost all of the work was produced in the then small, peripheral country of England. A rising tide of literature swept over Europe after the adoption of the printing press, but this particular river ran through only one nation. The Dutch were the economic powerhouse of Europe at the time, but they produced very little economic thought. France's great contributions to economic theory came a century later with the work of the physiocrats. German cameralism, a policy-heavy state-driven mode of economic thought, did not really pick up until the eighteenth century.[11] Spain's and Italy's great contributions were earlier and belonged to the scholastic mode of inquiry.[12]

The lack of parallel developments in other parts of Europe casts doubt on many existing theories as to what caused the shift in economic theory.[13] One of the primary theories attributes advances in economic knowledge to rapid economic growth.[14] Others have suggested that the particularly difficult logistical complexities of overseas trade were an important trigger for more complex economic thinking.[15] England was experiencing a notable expansion in overseas trade, but the size and speed of expansion paled in comparison to the global trade of the Dutch. Using these explanations, it

---

11. Schumpeter, *Economic Doctrine and Method*, 32; Keith Tribe, *Governing Economy: The Reformation of German Economic Discourse, 1750–1840* (Cambridge: Cambridge University Press, 1988); and Příbram, *History of Economic Reasoning*.

12. Barry Gordon, *Economic Analysis Before Adam Smith: Hesiod to Lessius* (London: Macmillan, 1975); Larraz, *La época del mercantilismo*; Grice-Hutchinson, *The School of Salamanca*; Marjorie Grice-Hutchinson, *Economic Thought in Spain: Selected Essays of Marjorie Grice-Hutchinson*, ed. Laurence S. Moss and Christopher K. Ryan (Aldershot, UK: E. Elgar, 1993).

13. As noted further in the conclusion, many of these works do not take the development of economic theory as their primary explanandum but are instead more interested in describing the contents of economic thought.

14. Appleby, *Economic Thought and Ideology*, 3–5; and Guy Routh, *The Origin of Economic Ideas* (Basingstoke, UK: Macmillan, 1975), 32.

15. Parakunnel Joseph Thomas, *Mercantilism and the East India Trade: An Early Phase of the Protection v. Free Trade Controversy* (1926; repr., Mansfield Center, CT: Martino Publishing, 2009); William J. Barber, *British Economic Thought and India, 1600–1858: A Study in the History of Development Economics* (Oxford: Clarendon Press, 1975); and Lynn Zastopuil, *John Stuart Mill and India* (Stanford, CA: Stanford University Press, 1994).

is difficult to reconcile why similar advances did not occur in other areas of Europe. Erik Reinert, Sophus Reinert, and Pernille Røge have argued that it was the example of the Dutch, envied by the English, that spurred further public reflection, emphasizing in particular the role of international competition between nations in stimulating early modern economic discourse.[16] But this argument does little to explain why the other nations of Europe would not have experienced similar changes in how they conceived and wrote about economic matters.

Another type of theory has emphasized the role of depression and economic turmoil, which numerous scholars have considered primary engines of economic theory in general and as crucial to the developments in seventeenth-century English economic theory in particular.[17] In these explanations, the doubt and confusion raised by specific episodes of crisis sow the seeds of thought and intellectual advancement. The insight is compelling, but does not explain why only seventeenth-century English economic downturns would have had such a special impact.

Other scholars have argued that these factors of growth and disruption generated new economic thought because they took place within the unique context of the rise of the nation-state. The seventeenth century falls

16. Erik S. Reinert and Sophus A. Reinert, "Mercantilism and Economic Development: Schumpeterian Dynamics, Institution-Building and International Benchmarking," in *The Origins of Development Economics: How Schools of Economics Thought Have Addressed Development*, ed. Jomo K. S. and Erik S. Reinert, 1–23 (New Delhi: Tulika Books; London: Zed Books, 2005); and Sophus A. Reinert and Pernille Røge, eds., *The Political Economy of Empire in the Early Modern World* (Basingstoke, UK: Palgrave Macmillan, 2013).

17. For those who consider them primary engines of economic theory, see Robert Eagly, *Events, Ideology, and Economic Theory: The Determinants of Progress in the Development of Economic Analysis* (Detroit, MI: Wayne State University Press, 1968); Mary O. Furner and Barry Supple, eds., *The State and Economic Knowledge: The American and British Experiences* (Cambridge: Cambridge University Press, 2002); Johnson, *Predecessors of Adam Smith*; J. D. Gould, "The Trade Crisis of the Early 1620's and English Economic Thought," *Journal of Economic History* 15, no. 2 (June 1955): 121–33; Jonathan Israel, "England's Mercantilist Response to Dutch World Trade Primacy, 1647–1674," in *State and Trade: Government and the Economy in Britain and the Netherlands Since the Middle Ages*, ed. Simon Groenveld and Michael Joseph Wintle, 50–61 (Zutphen: Walburg Pers, 1992); Magnusson, *Mercantilism*, 60–62; Barry E. Supple, "Currency and Commerce in the Early Seventeenth Century," *Economic History Review* 10, no. 2 (1957): 239–55, https://doi.org/10.2307/2590860; and Barry E. Supple, *Commercial Crisis and Change in England, 1600–1642: A Study in the Instability of a Mercantile Economy* (Cambridge: Cambridge University Press, 1959). For those who see them specifically as crucial to developments in seventeenth-century English economic theory, see Slack, *The Invention of Improvement*; and Carl Wennerlind, *Casualties of Credit: The English Financial Revolution, 1620–1720* (Cambridge, MA: Harvard University Press, 2011).

squarely within the era of mercantilism, which can be broadly characterized by the twin pursuits of power and plenty in early European nations—and in particular the attempt to amass increased political power through commercial expansion.[18] The term "mercantilism" refers to both state policy and economic thought produced across Europe from the end of the medieval period until publication of *The Wealth of Nations* (1776) and the onset of the Industrial Revolution.[19] Classic works on mercantilism are focused not on why new economic ideas emerged and multiplied in this particular era, but instead on how these ideas can or cannot explain shifts in state policy.[20] The implication, however, is that economic thought is a by-product of the state policy formation process.

A version of this view argues that in their need for greater financial resources, early nation-states encouraged and commissioned actors to produce new ideas and information useful for increasing its revenue base. This position is the one that Joseph Schumpeter takes, for example, in the introduction to his *History of Economic Analysis* (1954). Another similar interpretation emphasizes the role of state rivalries in the international setting as a motivating factor behind the production and publication of the many texts. Paul McNulty, for example, argues that a central force behind these texts was "the desire to enhance the wealth, power, and prestige of the national state, and in the process weaken the positions of the other states."[21] Lars Magnusson has made a similar argument.[22] And the position is similar to the one held by Reinert and Røge, with a subtle shift in emphasis from international competition to

18. Many controversies plague the use of the term "mercantilism." While it is perhaps best used to refer only to a specific era rather than to a dogma because of all the controversies and contrary positions included in mercantilist works, the broad contours generally agreed upon are present in the main works. An additional emphasis would be on the importance and value of bullion. Overviews are available in Steve Pincus, "Rethinking Mercantilism: Political Economy, the British Empire, and the Atlantic World in the Seventeenth and Eighteenth Centuries," *William and Mary Quarterly* 69, no. 1 (January 2012): 3–34, https://doi.org/10.5309/willmaryquar.69.1.0003; Stern and Wennerlind, *Mercantilism Reimagined*; and Roscher, *Principles of Political Economy*.

19. Smith, *Wealth of Nations*.

20. Eli Heckscher, *Mercantilism* (London: George Allen & Unwin, 1935); Schmoller, *The Mercantile System*; William Cunningham, *The Growth of English Industry and Commerce* (Cambridge: At the University Press, 1882); and W[illiam] J. Ashley, *An Introduction to English Economic History and Theory* (New York: Kelley, 1966).

21. McNulty, *Origins and Development*, 26.

22. Magnusson, *Mercantilism*, 96.

state power.[23] The problem with this explanation is, again, there were many rising nation-states experiencing international competition and only one real site in which new economic thought was taking root. And in that site, the evidence does not indicate that state actors were producing most of these texts. Instead, merchants authored a much higher proportion.

Recognizing the importance of merchant authorship to the growth of the English economic literature, Perry Gauci has argued that the new literature was driven by the status aspirations of the merchant class. Merchants were becoming more prosperous as avenues into overseas trade increased, but for most of the century they still lagged behind in terms of political representation, and their social status remained low. Gauci contends that they wrote so many texts about economic matters in an attempt to prove the value of their profession to the rest of society and thereby raise their social position. He sees the central underlying theme of political economy in the seventeenth century as the moral status of merchants.[24] This argument is compelling in the context of England, but again the low status of merchants was not a singularly English phenomenon.

These arguments all make extremely valuable contributions in exploring the problem space. Trade depressions, economic dislocation, growth and development, the rise of the nation-state, and the rise of merchants all were important to the emergence of this new literature. In light of the comparative context, however, they appear to have been insufficient to have brought about the change by themselves.

My approach in this book has been to take an analytical and methodologically diverse approach to evaluating the causes motivating merchant authorship of the new economic discourse. I first describe what changed in chapters 1 and 2. These chapters do not break entirely new substantive ground. The rise of a new mode of "mercantilist" economic thought in the seventeenth century has already been documented and discussed extensively. However, I apply new methods of computationally assisted text analysis—topic modeling—to conduct a more comprehensive analysis of the corpus than has been previously undertaken. In chapter 3, I propose

---

23. Sophus A. Reinert and Røge, *Political Economy of Empire*.

24. Perry Gauci, *The Politics of Trade: The Overseas Merchant in State and Society, 1660–1720* (Oxford: Oxford University Press, 2001), 171.

a new explanation for why this economic literature changed so dramatically in England. In chapters 4 through 6, I identify and rigorously assess this theory. I apply a range of methods to explore whether my explanation is correct and consider alternative hypotheses through statistical and comparative analyses. Such an approach has not been taken in the past within this subject area. The evidence uncovered in these chapters strongly suggests that merchant-state relations—and, in particular, two aspects of those relations—were central to the emergence of the new economic literature. In the next two sections, I describe these two elements: the chartering process and the marginalization of merchants in the state. I then turn to their qualitative impacts—how these factors not only stimulated debate but also shaped its contents. Merchant marginalization not only pushed debate into the public sphere, but it also promoted the reframing of economic thought in an attempt to appeal to political elites. The public sphere imposed its own discipline and encouraged a more rigorously logical and empirical approach to explanation, which was ultimately to the benefit of all.

THE INITIAL OVERTURE: CHARTERING

English society of the early modern era was becoming increasingly organized. Not only was the state expanding and beginning to adopt administrative structures, but formal commercial organizations also began to dot the economic landscape. In the medieval period, most commerce was conducted via guilds, partnerships, and independent merchants. In the sixteenth century, chartered companies began to take control over key areas of English overseas trade. In 1555, the Muscovy Company was granted a Crown charter that gave them exclusive rights to trade with the principality of Moscow and tsardom of Russia. The chartering process formalized the company's relationship to the state, specified features of internal organization such as a governing body and rules for pooling capital, and established formal conditions of membership. It brought a certain order to a part of English overseas trade by assigning it to a relatively small group of traders who had agreed to abide by the company's regulations and procedures. Achieving order in an otherwise chaotic market and in trade with a potentially threatening rival power was one of the Crown's goals in granting the charter and thereby sponsoring the formation of the company, but more pecuniary interests were also gratified by the transfer of money from the merchants to the Crown in return for their exclusive privileges.

Queen Elizabeth chartered the Muscovy Company, and she favored the approach of awarding privileges as a means of raising funds for the state. Soon after, she granted a new charter to the Merchant Adventurers of London, the Merchant Adventurers for Guinie, Hawkins's Voyages, the Kathai Company, the Mines Royal, and the Mineral and Battery Works.[25] Increasingly large sections of England's overseas trade began to fall under the purview of these corporate bodies. Other European nations at this time had a few large companies—notably, several different East India companies existed across the continent—but their prevalence was much lower than in England. The country with the second largest number of formally constituted commercial corporations was the Dutch Republic.[26] They had only five chartered companies. Outside of Europe, companies were not adopted until the nineteenth century.

This new locus of organizational capacity in society had intended and unintended consequences. The intent behind forming the companies was first and foremost to enrich the participants. The companies were also intended to expand trade into new areas, stabilize markets, increase Crown revenue, and bring goods to market. Accomplishing these sizable goals required the management of a significant degree of logistical complexity that was accomplished through the adoption of bureaucratic administration, a degree of hierarchical organization, and routinization of procedures. These elements of corporate organization had unintended consequences. By setting themselves off from the rest of society and relying on the creation of sets of routine procedures and roles, they created distinct internal organizational cultures.[27]

Both the intended outcomes and the introduction of new organizational cultures of the companies created shock waves in the culture of the

25. George Cawston and Augustus Henry Keane, *The Early Chartered Companies (A.D. 1296–1858)* (London: Edward Arnold, 1896); and William Robert Scott, *The Constitution and Finance of English, Scottish and Irish Joint-Stock Companies to 1720*, 3 vols. (Cambridge: At the University Press, 1912).

26. Ron Harris, *Going the Distance: Eurasian Trade and the Rise of the Business Corporation, 1400–1700* (Princeton, NJ: Princeton University Press, 2020), 323–28.

27. The canonical exploration of these processes is in Max Weber, "Bureaucracy," in *From Max Weber: Essays in Sociology*, ed. Hans Gerth and C. Wright Mills (New York: Oxford University Press), 196–240.

society around them. That this might happen should not be difficult to imagine. Consider, for example, the twenty-first-century impact of social media firms on privacy concerns, political polarization, and election processes, as well as the distinct impact that the unique organizational culture of Silicon Valley has had on U.S. society at large. The introduction of the corporation itself as a new vehicle for commerce and trade can be expected to have had similarly large consequences. Both the internal system of governance created to manage company operations and the monopoly privileges accorded to the companies by the state stimulated debate. English companies were created with internal courts for the establishment and dissemination of company policy. The external boundaries of the companies were heavily patrolled. Gaining membership was not an easy task and usually required the sponsorship of an existing member. But once inside, the court was a remarkably democratic space. The full contingent of members had voting rights, and there was a vigorous culture of debate within company halls. This culture produced individuals skilled at rhetoric, persuasion, and argumentation.[28] Debate was a strength of company merchants.

Debate, however, is never one-sided. The monopoly privileges granted to the companies by the Crown and Parliament guaranteed that there would be another side to issues raised by the companies. Weberian organizations are in part defined by the existence of formal boundaries that mark off those that are in from those that are out. The granting of monopoly privileges to the new corporations meant that a sizable body of merchants were excluded from new and potentially very profitable areas of trade. These merchants were ready to take up arms against the companies and the very idea of monopoly rights. And it was not only independent merchants who vocalized opposition. Customs officers, masters of the mint, fisherman, weavers, and producers of all types resented the potential reduction in trade resulting from monopolistic exclusion. The companies reignited old feuds and created new ones. Immense profits could be made in the risky arenas of overseas commerce. Both sides were deeply invested in persuading the government to enact policies that favored their interests.

28. Phil Withington, "Public Discourse, Corporate Citizenship, and State Formation in Early Modern England," *American Historical Review* 112, no. 4 (October 2006): 1016–38.

THE MERCHANT'S RESPONSE: PUBLISHING

With the financial stakes high, merchants jockeyed with each other to influence state policy. One way to guide state policy is participate in—and ideally control—the state directly. Because elements of representative government were present in England in the seventeenth century, direct influence for merchants was a possibility. The Crown held most power in the first half of the century, but Parliament was even then a significant governing body, and it became more powerful after the Glorious Revolution of 1688. But even though there was a long history of merchants serving in Parliament, they never approached a majority position. Under Queen Elizabeth, they made up nearly 15 percent of parliamentary seats, which turned out to be the high point for more than a century to come. As parliamentary power increased, more landed elites seem to have seen government service as a means to increase their influence, and lawyers increased their participation. In order to win a seat, merchants faced greater competition. The proportion of seats held by merchants declined over most of the century, reaching as low as 4 percent in 1625.[29] The Crown and Parliament began sporadically to call to order councils and committees on trade to serve in advisory roles, but even these contained few merchants. A number of economic publications of the time noted this fact and pleaded for regular advisory boards composed of experienced traders and financiers.[30]

29. David Hayton, Eveline Cruickshanks, and Stuart Handley, eds., *The House of Commons, 1690–1715*, 5 vols. (Cambridge: Published for the History of Parliament Trust by Cambridge University Press, 2002); P. W. Hasler, ed., *The House of Commons, 1558–1603*, 3 vols. (London: Published for the History of Parliament Trust by Her Majesty's Stationery Office, 1981); Basil Duke Henning, ed., *The House of Commons, 1660–1690* (London: Published for the History of Parliament Trust by Secker & Warburg, 1983); Romney Sedgwick, *The House of Commons 1715–1754*, 2 vols. (London: Her Majesty's Stationery Office, 1970); Andrew Thrush and John P. Ferris, eds., *The House of Commons, 1604–1629*, 6 vols. (Cambridge: Published for the History of Parliament Trust by Cambridge University Press, 2010).

30. Charles Davenant, *Discourses on the Publick Revenues, and on the Trade of England. In Two Parts* (London: Printed for James Knapton, 1698), Making of the Modern World; Charles M. Andrews, *British Committees, Commissions, and Councils of Trade and Plantations, 1622–1675* (Baltimore: Johns Hopkins Press, 1908), http://archive.org/details/britishcommitteooandrgoog; Henry Robinson, *Englands Safety, in Trades Encrease. Most humbly presented to the High Court of Parliament* (London: Printed by E. P. for Nicholas Bourne, 1641), Making of the Modern World; Thomas Violet, *The Advancement of Merchandize: or, Certain Propositions For the Improvment of the Trade of this Common-wealth, humbly presented to the Right Honorable the Council of State* (London: W. DuGard, Printer to the Council of State, 1651), Making of the Modern World; Slingsby Bethel, *The Present Interest of England Stated. By a Lover of his King and Countrey* (London: Printed for D. B., 1671), Making of the Modern World; and John Cary, *An Essay, on the Coyn and Credit of England: As they stand with Respect to its Trade* (Bristol: Will. Bonny, 1696), Making of the Modern World.

The tenuous nature of merchants' hold on power in England—marginality in the context of representation—was uncommon for the era. Most other nations lacked representative institutions, so public lobbying was unlikely to have significant influence. At the other end of the spectrum lay the Dutch Republic. The Dutch had representative institutions prior to England, but in contrast to England, merchants in the Dutch Republic were the majority power holders. If the relationship between the state and merchants in England was a courtship, in the Netherlands they were an old married couple. Seated at the helm of the States-General and provincial authorities, Dutch merchants could directly implement policy. In England, more indirect means were necessary. There were successful merchant lobbies who approached the Crown and members of Parliament; the East India Company had a particularly effective operation.[31] But lobbying did not always produce the desired outcome, and merchants wanted methods to amplify their influence. As relatively marginal figures in the hallways of government, merchants needed to find alternative avenues through which to influence trade policy.

When individuals need to communicate information, they talk to each other or write a letter, email, or text. When academics want to bring attention to a particular problem and promote policy change, they are generally talking not to another individual, but instead to an institution or organization—often the state. If it is an important issue, they might write a book. They do this because a book published in the public domain amplifies any one person's voice and, if they are lucky or influential, builds a popular base of support for the cause for which they are advocating.

The merchant class in England was sufficiently marginalized that they could not simply implement their preferences in state policy. On the other hand, they had become influential enough to have a decent chance of affecting state policy. Otherwise, there would have been little reason to take the time to write and publish. They chose to exercise the option of voice.[32] But it was more than just the agency of the merchants that led to this outcome. It was the attenuated relationship between a merchant class

31. Arnold A. Sherman, "Pressure from Leadenhall: The East India Company Lobby, 1660–1678," *Business History Review* 50, no. 3 (Autumn 1976): 329–55, https://doi.org/10.2307/3112999.

32. Albert O. Hirschman, *Exit, Voice, and Loyalty: Responses to Decline in Firms, Organizations, and States* (Cambridge, MA: Harvard University Press, 1970).

roiled by internal divisions and the state that led to publications. Neither states nor markets alone stimulated the development of this new literature. It was instead a result of an attempt to build a bridge between the two. In social network terms, this would be referred to as a particular type of cultural hole: a generative incommensurability separating different institutional logics.[33] In such cases, different populations inhabiting different logics create new forms of discourse in their attempt to communicate across domains.[34]

Low levels of merchant representation and the problematic and sometimes troubled relationship among the merchants, the companies, and the Crown and Parliament encouraged the creation of a new discourse about commerce, trade, finance, and industry. The rifts that divided the state and merchant class may have impeded short-term economic productivity, but they accelerated the development of a new area of economic inquiry and shaped its trajectory.

REFRAMING

One of the most significant shifts in economic thought produced in this institutional configuration was the turn away from the kinds of concerns we now group under the heading of "inequality" to a fairly restricted attention to economic growth. The underlying moral framework that had guided the work of the scholastics and derived from the mission of the church had encouraged the protection of the poor and stigmatized financial practices, such as usury, that were understood to be unjust. While this orientation made the development of capital markets more difficult than it should have

33. Mark A. Pachucki and Ronald L. Breiger, "Cultural Holes: Beyond Relationality in Social Networks and Culture," *Annual Review of Sociology* 36 (2010): 205–24, https://doi.org/10.1146/annurev.soc.012809.102615.

34. Pachucki and Breiger, "Cultural Holes," 216; Roger Friedland, "The Endless Fields of Pierre Bourdieu," *Organization* 16, no. 6 (November 2009): 887–917, https://doi.org/10.1177/1350508409341115; Jennifer C. Lena and Mark C. Pachucki, "The Sincerest Form of Flattery: Innovation, Repetition, and Status in an Art Movement," *Poetics* 41, no. 3 (June 2013): 236–64, https://doi.org/10.1016/j.poetic.2013.02.002; John Padgett and Walter W. Powell, *The Emergence of Organizations and Markets* (Princeton, NJ: Princeton University Press, 2012); Harrison C. White and Frédéric Godart, "Stories from Identity and Control," *Sociologica* 1, no. 3 (November–December 2007): 1–17, https://www.rivisteweb.it/doi/10.2383/25960; and John W. Mohr and Harrison C. White, "How to Model an Institution," *Theory and Society* 37, no. 5 (October 2008): 485–512, https://doi.org/10.1007/s11186-008-9066-0.

been, there were trade-offs. For example, predatory lending (understood then through the larger category of usury) was arguably less publicly tolerated than it is now.

The battles being fought in the new literature over company privileges and overseas trade simply did not intersect with the problem of the salvation of the human soul. Merchants and financiers cared little for the moral condemnation of commerce that had been a hallmark of the works produced from within the church. They were not proselytizing. Their goals were immediate and practical. The authors were explicit in text after text that they wrote in the attempt to persuade the state to adopt certain commercial policies. Max Beer described the corpus they created as "one long campaign for the political control of trade and commerce by the merchant class."[35] Robert Ekelund and Robert Tollison saw the literature as a collection of post hoc justifications and an apologia for an extractive regime privileging state actors, monopolists, and cartel schemes.[36] Contemporaries well versed in the financial and commercial landscape of the time were just as skeptical.

For these reasons, the authors often attempted to obscure their own personal financial stake in these policy decisions. It is, after all, difficult to win an argument about public policy by asserting that I personally will profit greatly from this arrangement. In order to persuade the public and the state, the authors had to construct a new moral framework that could legitimate their positions. Perhaps drawing from the communal basis of the company form, they began to ground their arguments in the idea of how different commercial practices contributed to the larger public benefit—the health of the Crown, the state of the commonweal, and the wealth of the nation.[37]

In a bellwether 1621 tract, Thomas Culpeper the Elder (not to be confused with the doomed paramour of Queen Catherine) argued that it was no longer convincing to condemn usury as a sin; instead, arguments had to evaluate the impact of high interest rates on the development of commerce

35. Max Beer, *Early British Economics from the XIIIth to the Middle of the XVIIIth Century* (London: George Allen & Unwin, 1938), 186.

36. Robert B. Ekelund Jr. and Robert D. Tollison, *Mercantilism as a Rent-Seeking Society: Economic Regulation in Historical Perspective* (College Station: Texas A&M University Press, 1981).

37. Paul McNulty referred to the era as distinct from the previous in its adherence to a new type of economic nationalism. McNulty, *Origins and Development*.

and trade.[38] The era of this new economic nationalism forsook the problems of justice and equity and embraced what was to be an exceptionally long turn to addressing the roots of economic growth. From where we now sit, these two issues—fair exchange and growth—are not in clear opposition. Yet we still have trouble conceptually integrating the two issues into one research program. Indeed, one could argue that sociology has taken on the problem of fair exchange in the study of inequality, and economics has taken on the study of growth and market performance. This split is at least in part a legacy of the seventeenth century, where they served as competing moral frameworks—when attention to the problems of development could only come at the expense of scholastic economic concerns.

THE DISCIPLINE OF THE PUBLIC SPHERE

The further development of the economic literature was linked to another major historical transition associated with the emergence of democracy and capitalism: the rise of the public sphere. The merchants' attempts to solve their legitimacy problem were necessary because of the context in which they were making the arguments. Merchants excluded from the discursive space of the companies or attempting to influence government commercial policies needed an arena that bridged different merchant associations, the state, and other elite actors. The public sphere is the quintessential bridging space. As Margaret Somers wrote, it "denotes a contested participatory site in which actors with overlapping identities as legal subjects, citizens, economic actors, and family and community members, form a public body and engage in negotiations and contestations over political and social life."[39]

Because it lay at the intersection of so many different actors, the public sphere presented a hostile environment for narrow appeals to personal

---

38. Thomas Culpeper, *A Tract Against Vsvrie* (London: Printed by W. I. for Walter Burre, 1621), Making of the Modern World; William Letwin, *Sir Josiah Child: Merchant Economist*, Kress Library of Business and Economics 14 (Boston: Baker Library; Harvard Graduate School of Business Administration, 1959), 82; and Geoffrey Poitras, *The Early History of Financial Economics, 1478–1776: From Commercial Arithmetic to Life Annuities and Joint Stocks* (Cheltenham, UK: Edward Elgar, 2000), 420.

39. Margaret R. Somers, "Citizenship and the Place of the Public Sphere: Law, Community, and Political Culture in the Transition to Democracy," *American Sociological Review* 58, no. 5 (October 1993): 587–620, https://doi.org/10.2307/2096277.

interest. In the private meetings between government officials and company lobbyists, deals could be struck without reference to the benefit of the nation as a whole. The chartered companies came into existence because of the congruence between the desires of wealthy merchants to control certain areas of trade and the needs of the Crown to fill its coffers. It was the justification of these arrangements to the wider public, outport merchants, and hostile elites that led proponents to belatedly justify the arrangements by claiming that companies imposed a beneficial order on trade. In a strictly private series of patron-client relations, the relationship to the public benefit or larger considerations of economic order would probably not have been central to the discussion. By eliminating—or at least reducing—the logic of quid pro quo, the public nature of the dialogue helped shift the conversation into a more rigorous interrogation of the problem of economic growth. By creating new spaces for public discussion that explored new topics, merchants made certain kinds of knowledge explicit and available in a way that lent itself to further elaboration.

The arguments were not just hung from a new frame. Most of the authors and reading public of the early modern era were not naïve enough to believe that simply claiming something was for the benefit of all necessarily meant it was not in reality for the benefit of the few. To counter suspicion and persuade their audience, the new authors introduced examples drawn from life and began to employ an abstract rhetoric evocative of laws of nature. The new arguments, bereft of religious overtones, were disembedded from moral and social concerns.[40] An abstract conceptualization of a world of self-regulating international flows of goods and bullion was introduced to the world.[41]

As William Letwin has previously argued, seventeenth-century authors were writing in pursuit of their own self-interest, advocating for policies and positions advantageous to their business pursuits; but in order to do so persuasively, they adopted a rhetorical position of a neutral and abstract scientific investigation.[42] A by-product was a turn to empirics and logic and, ultimately, the production of real insight into economic matters.

40. Appleby, *Economic Thought and Ideology*; Magnusson, *Mercantilism*.

41. Schumpeter, *History of Economic Analysis*, 347–53.

42. William Letwin, *The Origins of Scientific Economics: English Economic Thought, 1660–1776* (London: Methuen, 1963), 97.

Eventually, the discursive and rhetorical format created by these authors took on a life of its own, encouraging further scientific inquiry.

As Letwin notes, commercial pursuits ranked very low in the status orderings of the medieval and premodern European world. The motives of merchants were particularly suspect as they had been corrupted by monetary interests that diverged from the morality of the church. Thus, arguments arising from the pens of merchants about what kinds of economic policies would benefit the nation as a whole were widely regarded with mistrust. Some authors attempted to cloak their identity with anonymity. Another option was to employ logic and science to buttress their legitimacy. Roger North, for example, defended his brother Dudley North's treatise on trade on the grounds that it was conducted using the relatively new Cartesian principles of reasoned inquiry: "I find Trade here Treated at another rate, than usually hath been; I mean Philosophically: for the ordinary and vulgar conceits, being meer Husk and Rubbish, are waved; and he begins at the quick, from Principles indisputably true" and uses the new "Method of Reasoning hath been introduc'd with the new Philosophy."[43]

Abstraction also served to obscure private interests and elevate arguments into the loftier spheres of philosophical inquiry, but other trends also encouraged this tendency. Increasing abstraction went hand in hand with the broader political discourse that was emerging at this time. Peter Bearman has shown that religious rhetoric became more abstract in seventeenth-century England as gentry relations shifted from a local kin-based structure to a nationally embedded patronage-client pattern that transcended parochial interests.[44] Bridging across different counties meant a leveling up of the discourse from concrete issues between particular individuals to an ideologically driven rhetoric expansive enough to address similar conflicts cropping up throughout England under the rubrics of religious freedom or various points of dogma.

43. Dudley North, *Discourses upon Trade; Principally Directed to the Cases of the Interest, Coynage, Clipping, Increase of Money* (London: Printed for Tho. Basset, 1691), Making of the Modern World. Also noted by Letwin, *Origins of Scientific Economics*, 189–90.

44. Peter S. Bearman, *Relations Into Rhetorics: Local Elite Social Structure in Norfolk, England, 1540–1640*, Arnold and Caroline Rose Monograph Series of the American Sociological Association (New Brunswick, NJ: Rutgers University Press, 1993).

Although the economic debates were not intimately linked to the realignment of elite political networks, the emergence of the companies gave the issues a national dimension. Whereas guilds had traditionally entertained local privileges, the chartered companies were granted national monopolies. Most of the monopolies were given to London merchants with close ties to the Crown. Opponents were scattered across the countryside in the many and various outports; therefore, it was in their interest to coordinate opposition through abstract principles that could apply to and rally individuals across locales. The principle of free trade fit the bill very well.

The national implications of the controversies raised by the companies and the legitimation needs of the larger merchant class worked to increase the abstraction level of published works while encouraging the incorporation of empirical evidence, logic, and a scientific approach to long-standing problems. These elements are crucial to the long-lasting influence of the works produced in this era.

CONCLUSION

Though Adam Smith has been known for years as the founder of laissez-faire capitalism and the free trade doctrine, his reputation has undergone a significant revision in the first decades of the twenty-first century. Smith's originality—though not his genius—has been called into question. Many of Smith's most influential contributions are now widely known to have been made previously by other English authors. Mercantilists had called for the deregulation of trade more than a century before the publication of *The Wealth of Nations*. William Petty (1620–1687) is often credited with introducing the idea of laissez-faire economic policy in his use of the phrase *vadere sicut vult* ("let it go as it will"). Petty also developed a sophisticated labor theory of value well before Smith. Karl Marx, an avid reader of Smith and Petty, noted Petty's originality of thought and earlier crystallization of concepts that were to reappear in Smith.[45] One of Smith's most lauded achievements was to overturn the zero-sum model of overseas trade embraced by the early mercantilists. In this, he was following in the

---

45. Karl Marx, addenda to *Theories of Surplus-Value* [Volume 4 of *Capital*] (written 1862–63; originally part of the *Economic Manuscripts of 1861–1863*), 1350, https://www.marxists.org/archive/marx/works/1863/theories-surplus-value/add1.htm.

footsteps of Charles Davenant and Gardner, who had demonstrated the complementary benefits of overseas trade to trade partners in lucid prose a century prior. Even Smith's central contribution of recognizing the benefits of the international division of labor is evident in earlier works.[46]

Smith's real innovation lay elsewhere. As is well known, Smith was a professor of moral philosophy, not economics. In fairness, there were no departments of economics, but if there were, it is unlikely that Smith would have given up his position in moral philosophy to join one. It was *The Theory of Moral Sentiments* that Smith was revising on his deathbed, not *The Wealth of Nations*. Smith had not intended to begin the science of economics, but was instead engaged in a larger project combining philosophy, jurisprudence, and politics into a science of man.[47] Economics was just one aspect of his larger plan.

As has been noted, Smith was not against state regulation of trade—he was against the state regulation of trade that benefited the rich at the expense of the poor.[48] He agitated against state regulation because his default understanding was that state regulations were put in place to help the rich get richer, thereby impoverishing the rest of the population. He attacked monopolies, racketeering, tariffs, and bounties that raised the price of consumer goods; the practices of forced labor, sharecropping, and slavery; and the system of imperialism that extracted so much at such great cost from colonized lands and peoples.[49] *The Wealth of Nations* was "his attempt to marry the pursuit of the interests of the poor and the deprived with combined use of the market economy and well-chosen state intervention."[50]

In this, Smith was swimming against the tide of seventeenth-century works and accepted doctrine. Even the more advanced thinkers of the

---

46. Jacob Viner, *Studies in the Theory of International Trade* (New York: Harper & Brothers, 1937).

47. Ryan Patrick Hanley, ed., *Adam Smith: His Life, Thought, and Legacy* (Princeton, NJ: Princeton University Press, 2016).

48. Craig Muldrew, "From Commonwealth to Public Opulence: The Redefinition of Wealth and Government in Early Modern Britain," in *Remaking English Society: Social Relations and Social Change in Early Modern England*, ed. Steve Hindle, Alexandra Shepard, and John Walter, 317–40 (Woodbridge, UK: Boydell Press, 2015); Elizabeth Anderson, "Adam Smith on Equality," in Hanley, *Adam Smith*, 157–72; and Amartya Sen, "Adam Smith and Economic Development," in Hanley, *Adam Smith*, 281–302.

49. Elizabeth Anderson, "Adam Smith on Equality," 159.

50. Sen, "Adam Smith and Economic Development," 290.

seventeenth century believed that low wages were necessary to induce labor participation and secure good terms of trade overseas.[51] Their greatest concerns regarding the poor were to find means through which to coerce them into performing cheaper labor. This project was entirely opposite to the views of Smith, who repeatedly championed the rights of the poor and advocated for benevolence.[52]

For a reader familiar with the economic literature of the seventeenth and early eighteenth centuries, what is most striking about Smith was his reincorporation of philosophical and moral concerns—the problems of justice and sympathy—into a literature on trade that had left these matters by the wayside. He picked up the abstraction, the empiricism, the attention to the laws of economics, the importance of the flow of goods, and the difficulties involved in state intervention. He was exceedingly well versed in theories of value and specie flow—theories that had been developed in the previous two centuries. But remarkably, Smith seems to have been lionized in the historical record largely for what he drew from the mercantilists and not for his great innovation at the time, which was to reintroduce the problems of morality, equity, and benevolence into economic inquiry and ground them in a deep concern for the public benefit.

With few exceptions, later authors in the new field of political economy and economics seem to have sped past Smith's course correction. They followed the new line of thought planted initially by the mercantilists: empirical work on economic matters focused on the problems of growth and development.

51. Viner, *Theory of International Trade*, 56–57.
52. Muldrew, "Commonwealth to Public Opulence," 338–39.

Chapter One

THE DECLINING IMPORTANCE
OF FAIR EXCHANGE

Somewhere around 1550, near in time to the chartering of the Russian Company and the Company of Merchant Adventurers, *A Compendious or briefe examination of certayne ordinary complaints of diuers of our country men in these our days* (1581) was written.[1] It would not be published for another thirty years or so, and then under mysterious circumstances. The work was a dialogue that described what the author considered to be common complaints about the state of commerce, trade, industry, and all those various things that people do in order to make a living and get by. Some now refer to it by an alternate title, the "Discourse of the Common Weal." Figure 1.1 presents the ornate title page of this important work.

Though it is now recognized as a milestone, there is little evidence that it had a large audience in the sixteenth century. It first garnered historical attention through misattribution. As was the case for many of the texts in the corpus under consideration here, the author chose to publish anonymously. The initials "W.S." appear on the text, though they are likely to have belonged to the printer rather than author. An enterprising printer from the eighteenth century surmised that the author must have been William

---

1. Thomas Smith, *A Compendious or briefe examination of certayne ordinary complaints of diuers of our country men in these our days: which although they are in some part vniust & frivolous, [. . .]* (London: Thomas Marshe, 1581), Early English Books Online.

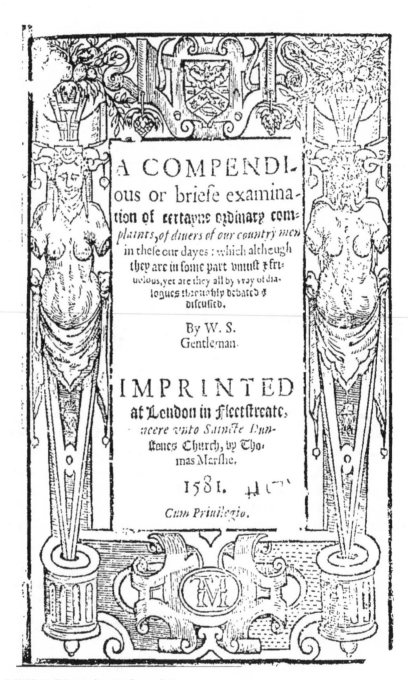

FIGURE 1.1. Title page from the *Compendious*

Shakespeare and included the text in a reissue of historical documents. Only later did historians of economic thought begin to piece together its origins. For years it was believed to have been written by John Hales,[2] a politician and administrator of the time. It is now more commonly attributed to Sir Thomas Smith, author of another important political text from the period, *De Republica Anglorum* (1583).[3]

The *Compendious* takes the form of a dinner conversation among a knight, a peasant, a capmaker, a merchant, and the esteemed Doctor Pandotheus. Over a meal of venison, the five characters air and argue various complaints about the economy, sharing one common sentiment familiar to most: everything is too expensive.[4] The peasant blames sheep—and, more specifically, the enclosures used to raise them—but his underlying concern is really with a decrease in the supply of land. The capper, a craftsman (and incipient Marxist), blames the existence of too many scholars. It is not scholarly activity itself that bothers the capper, but rather a scholar's lack of activity: "I would set you to the plough and carte, for the devil a whit of good yee doe with your studies."[5] The underlying diagnosis is labor shortage.

The other participants lend their sympathies to the peasant and the capper but reserve their judgment as to accuracy of their prognosis. The knight and the doctor provide long and carefully argued rebuttals to the peasant and the capper. The merchant is more successful in persuading the party. The merchant blames the economic malaise on the high prices pegged to foreign goods. Almost as an aside, he notes that high prices for foreign goods began with a debasement of coin that took place under King Henry VIII.

The doctor, who acts as the protagonist and voice of the author, notes the wisdom of merchants and zeros in on debasement as the root of the problem. According to him, the debasement caused foreign distrust of

---

2. Elizabeth Lamond and William Cunningham, eds., *A Discourse of the Common Weal of This Realm of England* (Cambridge: At the University Press, 1893), ix–x; Mary Dewar, "The Authorship of the 'Discourse of the Common Weal,'" *Economic History Review 19*, no. 2 (1966): 388–400.

3. Thomas Smith, comp., *De Republica Anglorum. The maner of Gouernement or policie of the Realme of England* (London: Printed by Henrie Midleton for Gregorie Seton, 1583), Early English Books Online.

4. Thomas Smith, *Compendious or briefe examination*, 33.

5. Thomas Smith, *Compendious or briefe examination*, 19.

English currency, counterfeiting of English coin, hoarding of English currency overseas, increasing rates of luxury imports, and bad terms of foreign exchange.[6] As a remedy to the malady, the doctor prescribes direct government intervention in overseas trade via a series of laws prohibiting and taxing foreign goods.[7]

The work is precocious in the sense that it contains in slightly disguised form themes that will continue to preoccupy authors for decades. The peasant, the capper, and the merchant essentially pick out the three major concerns of land, labor, and capital. Karl Marx was later to refer back to this work as an example of the differential class impact of currency depreciation.[8] An incipient economic nationalism based in zero-sum assumptions about foreign trade runs through the work. The English demand for French kerchiefs and fancy playing cards, for example, is denounced as detrimental to the good of the commonwealth.

Other features mark this text as quite distant from what we would expect from an economic work today. One is the quasi-literary form of the text. The dialogue format probably contributed to the mistaken notion that the text was a play (written by Shakespeare) rather than a serious economic work. Rhetorical skill and fluent argumentation—not evidence—are meant to convince the reader. A second revealing characteristic is the obsession in the text with the relationship between monetary value and the metallic properties of coinage. The properties of gold and silver are discussed at length and, more important, are central to the conclusion reached by the disputants that the ultimate cause of the economic depression was coin debasement. The strong line of bullionism and metalism underlying the judgment would seem irrational by the end of the seventeenth century.

A final significant difference that indicates the work belongs to a different, medieval universe of economic thought is the presence of strong moral overtones. The text devotes significant time to concern for the lower classes of society. The characters are at pains to acknowledge that economic woes place a particularly heavy burden on the shoulders of the poor. As the

6. Thomas Smith, *Compendious or briefe examination*, 73, 96.

7. Thomas Smith, *Compendious or briefe examination*, 61.

8. Karl Marx, *Capital: A Critique of Political Economy*, vol. 1, *Book One: The Process of Production of Capital*, ed. Frederick Engels, trans. Samuel Moore and Edward Aveling (Moscow: Progress Publishers, 1887; first German edition published 1867), chap. 29n2, https://www.marxists.org /archive/marx/works/1867-c1/ch29.htm.

doctor remarks, "hunger is bitter to bear." Commercial actions that make one person rich and another person poor are condemned: "for they may not purchase themselves profit by that which may be hurtfull to the other."[9] And noblemen that respond to the high price of wool by enclosing more lands for their sheep are not merely responding to market forces, they are driven by covetousness and avarice.[10] Most unusual to modern eyes, the text concludes its argument about economic problems with a long section on religious discord and schism. To a twenty-first-century reader, the link between the economic and religious arguments is elusive. No commercial, financial, or industrial practices are described in this section of the text. The doctor blames immorality for the irruption of religious discord: "we fell from the perfection of life, we grew out of credit, & the holy doctrine of Chryst sufferred slander by our sinful living. So we have gieven the fyrste occasion of this evil."[11] The spheres of commerce and religion are not held as distinct; instead, an implicit link ties material troubles to metaphysical struggles.

In comparison, consider one of the most advanced works of its time, Isaac Gervaise's *The System or Theory of the Trade of the World* (1720).[12] Gervaise was from a wealthy immigrant family of French Huguenots.[13] His wealth and standing derived from his family's involvement in one of the chartered companies of this era, the Royal Lustring Company. It is difficult to know how much influence Gervaise had among his contemporaries, but he had received significant attention for his writings by the mid-twentieth century and has been lauded as a true forerunner of formal economics by the influential figures Jacob Viner, Joseph Schumpeter, and Herbert Foxwell.[14]

Whereas the *Compendious* is a rambling 120 pages, *The System or Theory of the Trade of the World* is a concise 34. The language still has premodern characteristics, but there are no characters, no dialogue, and few literary flourishes or devices. Gervaise begins by defining his concepts: value, trade,

9. Thomas Smith, *Compendious or briefe examination*, 45–46.

10. Thomas Smith, *Compendious or briefe examination*, 84.

11. Thomas Smith, *Compendious or briefe examination*, 92.

12. Isaac Gervaise, *The System or Theory of the Trade of the World [. . .]* (London: H. Woodfall, 1720), Making of the Modern World.

13. Steven N. Durlauf and Lawrence Blume, eds., *The New Palgrave Dictionary of Economics* (Basingstoke, UK: Palgrave Macmillan, 2008).

14. Joseph Schumpeter, *History of Economic Analysis*, 366; Jacob Viner, foreword to *The System or Theory of the Trade of the World*, by Isaac Gervaise (Baltimore: Johns Hopkins Press, 1954), vi.

and labor. Much as in Thomas Hobbes or rational choice theory, he starts with an assumption about the fixed character of persons: "All men have, one with the other, an equal desire to draw them [the necessities of life] to themselves; which can be done, but by Labour only. And as Man naturally loves his Ease, the Possession of a part of them lessens his Desires, and causes him to labour less."[15] From these base propositions, Gervaise moves to construct early mathematical models linking credit, bullion, and value: "Credit the Cypher of the grand Denominator, losing its Value, as Gold and Silver vanish: And as in Arithmetick, Cyphers increase the Value of Numbers; in like manner, Credit increases the Denominator, and adds unto all things, and Increase of Denomination of Value, proportion'd to the Increase of the Denominatory by Credit."[16] These methods lead Gervaise to renounce the zero-sum, bilateral notion of trade that had been so prominent over the previous century. He instead embraced what looks very much like a theory of general equilibrium.[17] In his conception, "Trade causes a Vibration, or continual Ebbing and Flowing; which may be called the natural Ballance of Trade."[18]

As would follow from these observations, he rejects the bullionist obsession with gold for its own sake, saying "I never could reconcile myself, to that generally received Opinion."[19] He argues instead that gold will flow to nations based on their production levels. He explores and posits a relationship among production, consumption, and trade by considering a case in which a nation has somehow accumulated more than its natural share of gold or silver. As he puts it, this accumulation breaks the proportion of rich to poor in the population. What he means, given his proposition about the essential character of people, is that more people will be rich, and thus will work less. This change translates into a rise in consumption rates and a decrease in labor production. These trends in turn translate into increased imports, in order to satisfy the increased demand that cannot be supplied by a decreased production base. Those imports, however, will not be paid for in goods because all of the goods are already being absorbed in

15. Gervaise, *Trade of the World*, 5.

16. Gervaise, *Trade of the World*, 8.

17. Jacob Viner, *Studies in the Theory of International Trade* (New York: Harper & Brothers, 1937), 79–83.

18. Gervaise, *Trade of the World*, 10.

19. Gervaise, *Trade of the World*, 3.

the domestic market. Thus, goods must be paid for in bullion, which will produce a net outflow of bullion until the excess money is absorbed and distributed across all nations according to their production level.

This reasoning is quite sophisticated for the early eighteenth century—so much so that it has been written, well after the development and flourishing of twentieth-century economics, that "his treatment of income effects and his general equilibrium analysis of the international mechanism of adjustment are in many respects superior to those prevalent today."[20] Ultimately, the systematic and logical exposition of the balance among flows of specie, trade, and labor leads Gervaise to conclude that a system of free trade is most advantageous for all nations and parties.

There are few religious overtones in *The System or Theory of the Trade of the World*. God is mentioned only to posit that he made persons in order to labor.[21] Evil is used to refer to an imbalance in the amount of bullion a nation has accumulated.[22] Notably, for Gervaise, poverty is not a problem or a burden but is instead a natural and unchanging condition of humanity—one to be taken into account when constructing economic models of trade. Rather than seek to better men's souls, act in accordance with God's greater plan, or ensure equity in exchange, Gervaise instead considers what circumstances are best able to produce national profit. National economic growth is the central and only real concern.

MODELING CHANGES IN THE LITERATURE

Gervaise's text would not have been possible in the sixteenth century. The lack of Christian precepts and florid language mark it as culturally distinct from works of the sixteenth century—as if from a different world. The style of language, the terms of the argument, and the type of evidence presented would not have been compelling for a medieval audience. For a work like *The System or Theory of the Trade of the World* to make sense to its author and his readers, a major shift in expectations and audience was necessary. This shift took place largely over the course of the seventeenth century; it

---

20. J. M. Letiche, "Isaac Gervaise on the International Mechanism of Adjustment," *Journal of Political Economy* 60, no. 1 (February 1952): 34.

21. Gervaise, *Trade of the World*, 12.

22. Gervaise, *Trade of the World*, 18.

affected not just a few exceptional thinkers but also the larger set of readers, writers, and publishers. In this chapter, I use the tools of topic modeling to analyze this trend over the period from 1550 to 1720.

Computational approaches to text analysis are an exciting area of ongoing research. New advances are still being made, and more sophisticated analytical methods will almost certainly become available long after this book has made it into print. It is a vibrant field that uses machine learning and neural networks to classify and analyze large troves of data. In a world in which a huge amount of written documentation is continually being created by researchers, policy makers, bureaucrats, commercial businesses, and regular citizens through routine applications, forms, online interactions, and media of all types, it is impossible to get a grasp on all the accumulated knowledge simply by reading all the documents. No one person could take all the information in during one lifetime—or even in several lifetimes. Topic modeling is a statistical method for extracting information from large corpora—mountains of books, messages, and forms—without having to read through each document one by one.

One of the more tried-and-true approaches to topic modeling is Latent Dirichlet Allocation (LDA). LDA has been around since the early 2000s. It is no longer at the cutting edge of computational methods for text analysis. The advantage of that is that there is a good sense from previous history that it is a reliable approach. Latent Dirichlet Allocation is a Bayesian method based in word co-occurrence. Using the basics of which words appear with which other words, the method produces topics, which are common collections of words. For example, the words most likely to co-occur in the most prevalent topic (topic 21) are *men, well, honor, use, care, mean,* and *work.* Other words are also associated with the topic, but none of the words has to be included—particularly if all the other words are included. Documents are complex, and they usually discuss more than one topic. LDA assumes that most documents will be characterized by a small number of topics and that topics will be characterized by words that appear infrequently outside of their topics. The key result is that each document is associated with a likelihood that a topic is present. If there is a high likelihood, all the words in a given topic might not appear in each document that contains that topic, but an unlikely preponderance of those words must be present. The set of topics generated for a corpus functions as an inductively built categorization scheme that can be used to get a sense of what is being discussed in the thousands of documents you do not have time to read yourself. The method also has the benefit of assigning topics automatically, so that researchers cannot nudge marginal cases into categories where they do not fit because it suits their argument.

A great advantage of using topic modeling and automated text analysis methods more generally is the potential to reliably and systematically assess the prevalence of topics inductively built up from the corpus. Inductively built topics avoid the problem of researcher bias. They surmount the risk of using current ways of thinking about economic matters as a lens for interpreting and categorizing past works that were created within an entirely different *mentalité*. And although it is physically possible to read all the extant and available economic texts published in this era (indeed I have read many of them), it would be more difficult to systematically and consistently assess the prevalence of all the different topics that appear in all the different texts. Computational methods assist researchers by expanding the scope of the documents they can analyze and increasing the systematicity of their assessments.

CONSTRUCTING THE CORPUS

Before any computational analysis can begin, the corpus itself has to be constructed. The preeminent library of early economic history is the Kress Collection at Harvard University. The library defines economic works as those that cover the categories of "political economy, commerce, finance, taxation, money and banking trades and manufactures, transportation, labor, socialism, and the economic aspects of agriculture."[23] The Kress is the core collection of a digitized database, The Making of the Modern World, Part I, which also includes the early modern works on economic topics present in Goldsmith's Library at the University of London, the Butler Library at Columbia University, and the Sterling Library at Yale University. The database covers the period from 1450 to 1850, comprises more than 61,000 monographs and eleven million documents, and includes books as well as pamphlets, broadsides, serials, proclamations, and other ephemera.[24]

---

23. Ruth R. Rogers, "The Kress Library of Business and Economics," *Business History Review* 60, no. 2 (Summer 1986): 282, https://doi.org/10.2307/3115310.

24. The Making of the Modern World (database), Gale, https://www.gale.com/primary-sources /the-making-of-the-modern-world. Access to the database was granted by the Yale University Library system.

Although I consider only the English texts, it is a global collection: 31 percent of works are printed outside of England in another language.

Another exceptional database covering early modern England is the English Short Title Catalogue, which contains more than 480,000 titles published in England or English-speaking areas between 1473 and 1800.[25] The Short Title Catalogue is an ongoing and very successful project to catalog all English or English-language books that appeared in print during that period.

The initial stage of corpus collection consisted of merging the titles that appear in the Making of the Modern World database from 1580 to 1720 and the titles with subject headers that mark them as related to economic topics in the English Short Title Catalogue in the same period. Few titles were included in the Short Title Catalogue that were not already present in the Modern World database. The replications that were published in the same year were removed from the list of titles to avoid duplication. Titles published in different years were retained as they indicated reprints, an important marker of reader interest and increased circulation.[26] All together, 6,585 titles were amassed through this process.

Nearly all of these texts are available in some format through the database Early English Books Online (EEBO), which is an ongoing effort to digitize all texts printed in England, Ireland, Scotland, Wales, and North America from 1473 to 1700.[27] However, many of them are available only in early modern typeface. Figure 1.2 presents a snippet of *The bayte & snare of fortune* (1554), a text consisting of a dispute between the two characters Man and Money over the character of Money.[28] As is clear from the image, the text is legible—but barely. And although there are projects underway to create machine-based methods for reading in early modern typeface, the challenges in mechanically converting such inconsistent typeface, spelling, and punctuation are significant.

Most of these texts are therefore not available in a machine-readable format, and thus are difficult to subject to computational methods of analysis.

25. English Short Title Catalogue, British Library, http://estc.bl.uk/.

26. The contents and relevance of the texts were further verified, one by one, by manually checking titles, keywords, and short descriptions. In cases in which this was not sufficient to determine that the text actually addressed economic topics, the contents were read to verify relevance.

27. Early English Books Online (EEBO), ProQuest, https://eebo.chadwyck.com/home.

28. Robert Bieston, *The bayte & snare of fortune* (London: John Wayland, [1554?]), Making of the Modern World.

⸿ The Prologe.

Aynt Paule Doctor of veritie, sayeth that Auarice is the Roote and beginnyng of all euylles: Algates the men of this tyme present, be therto much enclined. For of all Estates fro the hyghest vnto the lowest, all geue theyr study vnto Iuarice, and euery one desyreth to haue golde and syluer: and for to haue the same they trauayle nyght and daye, by water and by lande, thynkyng therin to fynde quietnes and rest, whiche shal neuer be: for in ryches is neuer reast. The more that a man hath thereof the more he desyreth. For Auarice of the owne nature is vnsaciable, accordyng to the sayng of the Sage in the fift Chapter of Ecclesiastes. The couetous man is neuer satisfied. And Horace the Poete sayeth that the Couetous man is alwayes anhungred. And S. Ierome sayeth that the looue of worldely goodes is vnsaciable. And Boece in his thyrd booke of Consolacion sayeth that if the man whiche is auaricious had all the worlde in his dominacion, he woulde not be content: for euer he woulde desyer to haue worldly goodes more and more, and principally money, whiche neuer shoulde be noyous vnto man wer not his couetise, whiche euer brenneth mans harte: for God hath made the syluer as well as other thynges for the seruice of man, vnto whome he hath made all thing subiect. But whan the man letteth his appetite, and desyreth to get money otherwyse than by ryght and conscience, that may be called auarice whiche hath dominion vpon the man aboue reason: and so it appeareth that she whiche shoulde be maystres is the seruaunt, and she that should be subiecte, is the ladye, whiche is great blyndnes in man.

Thus is money maystres of the man, and man to money is subiecte, and is therwith so abused, that he doeth more therefore than for his maker, or for the health of his soule: O faulte of wisdome, o fault of reason, O faulse couetise thou art cause of the perdicion of many men, thou art cause that infinite euyls be dayly committed in this mortall worlde. And now to shew more playnly that men be enclyned to gather money, and consequently be subiecte to the same, I haue put here in wrytyng a question made bettwene Man and Money, by maner of a Disputacion, whiche vary in theyr wordes the one agaynst the other: for money woulde shewe his great power, and man speaketh agaynst hym. But after great disputa-cion the man abydeth banquished because of his couetous mynde, confessing that it is a great felicity to haue money in possessi-on.

(∵)   (∴)

A

There has, however, been a herculean effort to convert the books available in Early English Books Online into machine-readable format, the Text Creation Project (EEBO-TCP).[29] This project is a partnership with ProQuest and more than 150 libraries to transcribe the EEBO texts into machine-readable form. The EEBO collection contains roughly 132,000 texts. EEBO-TCP has converted roughly 60,000 of those texts into machine-ready format. It is a wonderful resource that continues to grow over time. These texts cover many topics other than economic matters. Between EEBO-TCP and the titles identified separately in the Making of the Modern World and the English Short Title Catalogue as covering economic topics, a final total of 2,353 texts that addressed economic matters in the time period in question are available in machine-readable format.

The second stage of corpus construction is cleaning and standardizing the text. Challenging in any context, this stage poses an even more formidable challenge in the early modern period. I used a combination of existing code, the Visualizing English Print (VEP) python suite, and my own corpus-specific list of regular language patterns and stop words to address the many irregularities of early modern print and spelling. This process corrected a long list of regular spelling variants—such as the interchangeable use of *mony* and *money*, *forraign* and *foreign*, and *ballance* and *balance*. Because this corpus is relatively small when compared to the universe of modern text data, I discarded stop words, focusing however on early modern variants such as *thee*, *unto*, *hath*, *doth*, and *doe*.

The last step of standardization was to convert the texts into comparable chunks for analysis. The texts themselves range from long books of hundreds of pages to relatively short proclamations limited to less than a page. Researchers have often solved this problem by using paragraphs, but in the early modern era paragraph use was not consistent. I chose instead to break the texts into overlapping segments of five hundred words each. Each segment was linked to information on the book, author, and year from which it was broken out. The segments overlap so that any contiguous words that were split apart in one case will be associated with each other in an overlapping segment. The end result consisted of 117,499 separate five-hundred-word documents cleaned and ready for analysis.

29. Early English Books Online Text Creation Partnership (EEBO-TCP), https://quod.lib.umich .edu/e/eebogroup/.

TOPIC MODELING RESULTS

Once the corpus was collected, cleaned, and standardized, modeling was possible. I used a package of tools created by Margaret Roberts, Brandon Stewart, and Dustin Tingley, called Structural Topic Model, for the analysis.[30] This package was designed to capture changes in topics over time, so it was ideal for my purposes, and it has a number of nice features, such as a simple routine that estimates the optimal number of topics to describe your data based on semantic coherence and word exclusivity. Topic modeling requires that the analyst predetermine the number of topics to be extracted from the data. This program simply runs a number of different models that begin with a different number of topics and picks the one with the highest semantic coherence and word exclusivity. Thus, the topics are consistent and tend to be defined by the use of words relatively unique to the topic.

In this case, the analysis returned sixty-six separate topics. Figure 1.3 presents the list of topics in order of prevalence across documents, with the most frequent words in the topics listed after the bar indicating prevalence.

Even though sixty-six is the optimal number of categories, it is difficult to think through so many trends at one time to get a large-scale sense of changes in the literature. To simplify the comparison, I grouped topics into themes, using a network clustering method. This approach preserves the high levels of coherence within topics, which treat many different subjects that we can still perceive as related to each other at a higher level of abstraction. For example, *parliament, speaker, court,* and *commons* are all political in nature and could belong to one topic, whereas *crown, king,* and *chamber* are also clearly political but can belong to another topic with little overlap between the two. They are different subjects, but are related—and therefore may be discussed in the same document. The coherent sixty-six topics, therefore, can be correlated by the likelihood that they will be discussed in the same document. I used this correlation between topics to produce a network of interlinked topics. Figure 1.4 presents this network. Nodes are sized by prevalence, such that a topic discussed in many documents will be bigger in size than those that do not appear in many documents. The width of the links between nodes is sized by the strength of the correlation

---

30. Molly Roberts, Brandon Stewart, and Dustin Tingley, stm: An R Package for the Structural Topic Model, https://www.structuraltopicmodel.com/.

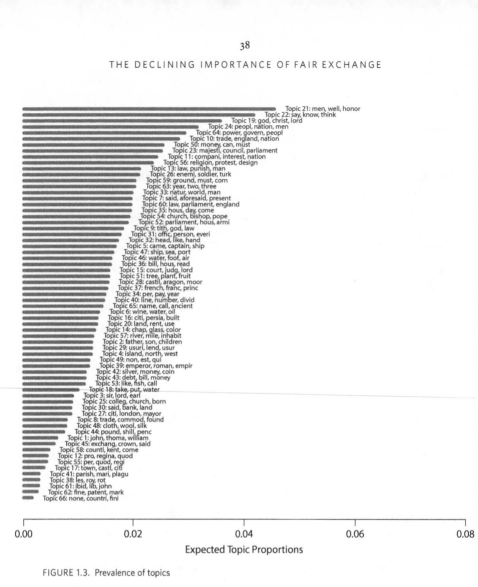

FIGURE 1.3. Prevalence of topics

between topics. The nodes are arranged in space by a spring algorithm that pulls nodes with higher correlations and nodes that are connected to the same topics closer together. If nodes have no common connections and a low correlation, they are pushed farther apart.

Converting the topics into a network may not immediately seem to improve clarity, but many methods have been invented to manage the complexity of networks that can be applied to make sense of the tangle of related topics. One class of tools is composed of different clustering algorithms. Just by eyeballing the network image in figure 1.4, it is possible to make out denser areas where topics seem to be more closely

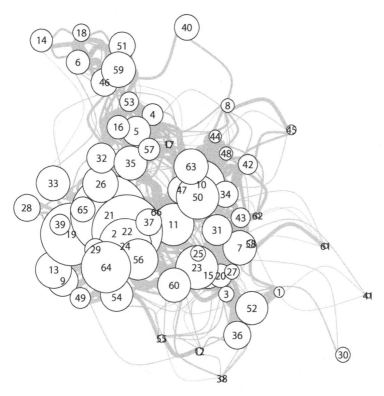

FIGURE 1.4. Network of topics

interrelated. For example, 56, 24, 22, 21, and 26 are fairly close, as are 50, 47, 34, 10, and 63.

Clustering algorithms use mathematical, computational, and graph theoretic approaches to identify areas of the network that are more densely interconnected—to produce clusters or, as they are sometimes called, communities within the larger network. My application of clustering methods here is built on the idea that themes are essentially clusters of topics. Therefore, if I cluster the network, I should be able to extract larger themes—clusters of related topics—that span the larger literature.

The correlation matrix between topics, or the measure of association, is weighted and undirected. The correlation can take on a range of values between zero and one, indicating a higher or lower likelihood of appearing in the same document. And the correlation is symmetric: the association between topic 21 and topic 22 is the same as the association between topic 22 and topic 21. Because walktrap algorithms are good at handling undirected weighted matrices, I used one here. The walktrap method for identifying clusters can be roughly described as sending out little exploratory sorties that traverse the network by moving from node to node across the edges that connect them. The path taken across the network is chosen at random. Because there are many recursive, overlapping, and redundant pathways in the denser portions of the network, the sorties tend to get caught in those areas—they get trapped. The likelihood of getting trapped in a certain area of the network based on the starting point of the sortie than becomes a means by which to identify different clusters.

Applying the walktrap algorithm to this network produces five clusters, which I refer to as themes. In figure 1.5, the themes are represented by five

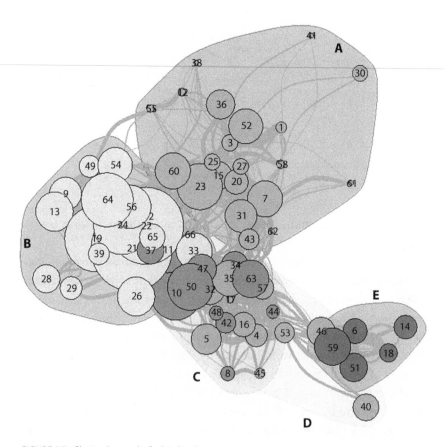

FIGURE 1.5. Clustered network of related topics

larger outlines, circular clouds that float outside of the group of nodes. The other characteristics of the network image are unchanged from the earlier figure.

These five themes have clearly recognizable subject areas. Each is marked by a letter. Cluster A, which contains the largest topic (21), is focused on religious and moral issues. Cluster B covers mainly political topics. Cluster C covers husbandry, Cluster D is travel, and Cluster E covers issues that are now more central to contemporary economic theory: trade, finance, and national prosperity.

The clustering algorithm is a terrifically useful first pass, but most of the best new computational methods combine human and algorithmic approaches to classification. I hand-coded the sixty-six topics by referring to high-frequency and highly representative words and cross-referencing them with the clusters produced by the walktrap algorithm. There was a fairly high convergence between the two methods. I agreed with the clusters more than 70 percent of the time. The remaining topics I reviewed once more, using several representative texts to get a deeper sense of what was at stake in the texts. A few times I even found that the algorithm had done a better job than I. Ultimately, eighteen topics were recoded, two of which I removed from the analysis because they were so idiosyncratic. One of these was a topic based around math terms; another appeared to be built from census reports. I then used these themes for further analysis of variation in topic prevalence over time. The presentation of the topics is descriptive only. The analysis helps to identify important trends. Once the trends are outlined, I move toward explaining them in subsequent chapters.

HUSBANDRY

Some of the themes produced may seem a little exotic to the modern ear— or perhaps a strange fit for a collection of works on economic topics. That is because authors began to concentrate increasingly on trade, finance, and national prosperity over the course of the seventeenth century, shifting their attention away from other, more traditional topic areas. Husbandry, for example, might seem like a strange topic for economic writings. Husbandry is defined as the care and feeding of fish, animals, and crops. In a more general sense, it is the study and practice of the management of property and natural resources. Medieval works were very concerned with the proper management of the household, manor, and demesne. This concern was not merely because it was useful. Scholarship on these issues had a very long tradition dating to Xenophon's classic work on the management of the household, *Oeconomicus*; a lesser work by a follower of Aristotle, *Oeconomica*; and Cato's manual, *De Agri Cultura*.[31]

While household management gravitated toward the realm of the female in Europe after the Industrial Revolution, in Ancient Greece the household was conceived as the domain of a male slaveholder. Xenophon's work is in the form of a dialogue, first between Socrates and Critobulus and later between Socrates and Isomachus. In the first lines of the work, the interlocuters agree that household management is a distinct branch of knowledge. The rest of the work fleshes out the various topics it should include, such as a division of labor between husband and wife, seasonal home decoration, exercise, overseeing servants, and discerning the quality of soil.

By the sixteenth and seventeenth centuries, a typical work in this vein might remind a contemporary reader of a Farmer's Almanac. Aphorisms and anecdotes were interwoven with practical advice on improving farming yield, increasing fish stocks, and raising healthy sheep. *The Jewel House of Art and Nature* (1594) described various new inventions and improvements.[32] Francis Bacon's *Sylva Sylvarum* (1626), published posthumously in the year of his death, included new and innovative techniques for agricultural improvement and the tending of livestock.[33] Some of the works targeted the feminine domain, such as *Covntry Contentments, or The English Huswife* (1615).[34] This book considered the interior rather than exterior of the household, covering topics such as healing, medicine, and surgery as well as cooking, distilling, vinting, malting, and weaving, among others. A typical passage—that is, one highly associated with the topic in the model—gives advice for storing rye: "for it is a common saying amongst husbandmen that rye will be drowned in the hopper that is if a shower of rain should but fall in the hopper or seed-basket whilst you were sowing it that shower

31. Moses I. Finley, *The Ancient Economy* (Berkeley: University of California Press, 1973), 17–34.

32. Hugh Plat, *The Jewel House of Art and Nature. Containing diuers rare and profitable Inventions, together with sundry new experimentes in the Art of Husbandry, Distillation, and Moulding* (London: Peter Short, 1594), Early English Books Online.

33. Francis Bacon, *Sylva Sylvarum: or, A Naturall Historie* (London: Printed by J. H. for William Lee, 1626), Making of the Modern World.

34. Gervase Markham, *Covntry Contentments, or The English Huswife* (London: Printed by I. B. for R. Jackson, 1623; originally published as the second book of the two-volume *Covntrey Contentments* [London: Printed by I. B. for R. Jackson, 1615]), Early English Books Online.

would drown it and the rye would hardly grow after: therefore your greatest care must be a fair season and a dry mould; for the contrary kills it."[35]

While they may seem quaint, these texts had a wide readership and significant staying power. Thomas Tusser, for example, seems to have been largely responsible for the dissemination of the ever-green phrase "Sweet April Showers, Doo spring Maie flowers." It appears in his most famous work, *Fiue hundreth pointes of good husbandry* (1579), which was an expanded edition of the popular *A hundreth good pointes of husbandrie* (1557).[36] Works of this type never disappear, but they also do not form the basis of modern or classical economics. As M. I. Finley points out, Adam Smith's mentor Francis Hutcheson was still publishing in this vein in 1742. But despite their personal relationship, "there was no road from the 'oeconomics' of Francis Hutcheson to the Wealth of Nations of Adam Smith published twenty-four years later."[37] The trajectory of these works was instead toward gardening, interior design, and cooking—all still supremely popular, though they have lost the former association with wealth accumulation and management and have instead increasingly been regarded as parts of leisure activity and conspicuous consumption.

Figure 1.6 presents a smoothed estimate of the trend in the likelihood of the eight husbandry topics appearing in a document over time

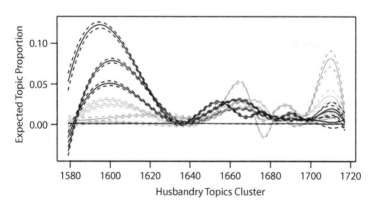

FIGURE 1.6. Husbandry topics over time

35. Markham, *Covntry Contentments*, 79.

36. Thomas Tusser, *A hundreth good pointes of husbandrie* (London: Richard Tottel, 1557), Early English Books Online; and Thomas Tusser, *Fiue hundreth pointes of good husbandry vnited to as many of good huswiferie [. . .]* (London: Richard Tottill, 15730, Early English Books Online.

37. Finley, *Ancient Economy*, 20.

from 1580 to 1720. Since the corpus of machine-readable texts ends in texts originally published prior to 1700, only reprints are included in the analysis from 1700 to 1720. Five unique topics are present in the cluster, characterized by words tied to evocative materials-based descriptions and directions: *wine, water, oil; glass, color, mine;* and *cream, rosewater, almond milk.* As is evident in the figure, the larger theme declines in prevalence over time, as do most of the topics. One notable exception is topic 14, which begins a sharp incline in 1700. This topic is closely linked to mining and smelting practices. Aqua fort, the extraction of gold from silver, the separation of manganese from salt, and the creation of brass are all covered in great detail in these passages. For example, readers learn that lead comes from ore "beaten raw as small as half an hazel nut then set the upon a little oven . . . and gently roasted and then beaten again and roasted again that its great wildness may come off and so the lead will easily separate from the slacks."[38] The surge in popularity of works on mining and smelting are very likely linked to the dissolution of the monopoly of the Society of the Mines Royal, one of the early chartered companies, in 1690. One might also consider this topic a transitional stage to the problems of industry, which grow significantly in importance over the course of the next two centuries but are still in an incipient mode in the seventeenth.

The heyday of husbandry was in the medieval era. The most popular works, such as Tusser's *volumes* and Conrad Heresbach's *The Whole Art and Trade of Hvsbandry,* were first published in the sixteenth century.[39] These works, as well as *Markhams farewell to Hvsbandry, Country Contentments: Or, The Husbandmans Recreations* and others, continued to be published and reprinted well into the eighteenth century.[40] But while the absolute

38. Lazarus Ercker and John Pettus, *Fleta Minor, Or, The Laws of Art and Nature, in Knowing, Judging, Assaying, Fining, Refining and Inlarging the Bodies of confin'd Metals* (London: Printed for the Author, by Thomas Dawks, 1683), Making of the Modern World.

39. Conrad Heresbach, *The Whole Art and Trade of Hvsbandry, contained In foure Bookes* (London: Printed by T. S. for Richard More, 1614), Making of the Modern World (Gale Document Number U0100089077).

40. Gervase Markham, *Country Contentments: Or, The Husbandmans Recreations,* 4th ed. (London: Printed by Nicholas Okes for Iohn Harison, 1631), Making of the Modern World; and Gervase Markham, *Markhams farewell to Hvsbandry or, The enriching of all sorts of Barren and Sterile grounds in our Kingdome, to be as fruitfull in all manner of Graine, Pulse, and Grasse, as the best grounds whatsoeuer [. . .],* 3rd ed. (London: Printed by Nicholas Okes for Iohn Harison, 1631), Making of the Modern World.

numbers of this type of work do not decline into the early modern era, they do diminish in proportion to the very large increase in other types of texts—particularly those on trade, commerce, and finance.

RELIGION AND MORALITY

Another declining topic area marks an even more significant shift in the cultural framing of economic thought. Figure 1.7 presents the trend over time for religious topics, the second largest theme contained in the corpus.

As can be seen in the network images of figures 1.4 and 1.5, topic 21 is one of the largest nodes in the network. It is the most prevalent topic in the data, and its fate over the century is charted by the line that begins second highest on the y-axis and peaks in 1640. The words *man, well, honor, use, care, mean,* and *work* occur with greatest frequency in this topic. The following is a representative passage:

> Others there are that in dalliance and sporting waste their time: and another sort there are who are so vehemently satirical that they will not spare any person no not the prince although thereby they incurr the hazard and penalty of loosing their heads, some are unapt to manage public affairs as being of a sullen and solitary humor or of a slack and slow disposition; and others as unfit for all employment as any of the aforementioned for that they be

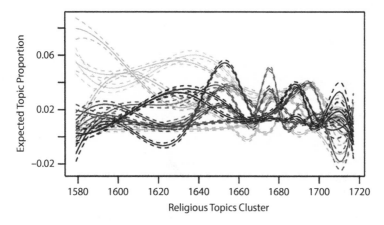

FIGURE 1.7. Religious topics over time

either obstinate in opinion or discourteous and boorish in their behavior and carriage.[41]

The passage is notable for its negativity, but stands out further for the way it evaluates and judges behavior at the level of the individual—not in terms of productivity but instead on the basis of character. Topic 21 captures documents with a high likelihood of condemning or criticizing individual behavior in works that are otherwise concerned with economic matters. They are moralizing in tone. In this sense, they are a continuation of a long tradition of medieval scholarship on economics that framed its descriptions, investigations, and interpretations of commercial behavior through the lens of Christian theology.

The scholastic tradition of writing on economic matters was an investigation of exchange and commerce undertaken from the perspective of the church, which is to say that the ultimate question under consideration was whether a given behavior was righteous or sinful. This distinction was understood to hinge largely upon the question of whether the exchange was equitable. Part of the inspiration for these works came again from Aristotle and his oversize place in the pantheon of medieval knowledge. While the management and increase of household wealth belong to *Oeconomica*, Aristotle discusses trade and commerce in the *Nicomachean Ethics*.[42] For him, trade and commerce are ethical issues—not problems of maximization.

The scholastics offered many sophisticated analyses of economic phenomena, including currency exchange, price formation, and the cost of risk. They always did so, however, from the perspective of a moral standpoint. One must understand how prices are formed and the cost of risk, for example, in order to understand whether a just price has been reached— or whether one party is profiting unfairly at the expense of another. The continuing obsession with the practice of usury, or charging interest for loans, derived from a concern that an exchange between two parties in

41. Thomas Manley, *The Sollicitor. Exactly and plainly declaring, Both as to Knowledge and Practice, how such an Undertaker ought to be qualified. [. . .]* (London: J. Streater, 1663), 2, Early English Books Online. Representative texts are drawn from the cleaned documents, so period capitalization and spelling have been lost.

42. Aristotle, *Nicomachean Ethics*, trans. H. Rackham, 2nd ed. (Cambridge, MA: Harvard University Press, 1934); and Aristotle, *Oeconomica* (Oxford: Clarendon Press, 1920).

which one charges interest is unbalanced—one party receives more than is fair—and therefore immoral.[43] It was from this perspective that Thomas Aquinas interpreted usury in *De malo* (1269–70) and *Summa theologicae* (1265–74).[44]

Less well known, but perhaps more sophisticated in his economic analysis, the Franciscan monk Peter John Olivi produced complex and insightful interpretations of the workings of contract, credit, risk, capital, and temporality that advanced economic understanding at the time. But his works were based on very different principles than modern economic theory because they were always written from the standpoint of Christian theology. The medieval historian of economic thought Joel Kaye summarized: "Olivi is most concerned with the question of whether the economic activities of men and the economic contracts they devise can (or cannot) be integrated into a governing reason or *ratio* consistent with God's plan for mankind."[45]

This intimate relationship between religiosity and interpretation in this strand of economic thought can be confirmed by referring back to the network image in figures 1.4 and 1.5. The nagging tone of topic 21 is highly correlated with the supernatural terms of topic 19. The high correlation means the topics have a high rate of co-occurrence in documents. Topic 19 is characterized by the words *god, christ, sin, heaven, hear, lord, hell,* and *wrath.* Representative passages describe the temptations of the devil and the succor of Christ. Another topic frequently mentions *tithes, god, gospel,* and *priests;* another uses the terms *bishop, school,* and *sermon;* another, more hopeful topic often refers to *nature, world, perfect,* and *mankind;* and

43. Robert Ekelund, Robert Hébert, and Robert Tollison have argued that the Catholic Church was more concerned with the status of its debts and loans, and that concerns for just treatment and equality had a stronger material basis than would have been admitted by many of the authors, whose written goals were much loftier. Robert B. Ekelund Jr., Robert F. Hébert, and Robert D. Tollison, "An Economic Model of the Medieval Church: Usury as a Form of Rent Seeking," *Journal of Law, Economics, & Organization* 5, no. 2 (Autumn 1989): 307–31.

44. Thomas Aquinas, *The "De Malo" of Thomas Aquinas,* ed. Brian Davies, trans. Richard Regan (Oxford: Oxford University Press, 2001); and Thomas Aquinas, *Summa theologicae tertia pars* (Venice: B. Stagninus, 1486), Making of the Modern World. Joel Kaye offers a much more in-depth interpretation and analysis of this aspect of Thomas Aquinas's work as well as other medieval scholarship, focusing on changes in the way balance and equity were conceptualized and conceived in this era. Joel Kaye, *A History of Balance, 1250–1375: The Emergence of a New Model of Equilibrium and Its Impact on Thought* (New York: Cambridge University Press, 2014).

45. Kaye, *A History of Balance,* 57.

another easily interpretable topic often uses the terms *usury, lend, law, borrow,* and *gain.* The documents in this theme come from works like Henry Bedel's *A Sermon exhortyng to pitie the poore* (1572), Thomas Lodge's *An Alarum against Usurers* (1584), Thomas Wilson's *A Discovrse vpon vsurie* (1584), Charles Miller's *Three Sermons, Or Homilies, to move compassion towards The Poor and Needy* (1596), and *The Death of Vsvry, or, the Disgrace of Vsvrers* (1594).[46]

The decline of religion in economic literature was an extremely important shift. It is hard to imagine contemporary economics being conducted with the salvation of the immortal soul and the wrath of God as central concerns. But the impact of this shift does not lie only in making economic work seem more contemporary simply because it has dropped the language of sin. When commerce is approached from a moral framework, behaviors are evaluated at the individual level. Just price and equity can be evaluated at a transactional level, exchange by exchange. The analyses are constrained to operate at the micro level, so it is difficult to think about the larger systemic properties and their impact not on the individual but on the larger social group. The decline in Christianity's influence on the literature opened up conceptual space for evaluating commerce and trade in a new way that could engage and conceptualize macrostructural, system-level properties with a new clarity. In addition, the new authors operating from outside of the scholastic tradition engaged in an analysis of economic life for its own sake and through the principles of commercial life itself. Profit and plenty could be considered as goods in themselves and as measures by which to evaluate trade. Such an approach was a far cry from the medieval position that money and commerce were necessary evils to be tolerated and held in abeyance. It also meant that works on commerce and trade were no longer merely collateral projects inquiring into the roots of moral behavior. They were becoming important topics in themselves.

---

46. Henry Bedel, *A Sermon exhortyng to pitie the poore* (London: Iohn Awdely, [1572?]), Making of the Modern World; Thomas Lodge, *An Alarum against Usurers* (London: Imprinted by T. Este for Sampson Clarke, 1584), Making of the Modern World; Thomas Wilson, *A Discovrse vpon vsurie, by waie of Dialogue and oracions, for the better varietie, and more delight of all those, that shall read this treatise* (London: Roger Warde, 1584), Making of the Modern World; Charles Miller, *Three Sermons, Or Homilies, to move compassion towards The Poor and Needy,* set forth by authority, A.D. 1596, new ed. (London: Printed for J. G. F. & J. Rivington, 1842; originally published 1596), Making of the Modern World; and *The Death of Vsvry, or, the Disgrace of Vsvrers* (Cambridge: John Legatt, Printer to the University of Cambridge, 1594), Making of the Modern World.

Although these shifts encouraged advances in economic thinking, there were also potentially negative consequences. It was the religiously inflected works that cared whether commerce was fair, that the poor were not taken advantage of, and that the wealthy did not wield undue power over others by virtue of possessing money alone. These moral concerns disappeared from most of the advanced works on economic matters over the course of the century. They were not to make a significant reappearance until Adam's Smith's failed attempt to reinsert moral concerns into what had become a systematic and empirical investigation into the commercial roots of national advantage.

POLITICS AND THE NATION

As religion declined in the literature, politics dramatically increased. Figure 1.8 presents political topics over the period of interest. Topics 23, 52, and 7 were the most prevalent political topics. Some of the increased interest must have been the result of the tumultuous events occurring in England at the time. For example, topic 52, which can be identified by its singular peak in the 1680s, is characterized by the frequent use of *cromwell, whitelocke, colonel, fairfax,* and *vote*. Its sudden prominence is a result of an increase in published works recounting specific political events with large-scale economic and political consequences and economic antecedents. Topic 7 is concerned with estate transfers and inheritance law. It is, in strict terms, more legal in nature than political. Its increases come in two humps,

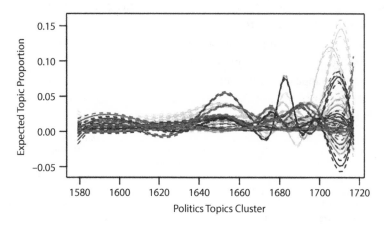

FIGURE 1.8. Political topics over time

Bactrian-style, a smaller one in the 1670s and a larger one in the 1700s. Its increasing prevalence might be seen as a sign of the evolution of English law taking place over this time.

The line that has the second highest peak of the group (peaking at roughly 1705) represents topic 23, which shows a more gradual increase and ultimately a decrease at the end of the period. This topic gives a key understanding of the changing audience and stakes of the emerging new literature on economics. The most common words in this topic are *majesty, council, parliament, lord, high, honor,* and *humble*. A representative passage might include text from a king's proclamation. More tellingly, representative passages also include moments in which the author addresses the Crown directly, as in this instance: "I shall print the aforesaid narrative or deliver it to your majesty's privy council in writing to the end these abuses in the custom house may be prevented for the future; as your majesty please to command me that I will perform and ever rest your majesty's most dutiful and obedient subject as long as I live."[47] The prevalence of this topic reveals the audience for these new works. The authors of these documents are not addressing church fathers or their flock. They are attempting to persuade the holders of legitimate political power of their interpretation and analysis of economic affairs—such as the potentially ruinous impact of corruption and exorbitant fees at customs houses and on overseas trade. Understandably, the language changes after the Glorious Revolution of 1688 and the resulting change in the balance of power among the executive, legislative, and judicial branches of government. Topics characterized by words like *bill, house, lord,* and *committee; law, parliament,* and *england;* and *power, govern,* and *people* became more prominent.

Some of these topics appear in documents that are largely political in nature but have economic consequences. For example, collections of statutes and laws appear. Publications on the history of the laws of England, dating to Henry III and the Magna Carta, are present.[48] One book

47. Thomas Violet, *To the Kings most Excellent Majesty, And to the Lords Spiritual and Temporal; with the Commons Assembled in Parliament. A true Discovery of the great Damage His late Majesty King Charles the First received,* [. . .] (n.p., [1662?]), Making of the Modern World.

48. William Rastell, ed., *A colleccion of all the Statutes (from the begynning of Magna Carta vnto the yere of our Lorde, 1557) whiche were before that yere imprinted.* [. . .] (London, 1559), Making of the Modern World; and *In This Volvme Are Conteyned the Statutes, made and established from the time of Kinge Henrye the thirde, vnto the firste yeare of the reygne of our moste gracious and victorious soveraigne Lord, King Henry the viii* (n.p., 1577), Making of the Modern World.

presented the laws and statutes of Geneva.[49] These laws, of course, included decrees governing economic behavior. A notable political contribution was Thomas Smith's *De Republica Anglorum* (1583). While a significant contribution, Smith's work is concerned largely with the offices of governance and touches only lightly on economic issues. And several works were centrally concerned with various political rivalries, including those with France, Spain, and the Ottoman Empire. To be included, these texts would have also considered the economic consequences of competition and conflict, or used trade conflicts to motivate aggressive acts. But the growing presence of political themes also indicates a sea change in the moral framework of economic writing and thought. Rather than religion, authors promoted their opinions by associating them with national interests. This trend is very much evident in works that were otherwise concerned with the subject of overseas trade.

TRADE, FINANCE, AND COMPANIES

The theme of trade grew over the course of the seventeenth century. Figure 1.9 represents the prevalence of topics dealing with trade, commerce,

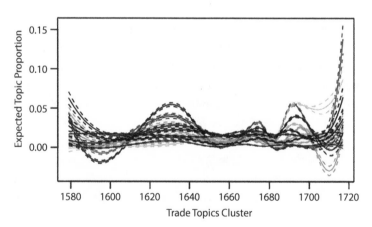

FIGURE 1.9. Trade topics over time

49. Robert Fills, trans., *The Lawes and Statutes of Geneua, as well concerning ecclesiastical discipline, as ciuill regiment, with certeine proclamations duly executed, whereby Gods religion is most purelie mainteined, and their common wealth quieth gouverned* (London: Rouland Hall, 1562), Making of the Modern World.

finance, and company operations—subjects we might now think of as the bread and butter of economics.

A few of the titles of seventeenth-century works on trade convey the extent of nationalist sentiment: *Englands Way To Win Wealth, The Advantages of the Kingdome of England, Englands Interest and Improvement, Englands Wants, England's Interest Asserted, England's Glory, England's Improvement Reviv'd, The Present Interest of England Stated, The Grand Concernments of England Ensured*, and many others with more and less colorful titles that put the welfare of the nation front and center, with economic prosperity as its central pillar.

The interests of England were foregrounded because the authors of these texts were most frequently attempting to persuade political elites to adopt policies favorable to their own commercial interests. As noted earlier, arguing that government policy works well for oneself is not very persuasive for policy makers; arguing that a policy would benefit the whole nation has a much better chance at success. The need to address and persuade government actors led to increasing attention to the political consequences of economic decisions, so that more political topics are interspersed through these texts. Many authors did not stop at using the language of national prosperity; they changed their entire mode of analysis.

The largest of the trade topics was 10, which was characterized by the words *trade, england, nation, foreign, commodity, country*, and *manufacture*. The temporal pattern for this topic is an early increase in the 1620s, just at the time that a famous debate over overseas trade and company privileges erupted in the public sphere, a dip in the 1640s, a rise in the 1670s, a sharp increase in the 1680s, and explosive growth in the 1700s. It is the topic that finishes out the era with the highest prevalence within the group of topics that makes up the larger theme. A representative passage runs this way: "i say this free admission of foreigners to import goods into england will more certainly enrich the nation than can be reasonably expected by the returns of the growths and manufactures of england and our plantations in foreign trade."[50] As can be surmised, these documents frequently addressed the subject of tariffs, particularly the relationship of a trade free of tariffs to

---

50. Roger Coke, *England's Improvements. In Two Parts* (London: Printed by J. C. for Henry Brome, 1675), Making of the Modern World.

the economic prosperity of the nation. In other words, early formulations of free trade theory make their appearance here. Topic 11, characterized by the words *company, interest, nation, english, design,* and *trade,* shows a similar meteoric ascent after the 1680s. It is represented by the line that finishes with the second highest prevalence.

The once common trade topics that declined over time included topic 50, characterized by the frequent use of the words *money, men, land, sell, interest,* and *price,* and topic 44, characterized by the words *pound, shill, pence, every,* and *worth.* Both these topics have more in common with the medieval model of individual-level commerce than the new formulations framing overseas trade in systemic terms and thinking through the national-level implications. These two topics had the highest prevalence at the onset of the period, in 1580.

Works fitting into the new rhetorical style had some diversity. It was rare, but female voices did enter the corpus. The "Shee-citizens" of London published a remonstrance in 1647 calling for free trade. Their goal was to end the exclusion of women from merchandising, citing the problems created by the lack of men left alive in the wake of the English Civil War.[51] The idea of a paper currency began to take root midcentury. *The Trades-Man's Jewel* (1650) and *The Key of Wealth* (1650) advocated for the creation of a paper currency backed by a land bank.[52] These texts often included sophisticated analyses of the intrinsic value of gold, the value of currency, and the relationships among price, supply, the number of traders, and the rate of trade.[53] The Great Fire swept London in 1666, destroying most of the city. In its wake, tracts devoted to insurance began to appear in small numbers. And the first publication on advertising, "observing how practical and advantagious to trade and business," appeared in 1675.

51. *A Remonstrance of the Shee-Citizens of London* ([London?], 1647), Early English Books Online.

52. William Potter, *The Key of Wealth: Or, A new Way, for Improving of Trade: Lawfull, Easie, Safe and Effectuall: Shewing how A few Tradesmen agreeing together, may (borrow wherewith to) double their Stocks, and the increase thereof, [. . .]* (London: R. A., 1650), Making of the Modern World; and William Potter, *The Trades-Man's Jewel: or A safe, easie, speedy and effectual Means, for the incredible advancement of Trade, And Multiplication of Riches; shewing How men of Indifferent Estates, may abundantly increase [. . .]* (London: Edward Husband and John Field, Printers to the Parliament of England, 1650), Making of the Modern World.

53. Potter, *The Key of Wealth*; and Potter, *The Trades-Man's Jewel.*

TRAVEL

A related theme with a mixed trajectory was travel. Travel was closely related to trade at this time. Tourism was, in practical terms, nonexistent. Only a relatively narrow part of the early modern population traveled in any significant way, and those who did travel were mainly overseas merchants. To those engaged in overseas trade, travelogues were an invaluable source of information on where markets were located, when they were open, what goods were for sale, which currencies were accepted, what taxes and tariffs were in place, and what other means of informally greasing the wheels of commerce might be effective in that region or port.

The passage most representative of topic 16, a prevalent travel topic located at the center of the cluster, was written by one of the most famous travelers in the history of European exploration. It describes a charming "little city whose situation the streams that water it the good fruits that grow there and particularly the excellent wine which it affords render a most pleasant mansion"[54]—just the place a merchant might like to purposefully include on his voyage.

Short descriptions and pages of financial details are copiously recorded in Lewes Roberts's exemplary and weighty 721-page tome, *The Marchants Mappe of Commerce* (1638).[55] As was the style at the time, the subtitle is both extremely long and informative:

> Wherein the Universal Manner and Matter of Trade is Compendiously Handled. The Standard and Current Coins of Sundry Princes observed. The Real and Imaginary Coins of Accounts and Exchanges expressed. The Natural and Artificial Commodities of all Countreys for Transportation declared. The *Weights* and Measures of all Eminent *Cities* and *Townes* of Traffick, collected and reduced one into another; and all to the *Meridian* of *Commerce* practiced in the Famous City of London.

---

54. John Baptista Tavernier, *The Six Voyages of John Baptista Tavernier, Baron of Aubonne; Through Turky, into Persia and the East-Indies, For the space of Forty Years. [. . .] To which is added, A new Description of the Seraglio*, trans. J. P. (London: Printed by William Godbid, for Robert Littlebury, 1677), Early English Books Online.

55. Lewes Roberts, *The Marchants Mappe of Commerce, wherein The Universall Manner and Matter of Trade is compendiously handled. [. . .]* ([London, 1638?]), Making of the Modern World.

Roberts tells us that in the seventeenth century, African currencies included shells, gold sand, iron, and salt-filled cakes. In Congo, male and female shellfishes were traded for gold. In Melinda, little balls of glass were exchanged for goods. In Cathay (China), something even more exotic and unheard of was in use: a kind of stamped paper.[56] He also tells us of the currency exchange rates in Seville, where exchange was based on the ducat, equal to 375 Marvedies, which was payable at a rate of 5 percent, which served as salary for the Banco. If you asked for payments in Ducato de Oro, you would be paid in full, but if you asked for payments in Carlins, you would lose between ½ and ¼ percent.[57] He goes into remarkable detail in describing the different systems of weights and measures, the rates of currency exchange, the availability of banks, assurances, and capital loans, and all the various fees and costs embedded in these types of exchange.

Earlier works were often more local in ambition. William Lambarde's *A Perambulation of Kent* described the nature of the soil, the woods of the forests, the fruits of the harvest, and the employment of the people.[58] Richard Verstegan's *The Post of the World* (1576) described Western Europe: "With their trade and traficke, with the wayes and distance of myles, from country to country, with the true and perfect knowledge of the Coynes, the places of their Mynts: with al their Martes and Fayres."[59] Each provided valuable commercial information. Many such books addressed their merchant readership directly in forewords.

Figure 1.10 presents the prevalence of travels topics over time. The ten topics frequently contain words like *island, north, west,* and *sea; ship, captain,* and *sail; persian, mosque,* and *basha;* and even *dance, music, kiss,* and *arm.* There is no clear trend. The most prevalent travel topic in the early sixteenth century and the most prevalent travel topic in the early eighteenth differ mainly in their regional focus: the first describes the Middle East and the second, the Indian subcontinent. The notable uptick in travel reprints after 1710 likely reflects a time when England came to more fully appreciate

56. Roberts, *Marchants Mappe,* 16.

57. Roberts, *Marchants Mappe,* 162.

58. William Lambarde, *A Perambulation of Kent: Conteining the Description, Hystorie, and Customes of That Shire* (Chatham, UK: Printed by W. Burrill; London: Published by Baldwin, Cradock, and Joy, 1826; originally written 1570; first published 1576), Making of the Modern World.

59. Richard Verstegan, *The Post of the World: Wherein is contayned the antiquities and originall of the most famous Cities in Europe* (London: Thomas East, [1576?]), Making of the Modern World.

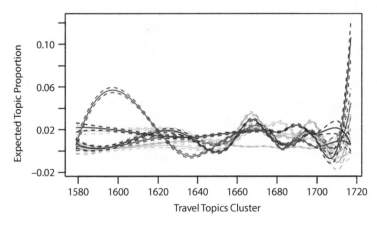

FIGURE 1.10. Travel topics over time

its newly powerful international situation. Publications containing detailed information about foreign markets continued to occupy an important position for at least another century. William Milburn's two-volume *Oriental Commerce*, for example, came out in 1813.[60]

PUBLICATIONS OVER TIME

Shifts in topics were related to shifts in publication patterns. To clarify how this trend is different from what has already been presented, consider that the topic model analyzes documents, which are small sections of books. Books are generally too long for a topic model to make sense of because there is too much co-occurrence of words. Additionally, the publications in the corpus vary greatly in length, making comparisons using a computational approach even more difficult. As noted earlier, the topic model applied here uses five-hundred-word overlapping chunks of publications for analysis. Latent Dirichlet Allocation, the topic modeling approach used, assumes that documents contain a small number of topics, but also assumes that they are usually composed of more than one topic. It follows that publications, which could be many hundreds of documents or thousands of words long, could contain a large number of topics. And they certainly did.

60. William Milburn, *Oriental Commerce; containing A Geographical Description of the principal places in The East Indies, China, and Japan, [. . .]; also, The Rise and Progress of the Trade of the various European nations with the Eastern world* (London: Printed for the Author, and published by Black, Parry, 1813), Making of the Modern World.

It is also true that books, though they may touch on many topics in the course of their narrative, are generally about one larger subject. Thomas Tusser's books might touch upon religion or travel at different points, but *Fiue hundreth pointes of good husbandry* is a text primarily about husbandry. Analysis at the publication level is less fine-grained than topic modeling for thinking about what interested the authors and consumers of texts, but it still presents an important part of the larger picture. Considering the subjects of books provides both corroboration of the trends evident in the results of the topic model and additional contextual information that can help make sense of the modeling results.

A simple count of the number of texts on economic topics published annually, presented in figure 1.11, gives a sense of the transformation that took place in the seventeenth century. The figure also includes the

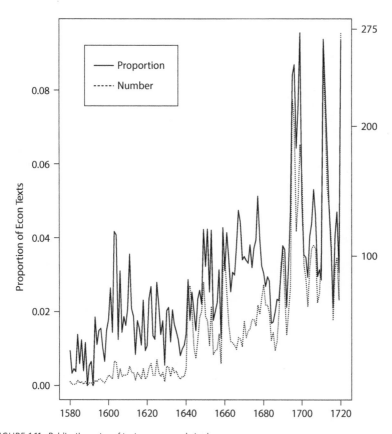

FIGURE 1.11. Publication rates of texts on economic topics

proportion of economic texts relative to all texts published in England and Scotland. The absolute count is represented by the stippled line, linked to the right axis, and the proportion is represented by the solid line, linked to the left axis. Publication rates pick up noticeably in the early 1600s, jump suddenly in 1640, and skyrocket in the 1690s. Readers will quickly note that big upticks occur around or near the dramatic political events then unfolding in England. Their relationship to the development of the new literature in economics will be discussed in more detail in later chapters.

Figure 1.12 represents subtopics within the economic literature and how they varied over time. It is a grouped histogram that allows for comparisons among the five subtopics, or themes, for seven different twenty-year periods. Different markings represent the different themes, which are presented

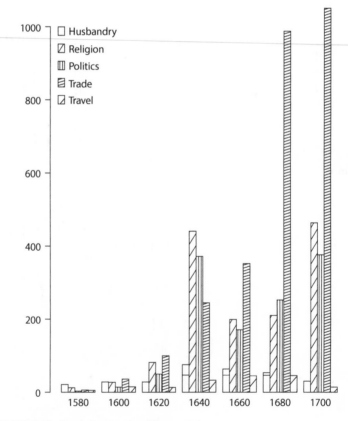

FIGURE 1.12. Publications by type over twenty-year periods

in the same order in the plot as they are listed in the legend. The publications were coded prior to undertaking the topic modeling, but very similar subject areas arose in that round of analysis as well. For ease of comparison and presentation, I collapsed some of the smaller categories into the five themes that I used to organize interpretation of the topic models. Religion counts combine subject areas I originally coded as "religious," "usury," and "the poor." In coding books, I originally used the category "husbandry," but this header also includes works coded as "agriculture/commons." Travel includes only publications coded under that title. Politics is more diverse, including works coded as "political," "colonies," "laws/statutes," "taxation," and "public debt." Trade includes works coded as "trade," "company/charters/patents," and "finance/bullion." A significant proportion of the texts fell into more than one of the finer-grained categories, while some did not fall into any of these broader currents of thought and instead addressed idiosyncratic topics. Table 1.1 provides a summary of the results of coding publications by subject area.

As can be seen from the table and the figure, the pattern is slightly—but not markedly—different for publications as opposed to the topics contained within those publications. Books on husbandry and travel decline. Religion has a brief zenith in the Civil War era of 1640 to 1659, but otherwise

TABLE 1.1
Publications by subject

	Religion	Husbandry	Politics	Travel	Trade	Total
1580–99	12	21	3	5	6	47
	(25.5%)	(44.7%)	(6.4%)	(10.6%)	(12.8%)	(100%)
1600–19	27	28	14	15	36	120
	(22.5%)	(23.3%)	(11.7%)	(12.5%)	(30%)	(100%)
1620–39	82	28	50	13	100	273
	(30%)	(10.2%)	(18.3%)	(4.8%)	(36.6%)	(100%)
1640–59	441	76	372	33	245	1167
	(37.8%)	(6.5%)	(31.9%)	(2.8%)	(20.9%)	(100%)
1660–79	199	64	171	45	352	831
	(23.9%)	(7.7%)	(20.6%)	(5.4%)	(42.4%)	(100%)
1680–99	210	54	253	46	988	1551
	(13.5%)	(3.5%)	(16.3%)	(3%)	(63.7%)	(100%)
1700–20	464	30	376	14	1051	1935
	(24%)	(1.6%)	(19.4%)	(.7%)	(54.3%)	(100%)

fluctuates between 20 and 30 percent for most of the period, with a slight cumulative decline over the last forty years. Politics similarly zigs and zags over the twenty-year segments, but shows a cumulative increase over time. The subject that shows the clearest increase is trade, which increases from 10 percent in the first full twenty-year period to well over 50 percent in the first decades of the eighteenth century. We can conclude that works on trade increased, and the changing prevalence of topics indicates that the way that people talked about trade altered significantly.

CONCLUSION

The seventeenth century was a major turning point for economic thought. Works changed dramatically from 1580 to 1720 along quantitative and qualitative dimensions. The increase in volume is striking in itself. The rate of publication for economic works grew more than a hundredfold from the sixteenth to the eighteenth centuries. The kinds of works and the topics that received the most attention in those works also changed. Religion and morality became less prevalent. Centering ideas around the household economy declined in importance. England's engagement with overseas was expanding rapidly, and public attention to topics that related to trade—such as company affairs, finance, and industry—was growing. The number of publications devoted to these subjects grew rapidly. While the general tide of works turned toward trade and politics, usury and poverty did not entirely disappear from the corpus. Instead, their numbers failed to increase. As publication rates rose, they began to take up smaller and smaller sections of the larger whole.

The transformation that occurred was not the product of any one person's influence. It was not confined to a few works of exceptional brilliance. Both renowned and obscure texts were drawing from new and different tropes. Insightful and mediocre texts began to frame their arguments in new ways. One of the interesting changes was the increase in trade publications and the concurrent increase in political topics within those trade publications. This tendency helps to explain why political topics seem to have had the greatest increase in prevalence, but trade books had the greatest increase in publication rates. Toward the end of the seventeenth century, trade matters were increasingly framed in political terms.

Mercantilism is known, for good reason, as the era of power and plenty, so the combination of economic concerns and nationalist sentiment should come as no surprise. What does challenge conventional wisdom is the timing. The onset of the era of mercantilism is usually dated to the 1500s or earlier, the corpus modeling shows that the combination of political and economic rhetoric began to dominate the larger discourse much later than this. Indeed, the most rapid increase in political topics takes place when the ideas that have been used to characterize mercantilism—such as unilateralism, corporatism, and bullionism—were being replaced by the free trade theories typical of classical economics. It would be remiss not to note the impact of the Civil War and the Glorious Revolution on these patterns, but it is also clear that consideration of the national impact of economic policies and practices became a standard refrain in public discourse at the inflection point when economic thought began to shed its medieval trappings.

The framework of political gains and national prosperity came at the expense of religious and moral valuations of economic behaviors. It may seem so natural now to think of economics in terms of GDP that it is hard to imagine how else commerce and trade might be evaluated. But this was not the lens applied in the medieval era. Then, trade, commerce, and money were commonly considered necessary evils. Money was a corrupting influence. Therefore, contact with money, through trade, finance, and industry, had to be carefully monitored by the church in order to reduce the potential damage to men's and women's souls. While it is true that the church itself may have been interested in regulating commerce to maximize its own wealth,[61] the public-facing side clearly presented itself as concerned with the moral impact on the human soul. The problem with usury was ultimately not about the impact of high interest rates on monetary circulation. In this framework, the problem with usury was that it was a sin.

One of the most significant consequences of the shift from this Christian moral theological framework was the shift away from the individual as the unit of analysis toward the nation. It seems very likely that the new emphasis on group outcomes, in the form of national prosperity, encouraged a system-level mindset that helped solidify and popularize concepts like "the system of trade" or, more pointedly, "the economy." These conceptions also encouraged the possibility of collecting together sets of lawlike

---

61. Ekelund, Hébert, and Tollison, "An Economic Model."

observations about economic behavior that began to underpin new beliefs about the benefits of free trade. And without the moral legitimacy provided by citing church doctrine or the work of Aristotle, authors had to invent new means of persuading their audience, which in this new literature often meant drawing upon their actual experience of trade. The result was a new injection of empiricism into the work.

While significant intellectual gains were made possible by refocusing inquiry from the soul to the nation, there were also costs. Just-price debates addressed whether exchange was fair for both parties. The new literature on the nation was not as concerned with this question. More important in the new framework was the question of whether this exchange contributed to the prosperity of all. This shift made it possible to conceive of arguments in which the impoverishment or even exploitation of a subset of the nation contributes to the larger prosperity of the whole. The principle of equity in exchange, which was one of the few protections for the poor and laboring classes, was diminished.

This about-face is hard to understand through internal discursive change alone. It seems unlikely that the logic of the existing discourse could have produced such a dramatic shift in the relevant moral framing of arguments. The economic works of the seventeenth century were so fundamentally different from medieval scholarship that it is hard to imagine how they could have evolved naturally from a focus on equity in exchange to a nationalistic and exclusionary discourse centered on national prosperity. The underlying values and central object of analysis were very different. These differences suggest that some external force or condition might have been responsible. The next chapter looks more closely at a smaller number of texts in order to begin to consider what external factors may have been involved in producing this change.

Chapter Two

TRANSFORMATIVE DEBATES

Many of the important works published in the seventeenth century were written in close dialogue with one another. In twenty-first-century academic publishing, writing a work in dialogue with another often signals respect for the earlier contribution—an acknowledgment of its influence and the importance of its contribution. In the seventeenth century, things were less polite. A large number of books were written in heated response to other publications. Vicious criticism was common, and few authors were above name-calling. Flurries of pamphlets and books broke out around different issues, Acts of Parliament, extensions of privileges, or company actions. Digging into the contexts and contents of these debates provides essential insights into both the causes and consequences of the transformation that took place between 1580 and 1720.

BULLIONISM AND THE BALANCE OF TRADE

Three authors, in particular, engaged in highly contentious and very public argument that had long-lasting significance. The key interlocutors were Gerard de Malynes, Edward Misselden, and Thomas Mun. Together they published a series of works in the early 1620s debating the export of bullion and the workings of overseas trade that was to influence economic theory for decades, if not centuries.[1]

In order to understand the importance of this debate to economic thought, it is useful to begin with a brief overview of the oldest of the three authors: Gerard de Malynes (fl. 1586–1641). Malynes was an independent merchant and a master of the mint. The earliest details of his biography indicate that he would have a talent for financial thought. Of English descent, he was born in Antwerp. His father, who was also an officer of the mint, returned to England in the 1560s in response to the call of Queen Elizabeth I for assistance in revaluing English currency under the direction of Sir Thomas Gresham. Malynes was a person of note, a prolific, learned, and well-respected author, and a slightly less successful merchant with a history of troubled ventures. In 1586 he was appointed to the position of trade commissioner of Antwerp, and "the next year he was back in England, buying pearls from Sir Francis Drake, and discussing mining proposals with Sir Walter Raleigh."[2] Malynes's fortunes took a serious turn for the worse after 1610, when he got involved with a coinage scheme that revolved around introducing a new copper farthing into common circulation. After his partner William Cockayne left the venture, Malynes found himself in possession of a great deal of worthless farthings and a continuing legal obligation to exchange those worthless farthings for silver coins—at great personal loss. Ultimately this situation drained Malynes of wealth and in 1619 landed him in prison for failure to repay debts.[3] Impressively, he was able to recover from this personal tragedy to the extent that by 1622 he was again advising the Crown and publishing new popular tracts on commerce.

As the last real medievalist in English economic thought, Malynes carried the torch of scholasticism to its sputtering end. His immersion in the problems and obsessions of this earlier era is most evident in *Saint George For England, Allegorically described* (1601).[4] In this narrative, an island of surpassing beauty, sweetness, and fecundity is ravaged by a foul beast. This

1. Mark Blaug, *The Early Mercantilists: Thomas Mun (1571–1641), Edward Misselden (1608–1634), Gerard de Malynes (1586–1623)* (Aldershot, UK: Elgar, 1991).

2. E. A. J. Johnson, "Gerard De Malynes and the Theory of the Foreign Exchanges," *American Economic Review* 23, no. 3 (September 1933): 443.

3. E. A. J. Johnson, "Gerard De Malynes."

4. Gerard de Malynes, *Saint George For England, Allegorically described* (London: Imprinted by Richard Field for William Tymme Stationer, 1601), Making of the Modern World.

dragon destroys trust, sympathy, virtue, and commerce. In an unusual turn for a mythical beast, it also turns overseas trade and finance into instruments that work against the interests of the citizens.

> By the meanes of his taile he maintaineth a league with forreine nations, and causeth them to serve his turne, by bringing in superfluous commodities at a deare rate, and they to feede uppon our native soile, to the common-wealthes destruction. He doth falsifie our weight and measure, and bringeth thereby inequality to our over-great hindrace, making of money a merchandize. He carieth out our treasure in bullion and money, empovershing our common-weale, in giving us chalk for cheese, making us like unto Aesops dog, going over a bridge to snatch at the shadow of the flesh, loosing the flesh itself.[5]

The dragon of the allegory is usury, which Malynes faults with a litany of social, moral, and economic woes over the course of his eighty-page text. Importantly, Malynes draws a link between usury and overseas trade. Usurers are blamed for the overvaluation of foreign goods, the consumption of luxury goods, false valuations of currency, and an imbalance in trade between England and its overseas trading partners that impoverishes the commonwealth.

This line of thought continues in *A Treatise of the Canker of Englands Common wealth*, also published in 1601.[6] Here Malynes takes aim at foreign exchange merchants. Beginning with the fact that England has no mines of gold and silver, Malynes argues that all specie in the country must be supplied through overseas trade. He then deduces from this proposition that the import and export of bullion in overseas trade determine the domestic supply of bullion and currency and that increases in the amount of bullion in circulation raise prices. On the one hand, this is a serious and logically grounded discussion of specie flow, price formation, and trade. Malynes also builds an empirical argument by including detailed lists of import and export prices for different commodities in the East Indies trade. On the other hand, Malynes concludes his argument by blaming England's economic woes on foreign merchants whom he believed were manipulating

---

5. Malynes, *Saint George For England*, 43.
6. Gerard de Malynes, *A Treatise of the Canker of Englands Common wealth* (London: Imprinted by Richard Field for William Iohnes printer, 1601), Making of the Modern World.

the currency exchange. The connection between moral behavior and economic outcomes that Malynes assumes ends up constraining his ability to logically investigate the problem. As in *Saint George For England*, bad outcomes are produced by bad people—be they usurers or foreign exchange merchants. The moralizing dimension, the focus on the evils of capital markets, and the assumption that the intentions of individuals, rather than the interactions of a commercial system, are causing the outcomes are all consistent with scholastic themes and moral framing.

E. A. J. Johnson wrote that Malynes's "stubborn dogmatism was paradoxically his chief virtue because it compelled his opponents to formulate their economic doctrines, and he must be given credit for crystallizing the views of a group of merchants who dissented from his oversimplified mediaevalism."[7] In this interpretation, Johnson repeats a common trope in the history of economic thought: the idea that wrongly held views necessarily call forth more accurate views.

Medieval, scholastic thought had persisted for quite some time without calling up noteworthy corrections or variations. However, a new perspective did arise in the 1620s that posed a significant challenge to scholastic economic doctrine. The circumstances through which Malynes's main interlocutors came to engage with him in the 1620s debate shed considerable light on the kinds of conditions necessary to produce a dramatic cultural shift in how people thought about economic matters. As will become clear, material interests and their relationship to the chartered companies played a large role in leading Malynes's opponents to crystallize their new perspective on these old issues.

While Malynes was encountering personal financial difficulties, England was heading toward a pronounced trade depression. The 1620s marked the beginning of a serious economic downturn, particularly pronounced in the cloth trade. The troubles were so widespread and so pronounced that James I took the unusual step in 1621 of calling to order a special commission on trade, which was to meet from 1622 to 1623. It was in this commission that Malynes encountered Thomas Mun.

Unlike Malynes, Mun was not known as a man of letters. His reputation was instead as a staid, sober, and plainspoken merchant. He wrote in straightforward prose devoid of Malynes's allegorical flourishes, the dialogic

7. E. A. J. Johnson, "Gerard De Malynes," 455.

structure of earlier works, and the literary allusions that populated other texts. Little is known of his education. Max Beer described him as "a merchant pure and simple, with no claim to scholarship."[8] Mun's father was a member of the Worshipful Company of Mercers, and Mun himself became a Mercer in 1596. He was very successful, amassed a great fortune, and was elected a director of the East India Company in 1615. It was in this role as the director of the East India Company that Mun found himself writing and publishing *A Discovrse of Trade, From England vnto the East-Indies.*[9]

General arguments about the evils of monopoly had been present for some time, but the East India Company was under a more immediate threat in the 1620s. The bullionist tenor of the time led to a widespread belief that the export of silver overseas was reducing the wealth of the nation, depressing the availability of currency, and causing prices to rise to unnatural heights. The East India Company, along with the Eastland Company, funded their trade by exporting bullion to buy goods in areas that lacked demand for English products. They were threatened by attempts to regulate foreign capital markets and under active attack by bullionists who blamed the companies for the dire economic circumstances of the country. As Mun indicated in the text, he wrote the tract to address the public outcry against the East India Company's practice of exporting bullion to buy goods in Asia.[10]

In doing so, Mun was following in the footsteps of other prominent company merchants. John Wheeler, a secretary of the Merchant Adventurers, is more properly credited with creating this new type of public defense. In 1601, Wheeler published *A Treatise of Commerce*, a lengthy and explicit defense of the practices of the Company of Merchant Adventurers.[11] He was responding to an intensification of pressure and criticism levied against the company over the course of the preceding decade. In the 1590s,

8. Max Beer, *Early British Economics from the XIIIth to the Middle of the XVIIIth Century* (London: George Allen & Unwin, 1938), 147.

9. Thomas Mun, *A Discovrse of Trade, From England vnto the East-Indies: Answering to diuerse Obiections which are vsvally made against the same* (London: Printed by Nicholas Okes for John Pyper, 1621), Making of the Modern World.

10. Mun, *A Discovrse of Trade*, 4.

11. John Wheeler, *A Treatise of Commerce, Wherein Are Shewed the Commodies Arising by a Wel Ordered, and Rvled Trade, Such as that of the Socieitie of Merchantes Adventurers is proved to bee, [. . .]* (Middleburgh: Richard Schilders, Printer to the States of Zeland, 1601), Making of the Modern World.

the Merchant Adventurers had beaten out the Hanseatic League and the Merchants of the Staple to become the most significant overseas trading organization operating in England. The Merchant Adventurers were a regulated company that specialized in the export of cloth. Because of their prominence, they were principally held to blame when trade decreased and depression struck. And there was reason to lay some blame at their feet.

In an attempt to drive up their profits in the face of the decreasing prospects of the 1590s, the company began to centralize their operations by restricting cloth markets to a few small English ports along the model of a staple market. These restrictions further depressed trade by restricting avenues for exchange. This prompted criticism from those who produced and sold the cloth domestically, who now had fewer options to vent their goods. It also angered members within the company itself, who quickly saw that such restrictions allowed interlopers to replace regular company operations.[12] Members of the company began to revolt by trading in restricted areas.[13] The company censured its member-interlopers in an internal memorandum.[14] Thomas Milles (c. 1550–1627), a customs officer, criticized the Merchant Adventurers and their role in these events in the book *The Cvstvmers Apology* (1599).[15] In short, the entire conflict spiraled out of control and gained the attention of Parliament, which began to reconsider the benefits of according monopoly privileges to chartered companies.

John Wheeler's defense revolved around an argument common to the time and to those who would defend monopoly privileges. His position was that beneficial trade had to be just and well-ordered and that company management supplied the necessary order. Wheeler was an advocate of the system of corporate governance developed under the Tudors. In an era in which there was an inherent distrust of merchants and their activities, there was widespread agreement that the selfish commercial pursuits of individual merchants had to be curbed and controlled in order for their activities to benefit the commonweal. The state did not have the capacity to

---

12. George Burton Hotchkiss, introduction to *A Treatise of Commerce*, by John Wheeler (Clark, NJ: Lawbook Exchange, 2004), 3–120.

13. Hotchkiss, introduction, 51.

14. Hotchkiss, introduction, 52.

15. Thomas Milles, *The Cvstvmers Apology. That is to say, A general Asnwere to Informers of all sortes, and their iniurouis complaints, against the honest reputation of the Collectors of her Maiesties Cvstvmes, specially in the Ovt-Portes of this Realme. [. . .]* ([London?], 1599), Making of the Modern World.

effectively control merchants' activities, and the companies were a compromise, a state-sanctioned means of coordinating merchant activity in order to curb competition between English merchants. Whether this lofty aspiration was indeed the motivation driving the formation of chartered companies and the widespread assignment of monopoly privileges under Queen Elizabeth I, or whether the practice was instead a venal attempt to increase state coffers, is less clear, but the rhetoric was an accepted and common mode of argumentation until at least the mid-century.

Wheeler's treatise does not make the same contributions as either Malynes or Mun to understanding the dynamics of specie flow or other principles of economic life under consideration in the period. It does, however, include a notable passage that should sound eerily familiar to readers of *The Wealth of Nations*: "For there is nothing in the world so ordinarie, and naturall unto men, as to contract, truck, merchandise, and trafficque one with an other, so that it is almost unpossible for three persons to converse together two houres, but they wil fall into talke of one bargaine or another."[16] The importance of Wheeler's work lay in its new mode of presentation. It was a published defense of the Merchant Adventurers meant to sway public opinion in their favor and thereby win the support of the Crown and Privy Council. The debate between Milles and Wheeler was an early instance of the heated arguments among merchants, excise officers, and financiers over the benefits and harms of chartered companies. As may be clear from the passage, so similar to Adam Smith's famous line on the "propensity to truck, barter, and exchange,"[17] the works were not published in a vacuum. They were read by others. Most important, they were read by people, Smith and his predecessors, who began to attempt building up a systematic picture of economic life. When Mun published *A Discovrse of Trade*, he was not only responding to specific circumstances but also drawing from and extending what was rapidly becoming an established genre of works on trade—largely informed by the experiences and controversies that swirled around the great chartered companies.

Mun began *A Discovrse of Trade* by responding to four common objections to overseas trade that had appeared in prior published work. This approach was common and usually produced a scattershot

16. Wheeler, *A Treatise of Commerce*, 6.
17. Adam Smith, *The Wealth of Nations* (New York: Bantam Classics, 2003; first published 1776).

of uncoordinated points. Mun, uncharacteristically for the time, managed to weave together a coherent argument out of his responses. The very first sentence directs the reader to the problem of national prosperity: "THe trade of Merchandize, is not onely that laudable practize whereby the entercourse of Nations is so worthily performed, but also (as I may terme it) the very Touchstone of a kingdomes prosperitie."[18] Mun argued that the East India Company brought goods into England at a lower price than if they had been passed along through the Levant route, thus both keeping silver out of the hands of the "infidels"—meaning the Turkish merchants and rulers who controlled that route—and lowering costs for English consumers. He noted that the trade encouraged the growth of shipping and employment among mariners. And he seems to have read Malynes previous works and acknowledged problems related to the abuse of currency exchange.

Mun's most important contribution in this text, however, was the way he advocated for a more general accounting for the losses and benefits incurred by England as a whole in the East India Company trade. He argued that the bullion used by the English East India Company was not lost but instead transmuted into goods, which were then exchanged for more bullion through the re-export trade. In an attempt to rebut the naïve bullionism of the day that placed value in the metallic properties of gold and silver, he wrote "money is the prize of wares, and wares are the proper use of money; so their Coherence is unseparable."[19] The value to the nation was doubly increased by this re-export trade, he argued, because it gained in the profits derived from the trade of Asian goods to other European nations and through the customs, imposts, and duties paid by the company to the state. He admonished critics to consider the overall balance of trade: "when the value of our commodyties exported doth overballance the worth of all those forraigne wares which are imported and consumed in this kingdome, then the remaynder of our stock which is sent forth, must of necessitie returne to us in Treasure."[20] Mun's formulation of the importance of the balance of trade was quickly picked up and echoed by authors for decades to come.

18. Mun, *A Discovrse of Trade*, 1.
19. Mun, *A Discovrse of Trade*, 26.
20. Mun, *A Discovrse of Trade*, 27.

A Discovrse of Trade was not just an extension of the new literature on commerce and trade; it was an improvement. Absent were the gratuitous allegations touching on the moral character of critics or merchants. In their place were facts and figures that Mun carefully marshaled to his side, including a table of the amount of spice, indigo, and silk bought for European markets in Aleppo, a comparison of the price of goods in the East and in England, a tally of the number of ships sent out by the East India Company, and a historical chart of the prices of spice and indigo. Even so, Mun's thinking advanced significantly over the next decade. His progress appears to have been closely tied to his experiences on the trade committee, which led him to a confrontation with Malynes and his more traditionally bound, scholastically inflected views on trade.

Mun's *Discovrse* reportedly played a role in his appointment to the king's Committee on Trade, which included many notable figures such as Viscount Mandeville, the Earl of Northampton, Sir Robert Cotton, and Dudley Digges.[21] The committee of 1622 had two parts, one led by Mun and one led by Malynes. The close quarters of the committee led to heated debates between Mun and Malynes, and it seems likely that Mun's opposition to Malynes solidified into a more systematic line of thought through the experience of repeatedly confronting him. The path through which this new position found expression in print was circuitous.

The first publication to arise out of the experiences of the committee was not the work of Mun, but instead of his associate Edward Misselden. Misselden nevertheless appears to have been deeply influenced by Muns's views and the *Discovrse*. He praised both Mun and Digges in his work.[22] Misselden was a deputy governor of the Merchant Adventurers and had done occasional work for the East India Company. He was hired by the East India Company in 1623 and appears to have been angling for that position while serving on the trade committee and writing his influential tract. It was the year before, in 1622, that Misselden published *Free Trade. Or, The Meanes to Make Trade Florish*. Misselden had a more literary bent than Mun. Beer reports that he "could quote Greek and Latin, Hebrew and

21. Beer, *British Economics*, 131–32.

22. Edward Misselden, *Free Trade. Or, The Meanes to Make Trade Florish. Wherein, The Causes of the Decay of Trade in this Kingdome, are discouered: And the Remedies also to remooue the same, are represented*, 2nd ed. (London: Printed by Iohn Legatt, for Simon Waterson, 1622), Making of the Modern World.

Rabbinic, and he took pleasure in displaying the jewels of his astonishingly wide scholarship on the foil of his opponent's alleged ignorance."[23] His work did have a vicious thread that was evident in his debates with Malynes over the years.

Misselden began with a premise similar to Mun's, that the path to domestic prosperity lay through a flourishing overseas trade. This premise happened to align with the business interests of the chartered companies with which Misselden was associated: the Merchant Adventurers and the East India Company. Misselden, however, also accepted the importance of domestically produced manufactures. In his florid prose, he referred to clothing and drapery made in England as the "Gold of our Ophir, the Milke & Hony of our Canaan, the Indies of England," which not only brought economic prosperity but also knit the subjects of the kingdom together into society itself.[24] He shared the bullionist concern for the loss and gain of gold and silver: "Money is the vitall spirit of trade, and if the Spirits faile, needes must the Body faint."[25] He attacked usury as detrimental to economic growth and even concurred that the undervaluation of coin in England was one of the central causes of the depression the nation then faced. And he believed that trade with European countries was fundamentally different from trade outside of Europe because trade with Christian countries remained within "the Circle of Christendome" which "commeth and goeth, and whirleth about."[26] In many ways he still shared, or at least drew from, what we would now think of as a medieval economic worldview.

Misselden was also an advocate of the philosophy of corporate governance, espoused earlier by Wheeler, though he was not necessarily consistent in how he deployed the idea. He both contested whether the chartered companies truly constituted monopolies and concluded that the "government and order" provided by the companies over their specific branches of trade more than made up in benefits for the loss of liberty their privileges entailed. "Trade without Order and Government, are like unto men, that makes Holes in the bottom of that Ship, wherein themselves are Passengers."[27]

23. Beer, *British Economics*, 147.
24. Misselden, *Free Trade*, 40.
25. Misselden, *Free Trade*, 28.
26. Misselden, *Free Trade*, 19.
27. Misselden, *Free Trade*, 84–85.

In much of this Misselden reads like an early mercantilist, not so different from Malynes in his adherence to scholastic ideas and assumptions. The central difference arose when Misselden argued that the secondary consequences of the East India Company trade more than made up for their export of bullion and when he dismissed Malynes's concern for the regulation of foreign exchange. As noted earlier, Malynes blamed individuals for corrupting the terms of exchange and was therefore in support of strong government regulation in this area. The rift between the two authors on these issues was to become more pronounced in continued iterations of the argument.

Malynes quickly published a response to Misselden, accusing him of neglecting one of the primary components of trade: "the Mystery of Exchange."[28] This was in *The Maintenance of Free Trade*, which had been intended as an accompaniment to a text that Malynes had been working on for some time but was published in the same year, *Consuetudo, Vel, Lex Mercatoria, or The Ancient Law-Merchant* (1622).[29] *Lex Mercatoria* was a compilation of ancient laws and documents that contributed to the debate over the role of the state in the development of rules of commerce. Malynes appears to have subtly altered *The Maintenance of Free Trade* to address Misselden's text, subtitling it "An Answer to a Treatise of Free Trade." Consistent with his previous work, Malynes identifies the root cause of depression in the abuse of exchange.[30] He criticizes Misselden for ignoring this crucial component of the system of trade. He describes its role in organic terms, "as the Liver (Money) doth minister Spirits to the heart (Commodities,) and the heart to the Braine (Exchange:) so doth the Brayne exchange minister to the whole Microcosme."[31] Malynes took a cautious approach to criticizing all the chartered companies but singled out the Merchant Adventurers and the East India Company (Misselden's affiliations) for

---

28. Gerard de Malynes, *The Maintenance of Free Trade, According to the Three Essentiall Parts of Traffique; Namely, Commodities, Moneys, and Exchange of Moneys, by Bills of Exchanges for other Countries. Or, An answer to a Treatise of Free Trade, or the meanes to make Trade flourish, lately Published* (London: Printed by I. K. for William Sheffard, 1622), foreword, Making of the Modern World.

29. Gerard [de] Malynes, *Consuetudo, Vel, Lex Mercatoria, or The Ancient Law-Merchant* (London: Printed by William Hunt, for Nicolas Bourne, 1656; first published 1622 by Adam Islip [London]), Making of the Modern World.

30. Malynes, *Maintenance of Free Trade*, 104.

31. Malynes, *Maintenance of Free Trade*, 38.

disparagement. He argued for government intervention and what we would now think of as protectionist policy, stating "merchants may easily commit errors, to the preiudice of the Common-wealth, albeit, it maketh for their private benefit."[32]

Misselden interpreted this comparatively tempered criticism as the literary equivalent of throwing down the gauntlet. He responded quickly with a biting essay full of personal attacks. Malynes had referred to himself metaphorically with an example drawn from Plutarch of a small fish that guides a large whale to safe waters. Misselden mercilessly poked fun at Malynes for this choice of words, repeatedly referring to him as the "little fish" throughout the 1623 response, *The Circle of Commerce. Or The Ballance of Trade, in defence of free Trade.*[33] Misselden's central argument was that the exchange of monies is not a form of trade, because money is not a proper good. In this way, Misselden was trying, somewhat wrongheadedly, to buttress the argument that the balance of trade affects the exchange of currency and that exchange of money cannot drive the balance of trade.

The role of the companies in all of this remains a central bone of contention, arguably driving the other more theoretical descriptions on the importance of currency exchange versus trade in goods. Misselden defended the companies against any and all criticisms found in Malynes and made the general charge—still heard today—that there is no one better qualified than the merchants themselves to tell whether or not they are getting good terms of exchange, and therefore are contributing to a healthy balance of trade at the national level. Memorably, he concludes this point by stating: "What else makes a Common-wealth, but the private-wealth."[34] Malynes responds somewhat in kind, but with less maliciousness, in *The Center of The Circle of Commerce* (1623), which asserts that the exchange of money is the center of the circle of commerce, which gives shape to the whole, and whose importance is sorely missing in Misselden's analysis.[35] This text concluded the public debate between Misselden and Malynes, but history has shown that

32. Malynes, *Maintenance of Free Trade*, 85.

33. Edward Misselden, *The Circle of Commerce. Or The Ballance of Trade, in defence of free Trade: Opposed To Malynes Little Fish and his Great Whale, poized against them in the Scale. [. . .]* (London: Printed by Iohn Dawson, for Nicholas Bourne, 1623), Making of the Modern World.

34. Misselden, *The Circle of Commerce*, 17.

35. Gerard [de] Malynes, *The Center of The Circle of Commerce. Or, A Refutation of a Treatise, Intituled The Circle of Commerce, or The Ballance of Trade, lately published by E.M.* (London: William Jones, 1623), Making of the Modern World.

Malynes lost the battle. This outcome, however, was due more to Mun than to Misselden. For generations after this exchange, the primacy of the balance of trade was unquestioned. It was Mun's final contribution, *England's Treasure by Forraign Trade*, not published until 1664 but written and privately circulated many decades earlier, that became accepted economic doctrine.[36]

The lasting impact of Mun's posthumous text is heightened by the organization of his argument. Whereas previous works often resembled laundry lists of loosely related points, Mun set out to make one overarching argument in a number of ways. Improving on his earlier *Discovrse*, this argument was a continuation of the debates with Malynes from the days of the committee on trade. Mun is believed to have written *England's Treasure* in the late 1620s,[37] after the committee and public debates between Malynes and Misselden had finally begun to wind down, but the text makes his position clear enough. In chapter 12, titled "The undervaluing of our Money which is delivered or received by Bills of Exchange here or beyond the seas, cannot decrease our treasure," Mun addresses Malynes central argument about the role of foreign exchange merchants in depressing English trade.[38] As in the *Discovrse*, Mun defends the East India Company trade. He addressed a range of topics, including the best qualities of merchants, Spanish treasure, foreign coin, the "Statute of Imployments," state revenues, and the price of land. All of these are considered in turn in order to affirm the central role of the balance of overseas trade in determining the nation's fortunes.[39]

> Let the Merchants exchange be at a high rate, or at a low rate, or at the *Par pro pari*, or put down altogether; Let Forraign Princes enhance their Coins, or debase their Standards, and let His Majesty do the like, or keep them constant as they now stand; Let forraign Coins pass current here in all payments at higher rates than they are worth at the Mint; Let the Statute

36. Lynn Muchmore, "A Note on Thomas Mun's 'England's Treasure by Forraign Trade,'" *Economic History Review* 23, no. 3 (December 1970): 498, https://doi.org/10.2307/2594618.

37. Paul Slack, "The Politics of English Political Economy in the 1620s," in *Popular Culture and Political Agency in Early Modern England and Ireland: Essays in Honour of John Walter*, ed. Michael J. Braddick and Phil Withington (Woodbridge, UK: Boydell Press, 2017), 55–72.

38. Thomas Mun, *England's Treasure by Forraign Trade. Or, The Ballance of our Forraign Trade is The Rule of our Treasure* (London: Printed by J. G. for Thomas Clark, 1664), Making of the Modern World.

39. Mun believed, along with his contemporaries, that trade within the nation could not affect its total wealth, as internal exchange, in his eyes, simply redistributed existing wealth within the nation.

for employments by Strangers stand in force or be repealed; Let the meer Exchanger do his worst; Let Princes oppress, Lawyers extort, Usurers bite, Prodigals wast, and lastly let Merchant carry out what mony they shall have occasion to use in traffique. Yet all these actions can work no other effects in the course of trade than is declared in this discourse. For so much Treasure only will be brought in or carried out of a Commonwealth, as the Forraign Trade doth over or under ballance in value.[40]

It would be hard to find stronger language to assert the primacy of the balance of trade over all other financial machinations and state regulations. Mun's worldview was one in which overseas trade dictated all other contours of economic life. Trade has a life and a course of its own, which should not be interrupted by ineffectual or possibly harmful government regulation. Whether or not Mun conceived of an "economy," he clearly saw trade as a system that operated according to its own principles, which he considered beyond government control. The balance of trade was one of the laws that explained its operations—for Mun, perhaps the only law. Mun's published work evolved from a principled defense of his own company's business practices into an early principle of economic theory.

In the end, the most unlikely of the three authors, Thomas Mun, became known as the key architect of mercantilist trade theory. Mun's formulation of the balance-of-trade theory became the guiding theoretical principle for serious works on commerce and trade for the remainder of the seventeenth century, Adam Smith cited him in *The Wealth of Nations*, and he remains one of the most famous of the authors of the period. The debate among the three, however, was crucial to the development and influence of his ideas and holds an important place in the history of mercantilist thought.[41]

CHARTERS, COTTON, AND CONFLICT

In June 1719, riots erupted on the streets of Spitalfields. It was reported that women were dragged from carriages and their clothes ripped from

---

40. Mun, *England's Treasure*, 218–19.

41. Joseph A. Schumpeter, *History of Economic Analysis: With a New Introduction*, rev. ed. (New York: Oxford University Press, 1954), 356; Blaug, *The Early Mercantilists*; and Slack, "English Political Economy."

them by angry mobs.[42] The targets of this mob violence were fashionable women. They were not targeted because they were fashionable or wealthy. They were targeted because they were wearing cotton.

The weavers of Spitalfields were reacting to the effect that cotton imports were having on their own woolens industry. As early as the 1660s, cotton imports from India began to take off in England's domestic market. Fashionable consumers switched from woolen goods to the lighter, cheaper, and more comfortable cotton textiles. In truth, the woolen industry in England was facing more than just new cotton goods. The Irish woolen industry was becoming increasingly competitive despite the complicated regulations imposed upon Irish exports.[43] One of the results was difficult times for the English weavers. In areas like Spitalfields, dedicated to the woolen industry, unemployment, poverty, and starvation spiked, and eventually the people turned to violent protest.

These problems quickly came to the attention of Parliament. A powerful woolen lobby had been formed in response to the perceived threat of the increasing cotton market.[44] Public pamphlets began to appear condemning the import of foreign cotton goods, and there was a widespread movement for a complete ban on cotton imports. A ban on cottons goods would have been devastating for the English East India Company, whose profits had soared on textiles from South Asia. The Indian subcontinent was at that time the leading textile manufacturer in the world, with a much higher capacity for quantity and quality than any place in Europe. The East India Company defended its right to import cotton textiles to Parliament and began to enlist authors to publish public works defending its trading practices.

Defenders—and critics—of the company who published public pamphlets and books were no longer inventing a new genre. They were stepping

---

42. Frank Lynn, *Crime and Punishment in Eighteenth-Century England* (Abingdon, UK: Routledge, 2013), 220; and Gitanjali Shahani, " 'A Foreigner by Birth': The Life of Indian Cloth in the Early Modern English Marketplace," in *Global Traffic: Discourses and Practices of Trade in English Literature and Culture from 1550 to 1700*, ed. Barbara Sebek and Stephen Deng (New York: Palgrave Macmillan, 2008), 193, SpringerLink.

43. Patrick Kelly, "The Irish Woollen Export Prohibition Act of 1699: Kearney Re-visited," *Irish Economic and Social History* 7, no. 1 (June 1980): 22–44, https://doi.org/10.1177/033248938000700103.

44. Patrick O'Brien, Trevor Griffiths, and Philip Hunt, "Political Components of the Industrial Revolution: Parliament and the English Cotton Textile Industry, 1660–1774," *Economic History Review* 44, no. 3 (August 1991): 397, https://doi.org/10.2307/2597536.

into an established line of discourse—the same one that Mun, Malynes, and Misselden had participated in decades earlier. But the defenders were placed in the particularly difficult position of explaining away the very evident damage that was being done to England's most central manufacturing industry, woolen textiles, and the severe economic distress that had resulted in areas like Spitalfields, in a context in which the very existence of the chartered companies was already a charged issue.

One of the first to enter the fray was the headstrong Josiah Child (1630–1699). Child was the son of a merchant who had made a large fortune supplying beer to the Royal Navy. He was a founding member of the Royal African Company and, early on, a private trader in the East Indies region. Unsatisfied with his small private share in the lucrative eastern trade, Child moved quickly to become a dominant figure in the East India Company. Within eight years, from 1671 to 1679, Child became the largest single shareholder and a powerful force within the company.[45] He served as governor from 1681 to 1683 and, in a second term, from 1686 to 1688. By most reports, he treated the company as his own personal fiefdom. His most disastrous act was to initiate an ill-conceived and entirely unsuccessful assault on the Mughal emperor Aurangzeb.

Child was not the most innovative of the authors and has not gone down in history as a great thinker,[46] but he did become one of the most popular authors of economic tracts in his time. Child had already begun his publishing career in the 1660s, prior to the onset of the debate on the cotton trade. The earlier works were *Brief Observations Concerning Trade, and Interest of Money* (1668) and *A Short Addition to the Observations Concerning Trade and Interest of Money* (1668).[47] In these publications, Child advocated for the lowering of interest rates.

In 1681, he moved into the cotton debates in a limited way with a full-throated defense of the East India Company. In *A Treatise Wherein is*

45. Richard Grassby, "North, Sir Dudley (1641–1691)," in *Oxford Dictionary of National Biography* (Oxford University Press, 2004; online ed., 2008), https://doi.org/10.1093/ref:odnb/20297.

46. William Letwin, *Sir Josiah Child: Merchant Economist*, Kress Library of Business and Economics 14 (Boston: Baker Library; Harvard Graduate School of Business Administration, 1959).

47. Josiah Child, *Brief Observations Concerning Trade, and Interest of Money* (London: Printed for Elizabeth Calvert, 1668), Making of the Modern World; and Josiah Child, *A Short Addition to the Observations Concerning Trade and Interest of Money* (London: Printed for Henry Mortlock, 1668), Making of the Modern World.

Demonstrated I. That the East-India Trade is the most National of all Foreign Trades, Child defended the company against both the woolen manufacturers and the Levant Company merchants, arguing that the value of the East India Company trade was greater than the losses incurred by the woolen or Turkey trade due to the monopoly restrictions over the eastern trade.[48] He made some concessions to the wool lobby by arguing that the East India Company had been trying its best to open new markets for English woolens in Japan and Indo-China, but defended its failures by complaining that the rising price of wool in the previous five years had made its sale on the domestic and international fronts more difficult.[49] He followed this book with a slightly shorter work, *A Discourse Concerning Trade*, also focused on explicitly defending the value of the East India Company to national interests.[50]

His next work took a slightly more devious route to pursuing the interests of the East India Company. Child was not very imaginative in his choice of titles, so please note that the new and longer work, *A Discourse About Trade* (1690),[51] was substantially different from *A Discourse Concerning Trade*. *A Discourse Concerning Trade*, however, was *not* substantially different from the later publication, *A New Discourse of Trade* (1693),[52] which was in fact not at all new because it mainly contained republications of Child's previous work—including large selections from *A Discourse Concerning Trade*. He was not the most forthright of men.

48. Josiah Child, *A Treatise Wherein is Demonstrated I. That the East-India Trade is the most National of all Foreign Trades [. . .]* (London: Printed by J. R. for the Honourable the East-India Company, 1681), Making of the Modern World.

49. This work was originally published under the pseudonym Philopatris. It was widely believed, however, that Josiah Child was the author. This attribution was persuasively contested by William Letwin, who is an expert on Child and his work. See William Letwin, *The Origins of Scientific Economics: English Economic Thought, 1660–1776* (London: Methuen, 1963), chap. 1. After very careful consideration, O'Brien and Darnell used a statistical analysis of the text and found that Child was indeed the author. D. P. O'Brien and A. C. Darnell, *Authorship Puzzles in the History of Economics: A Statistical Approach* (London: Macmillan, 1982), https://doi.org/10.1007/978-1-349 -05697-2. I follow that analysis here in the attribution of authorship. Child, *A Treatise Wherein is Demonstrated*, 8–9, 20.

50. Josiah Child, *A Discourse Concerning Trade, And that in particular of The East-Indies, Wherein several weighty Propositions are fully discussed, and the State of the East-India Company is faithfully stated* ([London: Andrew Sowle, 1689?]), Making of the Modern World.

51. Josiah Child, *A Discourse About Trade, Wherein the Reduction of Interest of Money to 4 l. per Centum, is Recommended* (London: A. Sowle, 1690), Making of the Modern World.

52. Josiah Child, *A New Discourse of Trade, Wherein is Recommended several weighty Points relating to Companies of Merchants* (London: John Everingham, 1693), Making of the Modern World.

In *A Discourse Concerning Trade* and *A New Discourse of Trade*, Child expanded upon a refrain he had developed earlier: the link between land values and interest. It is not entirely clear which work was written first because the preface of the 1690 discourse states that the book was written in the late 1660s, soon after the Great London Fire.[53] On the other hand, Child frequently misled his readers in order to distract from his intentions. Whatever he states, it is very likely that he published this work in 1690 to drum up support for a bill that would soon be introduced to Parliament proposing a reduction in interest rates.

In the 1668 work, Child had floated the idea that interest rates and land were like two buckets of a scale, where one goes up, the other goes down.[54] In the 1690s, he returned to this idea. Child clearly believed that lower rates would serve his personal interests and the interests of the East India Company. The challenge was to convince the Crown and landed gentry to vote in Parliament to lower rates. This was not necessarily an easy task because those groups feared that rate reductions would adversely impact the value of their land. Their resistance led Child to publish. Child was a powerful merchant, served in Parliament, and sat on the Committee for Trades and Plantations—yet he perceived that writing and publication offered a device for amplifying his opinions. And he tailored his arguments to his intended audience. Parliament was dominated by aristocratic elites with large stocks of land. Child undertook to persuade those elites that the policies he favored would benefit them as well by raising the price of land.[55] (Mun also took this tack in *England's Treasure.*)

It is unclear if making a spurious connection between interest and the value of land based on self-interested and clandestine motivations constitutes a contribution or advancement to economic thought. Yet Child's work was a significant stimulus to a work of much clearer value. None other than the philosopher John Locke was motivated by Child's public advocacy to print his own rebuttal. He did so in *Some Considerations of the*

---

53. Child, *A Discourse About Trade*, A2.
54. Child, *Brief Observations Concerning Trade*, 6, 13.
55. This argument is articulated at greater length in Edward J. Harpham, "Class, Commerce, and the State: Economic Discourse and Lockean Liberalism in the Seventeenth Century," *Western Political Quarterly* 38, no. 4 (December 1985): 565–82, https://doi.org/10.2307/448613.

Consequences of the Lowering of Interest, and Raising the Value of Money (1692).[56] This work returned to themes first developed in an earlier unpublished manuscript, *Some of the consequences that are like to follow upon the lessening of interest rates to 4 percent.*[57]

Locke strongly disagreed with Child's analysis. In the first place, Locke did not believe that interest rates could be set by the government. As he referred to it, "the price of money" cannot be regulated but is instead set by supply and vent, where the term "vent" should be understood as similar to our sense of demand and captures the number of buyers.[58] If the government sets the price of money—i.e., the rate of interest—at a point lower than determined by the number of buyers and sellers, the natural value of the good according to Locke, it would have the effect of decreasing the amount of money in circulation, because those who had money would have less incentive to loan it out. The decrease in money circulating would in turn depress trade and commerce and ultimately lower land values because the value of what is produced on land decreases as well. As pointed out by Edward Harpham, Locke was conceptually severing the relationship Child had posed between the merchant's short-term interest and the landowners' interests. Locke, however, appears to have made the argument not by virtue of his own self-interest but via a disciplined use of philosophical reasoning based on the idea of natural law. Locke's work was ultimately unsuccessful in its goal: the bill to lower interest was passed in 1692. Locke did, however, achieve an advancement in economic thought. As Harpham puts it, Locke based his argument in a well-developed microeconomic theory. His consideration of land values and interest rates was predicated on a theory of market forces. As Karen Vaughn noted, this microeconomic base allowed Locke to make the significant contribution of grounding his quantity theory of money, which was generally accepted but not theoretically supported, in a general theory of value.[59]

56. John Locke, *Some Considerations of the Consequences of the Lowering of Interest, and Raising the Value of Money* (London: Printed for Awnsham and John Churchill, 1692), Making of the Modern World.

57. Letwin recovered this manuscript and published it as an appendix to his 1963 book. Letwin, *Origins of Scientific Economics*, 273–300.

58. Vaughn points out the subtle importance of Locke's use of "vent" rather than "demand." Karen Iversen Vaughn, *John Locke, Economist and Social Scientist* (Chicago: University of Chicago Press, 1980), 19–21.

59. Harpham, "Class, Commerce," 571, 578–79; and Vaughn, *John Locke*, 32.

Whereas Child's bullish defense of his company's prerogatives egged Locke into important work, another aspect of Child's argument lay in his challenge to the balance-of-trade concept and related even more directly to the trade in cotton. While circumspectly acknowledging the former value of the idea of the balance of trade, Child argued that the idea had become outmoded. His arguments against it were not entirely original. He argued that the balance of trade was too difficult to calculate, that it did not capture all the ancillary benefits that come from certain trades (such as ship lading, for example), and that the concept treated each trade in isolation from each other when it should also consider the relationships between different types of trade (such as the Levant and East Indian trade). These two latter points had in fact been made by Mun himself when he first developed the concept decades earlier.

Still, there was an important intuition there. Child knew that his company, the East India Company, was importing more manufactured goods than it exported. The company was still exporting bullion to Asia mainly to buy finished goods. And the substitution that seemed to be occurring between English wool and Indian cotton was potentially doing further damage by reducing the market for goods manufactured in England. It could not have been helping the balance of trade as formulated by Mun. But he could also see clearly that the East India Company was thriving. From his perspective, the problems in the woolen industry should not have been laid at the feet of the English East India Company, and it would have been the height of folly to undercut a thriving trade in order to shore up a failing one. Instead, he argued that the economic growth of the nation depended upon the further enhancement of trade that had already proven to be highly profitable.[60] This idea, born of material interest, was powerful nonetheless. But it was up to other, less popular authors to offer clear articulations of the logic that would support overturning the balance-of-trade theory in favor of a freer trade.

It should not, however, be supposed that supporters of the woolen industry and critics of the East India Company were absent from the debate or did not also make significant contributions. John Cary was one of the significant voices at odds with Child. Cary was a prominent member of Bristol's Society of Merchant Venturers and an influential figure.[61] He was

60. Child, *A Discourse About Trade*, 135–61.

61. H. F. Kearney, "The Political Background to English Mercantilism, 1695–1700," *Economic History Review* 11, no. 3 (1959): 485.

a friend and correspondent of John Locke, who remarked favorably on his ideas and analysis. His work was also well received by the public. *An Essay on the State of England, In Relation to its Trade, Its Poor, and Its Taxes* (1695) was reissued in 1719 and 1745 and translated into French and Italian.[62]

The Bristol Venturers published Cary's book as a means through which to attack the privileges of the East India Company. The Bristol Venturers had a history of attacking the privileges of London chartered companies, which is understandable as outports such as Bristol were largely excluded from these lucrative arrangements. Contra Child, Cary defended the principle of the balance of trade. "Where the Exports of a Nation in product and Manufactures are outballanced by Imports fit only to be consumed at home, though one Man may get by the Luxury of another; the Wealth of that Nation must decay."[63] He portrayed the wealth of the East India Company as deriving from frivolous consumption that would weaken rather than strengthen the health of the nation. He was a strong proponent of trade regulations, tariffs, and bans. And, in a sign of how the terms of the debate were lining up, he attacked the idea that the undirected pursuit of self-interest might serve a public good. Cary's essay became grist for more complicated arguments that continued to grapple with the relationship among manufacturing, trade, and economic growth.

Charles Davenant (1656–1714) took up this task in his *An Essay on the East-India-Trade* (1696).[64] Davenant was originally a playwright. His semi-opera *Circe*, based on Euripides' romantic drama *Iphigenia in Tauris*, achieved some level of popularity. Henry Purcell composed music for a revival of the piece sometime in the 1680s. Nevertheless, Davenant left the world of theater to become an excise commissioner. He served as member of Parliament in 1685 but was left without a position or immediate prospects after the revolution. He managed to find sporadic employment with the East India Company, and his 1696 essay has been widely interpreted as an attempt to gain secure employment within the company. By 1703 he

---

62. John Cary, *An Essay on the State of England, In Relation to its Trade, Its Poor, and Its Taxes, For carrying on the present War against France* (Bristol: Printed by W. Bonny, for the Author, 1695), Making of the Modern World. For publication and translation details, see Kelly, "Irish Woollen Export," 27.

63. Cary, *Essay on the State of England*, 1.

64. Charles Davenant, *An Essay on the East-India-Trade. By the Author of The Essay upon Wayes and Means* (London, 1696), Making of the Modern World.

had taken the position of inspector-general of imports and exports, and by 1713 he was leading the economically focused newspaper the *Mercator, or, Commerce retrieved*.[65]

It makes sense then that Davenant began his 1696 essay with a rehearsal of the same defense of the East India Company offered by Mun, Child, and many others in the interim: trades cannot be considered in isolation, and the re-export trade in eastern goods alone overbalanced the supply of bullion into England. This defense addressed the early-seventeenth-century concern about the loss of bullion, but it did not address the more recent emphasis on the import/export balance of manufactured goods. Davenant confronted this problem in the second section of the book, breaking new ground as he did.

Davenant began by observing that England had a natural advantage over other nations in producing wool. This advantage, he asserted, was the source of the profit gained when wool is sold abroad. It follows that the more wool that is sold abroad, the more England profits. It also follows, however, that when wool is consumed within England, this consumption reduces the amount that is sent abroad for sale. Thus, the consumption of cotton goods, substituting for woolen goods, frees up more wool for sale overseas, contributing to the larger benefit of the nation. The best situation, he concludes, is the consumption of the cheapest foreign goods at home and the sale of the good England has the greatest natural advantage in producing abroad. This formulation is beginning to sound very much like the idea of absolute advantage and is a significant step away from the rigid calculation of gains and losses through which prior generations had viewed trade with other nations. Davenant concludes: "That the East-India Goods do something interefere with the Woollen Manufacture, must undoubtedly

65. While the worlds of theater and the market may seem very distant, there was a tighter link in this era than might be imagined. See Jean-Christophe Agnew, *Worlds Apart: The Market and the Theater in Anglo-American Thought, 1550–1750* (Cambridge: Cambridge University Press, 1986); Reinhard Strohm, "Iphigenia's Curious *Ménage à Trois* in Myth, Drama, and Opera," in *(Dis)embodying Myths in Ancien Régime Opera: Multidisciplinary Perspectives*, ed. Bruno Forment (Leuven, Belgium: Leuven University Press, 2012), 132; Julian Hoppit, "The Contexts and Contours of British Economic Literature, 1660–1760," *Historical Journal* 49, no. 1 (March 2006): 79–110, https://doi.org/10.1017/S0018246X05005066; David Waddell, "Charles Davenant (1656–1714): A Biographical Sketch," *Economic History Review* 11, no. 2 (December 1958): 279–88, http://doi.org/10.1111/j.1468-0289.1958.tb01641.x; and William Deringer, *Calculated Values: Finance, Politics, and the Quantitative Age* (Cambridge, MA: Harvard University Press, 2018), 116, 122.

be granted, but the Principal Matter to be Consider'd, is, Which way the Nation in General is more Cheaply supply'd."[66]

He also observes that forcing domestic consumption through laws and regulations will have the effect of artificially raising the price of wool, thereby decreasing its sales abroad—and reducing the benefit of the trade for the nation as a whole. As a rule, he stands firmly against government regulation. He argues that "[Trade] Laws are needless, unnatural, and can have no Effect conducive to the Publick Good"; that "The Natural Way of promoting the Woollen Manufacture, is not to force its Consumption at home, but by wholsome Laws to contrive, That it may be wrought cheaply in England, which consequently will enable us to command the Markets abroad"; and that the consumer demands of the public cannot be shaped by the state, but the state should ask instead "which Way the Folly of their People can be supply'd at the cheapest rate."[67]

As you may expect from his argument, Davenant's policy recommendations were for the deregulation of trade through the removal of tariffs and bans on certain goods. As he was an employee of the East India Company, it is perhaps unsurprising that he did not go so far as to advocate for removing chartered privileges. He further recommended expanding the labor force by reducing assistance to the poor.

In the same year Davenant's work was published, Nicholas Barbon wrote: "The Balance of Trade does so generally perplex all Debates concerning Trade. And that the Notion seems as if it were at first invented by some Merchants, on purpose to mislead Mens Reasons about Trade; because it is commonly us'd for an Argument against any flourishing Trade, That such a Trade is not for the Interest of the Nation."[68] Gardner advanced arguments very similar to Davenant's a year later in *Some Reflections on a Pamphlet, intituled, England and East-India Inconsistent in Their Manufactures* (1697).[69] In 1697, Henry Pollexfen responded with a different strategy,

66. Davenant, *Essay on the East-India-Trade*, 32.

67. Davenant, *Essay on the East-India-Trade*, 26, 27, 39.

68. Nicholas Barbon, *A Discourse Concerning Coining the New Money Lighter. In Answer to Mr. Lock's Considerations about raising the Value of Money* (London: Printed for Richard Chiswell, 1696), 52, Making of the Modern World.

69. [Gardner], *Some Reflections on a Pamphlet, intituled, England and East-India Inconsistent in Their Manufactures* (London, 1696 [1967?]), Making of the Modern World. Gardner's argument was so similar that it has been claimed that Davenant was in fact the author of this text rather than Gardner, but there is little evidence to support this idea. See David Waddell, "The Writings of Charles Davenant (1656–1714)," *The Library* s5-XI, no. 3 (September 1956): 206–12.

criticizing the East India Company on the grounds that the charter was a violation of the principles of the Magna Carta.[70] In 1701, Henry Martyn tied together these two strands of thought by bringing Davenant's, Gardner's, and Barbon's argument to the logical conclusion that each had assiduously avoided for reasons tied to the interests of the company they served.[71]

Martyn argued for the abolishment of chartered companies and their special privileges—singling out the East India Company in particular. Following Davenant and Gardner, he argued that the consumption of foreign manufactures was not more harmful to a nation than the consumption of domestic manufactures because the consumption of foreign goods frees up labor for the production of other domestic goods: "a Law to restrain us to use only English Manufactures, is to oblige us to make them first, is to oblige us to provide for our Consumption by the labour of many, what might as well be done by that of few; is to oblige us to consume the labour of many, what might as well be done by that of few."[72] He then observed that opening up overseas trade to all merchants would increase the volume of exchange with the East, further increasing the productive capacity of English labor. Finally, he argued that the multiplication of value through the efficient use of labor would increase national stores of bullion: "by such an universal Freedom of Trade, our Superfluities wou'd be multiply'd, our exportations wou'd be enlarg'd, our bullion wou'd be increas'd, and the more Money wou'd be still imploy'd in Trade."[73] Importantly, the rejection of the zero-sum model of overseas trade that had been implicit in this new perspective is made explicit by Martyn.[74]

These contributions were a step toward the theoretical framework of classical economics. The relevance of debates over company privileges in these works was so great that William Letwin has called it "the great chartering controversy."[75] The limitations of the balance-of-trade doctrine were

---

70. Henry Pollexfen, *A Discourse of Trade, Coyn, and Paper Credit: And of Ways and Means to Gain, and Retain Riches. To which is added the Argument of a Learned Counsel, upon an Action of the Case brought by the East-India-Company against Mr. Sands and Interloper* (London: Printed for Brabazon Aylmer, 1697), Making of the Modern World.

71. Henry Martyn, *Considerations on the East-India Trade* (London: Printed for J. Roberts, 1701), https://EconPapers.repec.org/RePEc:hay:hetboo:martyn1701.

72. Martyn, *Considerations*, 30.

73. Martyn, *Considerations*, 69.

74. Martyn, *Considerations*.

75. Letwin, *Origins of Scientific Economics*, 52.

being recognized and overcome. Liberal economic theory—in the sense of a new rejection of government interference—was taking shape.[76] And Davenant, Gardner, and Martyn's theories of trade were seeding the soil for David Ricardo's formulation of comparative advantage.[77] Fueled by the material interests of company merchants, the public debates over the cotton industry challenged existing notions and advanced knowledge and theory about commerce and trade.

THE CORPORATE ELEMENT

One element common to both episodes was the centrality of the large chartered companies. I have focused on the bullion and cotton controversies, in which the East India Company played a central role, but other companies were debated and other debates arose about even the East India Company. While Mun, Malynes, and Misselden focused on what the companies did, another thread in the literature debated the companies' right to exist.

Some authors simply hated certain companies, the way that some people now hate Amazon, Google, or Facebook. They have their reasons, but those reasons are not necessarily grounded in systematic economic thought. John May hated the East India Company for importing the "excrement of the worm"—aka silk—particularly compared with the superiority of the pure "fleece of the sheepe."[78] For him the root problem was moral: the East India Company flourished because of "the wicked practices of deceitfull people."[79] Robert Kayll believed that overseas trade companies were responsible for the domestic loss of forests, ships, and seamen. He argued they were all being destroyed in the unnecessarily dangerous voyages in exotic eastern waters and concluded that the companies "are strictly vsed to the eternall benefite of a few, and the wrong of all the residue."[80] Dudley Digges, an Oxford-educated descendant of an elite family and prominent company investor, called Kayll's argument the "vapours of an idle or corrupted

76. Schumpeter, History of Economic Analysis, 41, 365–73.

77. Douglas Irwin, Against the Tide: An Intellectual History of Free Trade (Princeton, NJ: Princeton University Press, 1996), 54–55.

78. John May, A Declaration of the Estate of Clothing Now Vsed Within This Realme Of England (London: Adam Islip, 1613), 3, Making of the Modern World.

79. May, A Declaration, 3–4.

80. Robert Kayll, The Trades Increase (London: Nicholas Okes, 1615), 52, Making of the Modern World.

braine," worthy of consideration only because of the effect it might have on those with "weake stomacks."[81]

These personalized attacks persisted, but newer, more general arguments about monopoly and free trade entered the lexicon in the 1640s. By the late 1640s, abstract arguments about commerce and national prosperity were appearing with increasing frequency. Lewes Roberts, merchant of the Levant Company, published *The Treasure of Traffike, or A Discourse of Forraigne Trade*, an extended epistle on the virtues of corporate governance with caveats for overly restrictive patents and monopolies, in 1641.[82] Henry Robinson, an associate of Samuel Hartlib and freeman of the Mercers' Company, made a similar argument in *Englands safety, in trades encrease* (1641).[83] Robinson returned to the problem of currency exchange and made several solid and sophisticated observations about the relationship between currency valuations and the price and quantity of imports and exports—in particular, that undervaluation of currency ultimately decreases the sale of goods abroad as they are sold at a higher price. Both the attacks and defenses of specific companies and the idea of chartered privileges were absorbed into the general argument about free trade, which had begun to sound more and more like a rallying cry. In 1645, the phrase 'freedom of trade' began to appear in the titles of different books. Those advocating freedom of trade, however, were usually arguing against the chartered privileges of the great companies rather than against government intervention through tariffs or bans. Indeed, it was the merchants of the great companies who argued the position that direct government interference of that sort hurt trade.

As with Misselden's writing, some of the discourse was unexpectedly acrimonious. In *A Discourse Consisting of Motives for The Enlargement and Freedome of Trade* (1645), Thomas Johnson compared the Merchant Adventurers to "an Ulcer upon the Body politique of this Kingdome a long time, which hath beene often rub'd and lanc'd, yet it clos'd againe and gatherd

81. Dudley Digges, *The Defence of Trade. In a Letter To Sir Thomas Smith Knight, Gouernour of the East-India Companie, &c.* (London: Printed by William Stansby for Iohn Barnes, 1615), 2–4, Making of the Modern World.

82. Lewes Roberts, *The Treasure of Traffike, or A Discourse of Forraigne Trade* (London: Printed by E. P. for Nicholas Bourne, 1641), Making of the Modern World.

83. Henry Robinson, *Englands Safety, in Trades Encrease. Most humbly presented to the High Court of Parliament* (London: Printed by E. P. for Nicholas Bourne, 1641), Making of the Modern World.

more corruption" and "Incubusses [that] doe suck the very vitall spirits, and drive into one veine that masse of blood which should cherish the whole body."[84] But along with these colorful metaphors, Johnson's critique led him into the terrain of price movements. The Merchant Adventurers' position at the time, and a widespread belief of early-period mercantilism, was that high prices were desirable because merchants made a greater profit on them. The idea was that the organization of merchant activities that the company made possible, through its regulations and restrictions, could preserve those high prices. Johnson observed to the contrary that "it is not the high prices but the plenty that propagates Trade"[85]—a position much closer in line with modern economic thinking.

Henry Parker took up the contrary side of the newly generalized argument about free trade. An associate of the Merchant Adventurers, he defended the company by critiquing trade conducted without the benefit of corporate organization. He offered this evocative metaphor: "Liberty therefore may well be compared to fresh waters, it is potable, and sweet whilst it endures a just confinement in the vaines and channells of the early. But when it once refundes it selfe into the bosome of the briny Ocean, it retaynes no longer its former rellish."[86] In other words, freedom is best experienced only within certain well-worn channels, and too much freedom causes confusion and conflict. To make his point, he offered one of the early versions of the tragedy-of-the-commons problem, in which individuals' self-interest leads them to take actions detrimental to both themselves and their greater whole over the long run.

Within a few years, other interest groups were picking up the free-trade refrain and support for the philosophy of corporate governance came under increasing scrutiny. Robinson walked back his support of corporations into a more tepid stance in a new book in which he wished that the enclosing of free trade "by Charters and Corporations, may be seriously debated and agreed on, that it may neither be quite ruined, for want of good

84. [Thomas Johnson], *A Discourse Consisting of Motives for The Enlargement and Freedome of Trade. Especially That of Cloth, and other Woollen Manufactures, [. . .]* (London: Printed by Richard Bishop for Stephen Rowtell, 1645), A4, Making of the Modern World.

85. Thomas Johnson, *A Discourse Consisting,* 25.

86. Henry Parker, *Of a Free Trade. A Discourse Seriously Recommending to our Nation the wonderfull benefits of Trade, especially of a rightly Governed, and Ordered Trade. [. . .]* (London: Printed by Fr: Neile for Robert Bostock, 1648), 7, Making of the Modern World.

Government; nor yet obstructed, no lesse then if monopolized, by colour of Corporation."[87] Thomas Violet advocated for free trade and criticized a series of chartered companies in *The Advancement of Merchandize* (1651).[88] To be clear, this was not the contemporary idea of free trade but freedom from chartered privileges. Indeed, Violet advocated for a long series of specific and severe acts of market regulation, such as requiring all women over the age of twelve to spin one pound of flax or hemp every month.[89] Violet wrote that his motivation for publishing what had originally been a report to the government's Council of Trade was to mobilize the public to take up his cause and petition Parliament and the council.

Despite increases in free-trade sentiments, companies persisted, and the controversies stirred up by company privileges continued to drive pamphlet wars and published debates. *The Grand concernments of England ensured* (1659) argued that the monarchy was bad for trade because of its attempts to control trade through the grant of monopoly privileges.[90] In one of the longest and most detailed documents produced in this period, *Trade revived*, John Bland argued the opposite: "the abolishing of Corporations and companies, whereby the Comerce is left without support, and open to all people, whose ignorance and want of experience hath not only suffered our native Commmodities to lose their value abroad, but at home, pulling up thereby the foundation of all Comerce."[91] Bland made a laundry list of other recommendations, including legally dividing trade into wholesale and retail, forming a convoy to protect merchants' ships in the Atlantic, reminting the shilling, and creating a bank to ease the currency problems faced in trade. Other of his ideas were simply repugnant:

---

87. Henry Robinson, *Briefe Considerations, Concerning the advancement of Trade and Navigation, Humbly tendred unto all ingenious Patriots; Purposely to incite them to endeavour the felicitie of this Nation, [. . .]* (London: Matthew Simmons, 1649), 9, Making of the Modern World.

88. Thomas Violet, *The Advancement of Merchandize: or, Certain Propositions For the Improvment of the Trade of this Common-wealth, humbly presented to the Right Honorable the Council of State* (London: W. DuGard, Printer to the Council of State, 1651), Making of the Modern World.

89. Violet, *The Advancement of Merchandize*, 20.

90. *The Grand Concernments of England Ensured: Viz. Liberty of Conscience, Extirpation of Popery, Defence of Property, [. . .], With a Sad Expostulation, and some smart Rebukes to the Army* (London, 1659), Making of the Modern World.

91. John Bland, *Trade Revived, Or a Way Proposed To Restore, Increase, Inrich, Strengthen and Preserve the Decayed and even Dying Trade of this our English Nation, in its Manufactories, Coin, Shiping and Revenue* (London: Printed for Thomas Holmwood for the use of the People of England, 1659), 2, Making of the Modern World.

he devoted several pages to a number of extremely anti-Semitic recommendations. Samuel Fortrey, son of a prominent silk merchant, defended the corporate organization of trade as well as the export of bullion (1663),[92] as did John Hodges, author of *The true and only causes of the want of money in these kingdoms* (1666).[93] William Petyt, a barrister and a Whig, argued against the chartering of trade, condemning monopolies and the export of bullion, while blaming the great overseas companies for what he considered to be the increasing cultivation of a detrimental taste in foreign luxury goods in England (1680).[94] Slingsby Bethel attacked the exclusiveness of the companies and argued that the English East India Company should not be exempted from such critiques because of the particularities of trade with Asia (1671).[95] Thomas Papillon defended the English East India Company, arguing that the company could not be blamed for the lack of available currency because it was pursuing a thriving trade that made money plentiful.[96]

In the aftermath of the Great Fire of London, Nicholas Barbon created one of the first insurance companies. When the City of London and the Friendly Society attempted to enter the new market for residential insurance, Barbon attacked them in print. His publications touched off a vicious pamphlet war that drew in William Hale, Henry Spelman, Thomas Papillon, and Dudley North.[97] Similar episodes were created by the debate over the introduction of "imaginary money"—meaning a paper currency. A central question was whether a state-supported chartered company should be

92. Samuel Fortrey, *Englands Interest and Improvement. Consisting in the increase of the store, and trade of this Kingdom* (Cambridge: John Field, Printer to the University, 1663), Making of the Modern World.

93. John Hodges, *The true and only Causes of the want of Money in these Kingdoms; And the Remedies. Mentioned in these General Assertions, in order to more particular Demonstrations, how these Kingdomes may yet be made the Richest, and most Powerful, Kingdoms in the World* (London, 1666), Making of the Modern World.

94. William Petyt, *Britannia Languens, or a Discourse of Trade: Shewing The Grounds and Reasons of the Increase and Decay of Land-Rents, National Wealth and Strength. With Application to the late and present State and Condition of England, France, and the United Provinces* (London: Printed for Tho. Dring and Sam. Crouch, 1680), Making of the Modern World.

95. Slingsby Bethel, *The Present Interest of England Stated. By a Lover of his King and Countre* (London: Printed for D. B., 1671), Making of the Modern World.

96. Thomas Papillon, *The East-India-Trade a most Profitable Trade to the Kingdom. And Best Secured and Improved in a Company, and a Joint-Stock. Represented In a Letter written upon the Occasion of two Letters lately published, insinuating the Contrary* (London, 1677), 4–5, Making of the Modern World.

97. Letwin, *Origins of Scientific Economics*, 53.

formed to back the paper currency. This argument was ultimately resolved in 1694 by the creation of the Bank of England. North, to whom the origin of equilibrium theory has been attributed, went on to write several more publications that furthered his interests as deputy governor of the Royal African Company and governor of the Muscovy Company.[98] Debates over the deregulation of the African slave trade generated nearly two hundred printed pamphlets in the 1690s, the majority of which were generated by independent traders opposing the monopoly of the Royal African Company.[99] Many other examples fill the corpus.

MORALITY AND SCIENCE

Many of the people involved in these debates were advancing arguments that served their material interests. This does not mean that the arguments were devoid of value or insight. It does mean that the authors faced a crisis of legitimacy that was very apparent to their contemporaries.

Nicholas Barbon, for example, characterized previous works on trade as a series of debates between different companies all arguing in such a way as to improve their business prospects: "The Turkey-Merchants Argue against the East-India Company, the Woollen-Draper against the Mercers, and the Upholster against the Cain Chair-Maker."[100] He was not alone in reading the debates this way. In order to be persuasive, the authors had to find some way of countering these criticisms.

Previous works claimed a moral high ground by deploying Christian precepts. The Christian worldview did not look favorably on merchants, and authors interested in defending trade, corporate or independent, had to look elsewhere for means to bolster their credibility. Condemnations of commerce, money, and the practice of usury—as well as injunctions to help the poor—also did not sit well with merchants deeply entrenched in the worlds of commerce and finance. Merchants were interested in profits and growth—not the state of the soul. While the occasional insult certainly

98. Grassby, "North, Sir Dudley."

99. William A. Pettigrew, *Freedom's Debt: The Royal African Company and the Politics of the Atlantic Slave Trade, 1672–1752* (Williamsburg, VA: Omohundro Institute of Early American History and Culture; Chapel Hill: University of North Carolina Press, 2013), 37.

100. Nicholas Barbon, *A Discourse of Trade* (London: Printed by Tho. Milbourn for the Author, 1690), A4–A5, Making of the Modern World.

found its way into many of the texts, moral attacks lost traction. Instead of blaming one wicked group of usurers, financiers, or company merchants, authors like Mun, Martyn, and Davenant began with the assumption that people were trying to do the best they could in whatever circumstances they found themselves—not that some people were good and some people were bad, and their good or evil intentions could explain the state of trade.

One strategy was simply to lie. Josiah Child used this tactic on several occasions. Child originally published both texts anonymously. The introduction to *A Discourse Concerning Trade* gives some insight into why he would have made such a choice, exactly what he was trying to hide, the legitimacy problems faced by company merchants, and the sometimes disingenuous ways that were used to attempt to circumvent them. In it, he wrote, "The Abstracter of the foregoing Treatise, is no East-India Merchant, nor any way concerned with the Company; Neither is he engaged in this work by any of them, but, being a great lover of his Native Country, he should be much grieved to see England lesser in Naval power and Trade."[101] And in the preface to *A Discourse About Trade*, the publisher (or Child) states that the manuscript fell into his hand "very accidentally" and was written by "no Trader" who "neither pays any Use for Money, but receives a great deal yearly, and hath to my knowledge a considerable Estate in Lands, and therefore the most invidious cannot conceive he had any private or selfish end in the following Discourses."[102]

Another method was to obscure one's own stake in an argument by taking a more general position. Instead of arguing for the importance of a specific company, one could argue for the importance of all companies. Instead of arguing about the injustice of being excluded from the Baltic trade, one could argue about the injustice of restricting free trade in all goods. The trend from personal to general in debates about the companies was an important one that had roots in material interests but ultimately increased the level of abstraction in the literature in conceptually helpful ways.

Yet another strategy was used in the introduction to Dudley North's *Discourses upon Trade*. The author was described as "of a temper different from most, who have medled with this Subject in Publick; for it is manifest, his Knowledge and Experience of Trade is considerable, which could not be

101. Child, *A Discourse Concerning Trade*, 11.
102. Child, *A Discourse About Trade*, A3.

attained, unless he were a Trader himself; and yet it is not to be collected from any thing he says, of what Nature his dealing hath been; for he speaks impartially of Trade in general, without warping to the Favour of any particular Interest."[103] North's defense is slightly different from Child's in that it contains a claim to expertise based on experience.

Experience was gaining traction in mid-seventeenth-century England. The strong moral overtones of medieval economic scholarship were related to the situation of the authors. Previous works on economics had been written mainly by scholastics, not merchants. Scholastics were men of the church, who operated at a distance from the world of commerce. Historians of the scholastics are often at pains to understand how cloistered ecclesiastics could have come to study and gain insight into commercial affairs.[104] Legitimacy in this era came from textual knowledge—largely, the Bible and Aristotle—rather than experience.

The new merchant authors drew from their own knowledge, which included detailed records of company trade accounts. The use of experience and data was a means through which merchants could bolster their legitimacy—but it was also a significant step forward in progress toward an empirical and scientific study of economic phenomenon.

William Petty introduced the idea of applying statistical analysis to economic and political data in his book *Political Arithmetick* (1690), thereby establishing new and influential standards for rigorous empirical approaches.[105] Petty himself was the son of a clothier and had turned to scholarship and scientific inquiry after an injury on board a merchant ship made him unfit for duty. Petty and North were influenced by the new scientific method of Francis Bacon. Petty was one of the founders of the Royal Society. He also was the author of the first clear explication of the labor theory of value. In *A Treatise of Taxes & Contributions* (1662), he proposed that the value of a good is the amount that a "single man can save within the same time, over and above his expence, if he imployed himself wholly to

103. North, *Discourses upon Trade*, A.

104. See, for example, Joel Kaye's penetrating dive into the works of Thomas Aquinas, Galen, and Nicolas Oresme in *A History of Balance, 1250–1375: The Emergence of a New Model of Equilibrium and Its Impact on Thought* (New York: Cambridge University Press, 2014).

105. William Petty, *Political Arithmetick, or A Discourse Concerning, The Extent and Value of Lands, People, Buildings; Husbandry, Manufacture, Commerce, Fishery, Artizans, Seamen, Soldiers; [. . .]* (London: Printed for Robert Clavel, 1690), Making of the Modern World (Gale Document Number U0100311687).

produce and make it," and concluded that all things should be valued by the amount of land and labor that go into them.[106] But both Petty and North were also following in the footsteps of merchant authors who had incorporated trade data and drew from their experience earlier in the century. The directionality of influence between merchant authors drawing from their account books and the emerging new self-consciously scientific use of data is hard to establish. Indeed, it has been argued that those early merchants were a significant influence on Bacon's empiricism.[107] Either way, the new discourse of scientific objectivity suited the needs of the authors of economic works, who were so often accused of serving their own narrow interests.

By the end of the seventeenth century, several economic authors had explicitly aligned themselves with philosophy and the scientific method. Dudley North and his brother Roger described this method as beginning true principles and proceeded to logically sound judgments—per the methods of philosophical reasoning. Henry Martyn similarly claimed that his opinions were based on the scientific methods and the logical deduction of systematic laws governing commerce and industry.[108]

Works increasingly drew in an explicit way from the scientific method, which had also become a part of public discourse by the middle of the century. Principles such as the balance of trade were widely accepted, circulated, and interrogated, so that authors began to recognize that an independent, common body of knowledge about trade was taking shape. Thomas Mun's lucid exposition of the idea of a balance of trade became a touchstone for authors. For the remaining years of the century, serious works on commerce inevitably considered his theory. Henry Martyn explicitly proposed using Petty's method of political arithmetic for investigations into economic matters.[109] In 1696, Nicholas Barbon referred to the accumulated body of works dealing with trade and specie flow as the "Theory

106. William Petty, *A Treatise of Taxes & Contributions. Shewing the Nature and Measures of [. . .]. The same being frequently applied to the present State and Affairs of Ireland* (London: Printed for N. Brooke, 1662), 24–25, Making of the Modern World.

107. Carl Wennerlind, "Money: Hartlibian Political Economy and the New Culture of Credit," in *Mercantilism Reimagined: Political Economy in Early Modern Britain and Its Empire*, ed. Philip J. Stern and Carl Wennerlind (New York: Oxford University Press, 2013), 74–96.

108. Martyn, *Considerations*.

109. Martyn, *Considerations*.

of Foreign Coins."[110] Daniel Defoe called it the field of "Universal Commerce."[111] Authors had become comfortable with discussing the abstraction they referred to as the "system of trade."[112] Progress was made in this extensive and heated dialogue. As Christopher Hill notes, economic thought had radically transformed over the course of the century: "The medieval ideas which underlay the great trading companies—restrict output, maintain quality and prices, still accepted at the beginning of the century—had been totally abandoned by the end."[113]

The field of economic literature was not just proliferating—as shown in the previous chapter—it was beginning to cohere as an independent entity. In the early seventeenth century, authors were regularly citing each other, as well as engaging in some heated and at times personal arguments. By the second half of the century, they were drawing from previous works in order to construct new arguments and elaborate on existing knowledge about the construction of value, specie flow, and the relationship between trade and land rents. By the 1690s, the authors had a theoretical domain—trade and finance—and a method through which to approach it: scientific reasoning and political arithmetic.

CONCLUSION

The bird's-eye view of the corpus presented in the previous chapter described the large cultural shift overtaking economic discourse. This chapter has focused in with a smaller lens on the literature, concentrating on two of the most transformative and generative debates of the era, as well as some more significant new features of the shifting discourse. This kind of close reading is an important supplement to any broad-brush corpus-wide assessment, particularly one that employs computational methods.

110. Barbon, *A Discourse Concerning Coining*, 19.

111. William Deringer, *Calculated Values: Finance, Politics, and the Quantitative Age* (Cambridge, MA: Harvard University Press, 2018), 132.

112. Isaac Gervaise, *The System or Theory of the Trade of the World* (Baltimore: Johns Hopkins Press, 1954); David Clayton, *A Short System of Trade: Or, An Account of What in Trade must necessarily be Advantageous to the Nation, and What must of Consequence be Detrimental* (London: Printed by R. Tookey for the Author, 1719), Making of the Modern World.

113. Christopher Hill, *The Century of Revolution, 1603–1714*, 2nd ed. (New York: Norton, 1961), 225.

A more detailed inspection contributes in at least two ways. First, while topic prevalence can provide evidence of secularization and nationalization in the economic discourse, it misses the intellectual contributions that were made by various authors. Those contributions were significant. The changes in the literature were systemic in the sense that they were not isolated acts of one uniquely brilliant man or woman. They were a result of institutional pressures that acted on larges classes of individuals. But this does not mean that there was not variation in the genius of individual responses. Individual breakthroughs require a larger discourse or milieu to support them. Still, those breakthroughs are important points in the larger progress toward greater collective knowledge. Because they are somewhat more significant than other contributions, they also serve as prime examples, which leads me to the second point.

Looking at two actual areas of debate makes the micro-mechanisms driving individuals' participation in the publication process clearer, making it is possible not only to observe the transformation but also to begin to understand the historical circumstances that produced it. The two most renowned and intellectually generative debates, about specie flow in the 1620s and manufacturing imports in the 1690s, are good cases to explore, not only because they were intellectual breakthroughs but also because they are representative of the larger class of debates. They were both directly tied to the practices of the some of the largest chartered companies, including the East India Company, the Eastland Company, and the Levant. This was far from uncommon.

Companies and their conduct were not the only subject of the new surge in economic writings. The excise tax drew considerable attention. Fishing rights were brought up here and there. There were even books on advertising and self-help. Usury, husbandry, and sermons to help the poor all appeared. But the chartered companies and their actions were at the heart of the most intellectually and theoretically generative debates of the century and were directly involved in an unusually large proportion of the new style of economic publications. The next chapter lays out contextual and theoretical reasons why this was the case.

Chapter Three

KEY ACTORS, INSTITUTIONS, AND RELATIONS

The economic literature of the seventeenth century was a turning point. Economic thought became markedly more sophisticated, empirical, and theoretical. It also became less concerned with fair exchange and more concerned with national prosperity. The chartered companies seemed to play an inordinately large role in its development. My central aim in this book is to supply an answer as to why these changes took place. A powerful clue lies in the intended audience for works.

Although they sometimes obscured their motivations, the authors were more explicit about their intentions. Thomas Mun, for example, wrote in the introduction to his *A Discovrse of Trade* that he was making his writings public "so these misunderstandings and errours may be made knowne unto the whole body of this Kindgome, which at this present time is most worthily represented in those noble assemblies of the high Courts of Parliament."[1] Henry Robinson, author of *Englands Safety, in Trades Encrease*, wrote, "My firste aime and pretence of penning this discourse, as you will finde perusing it, was, chiefly through brevitie to allure some one to cast an eye on't, who duly considering of what consequence the subject is,

---

1. Thomas Mun, *A Discovrse of Trade, From England vnto the East-Indies: Answering to diuerse Obiections which are vsvally made against the same* (London: Printed by Nicholas Okes for John Pyper, 1621), 4, Making of the Modern World.

might in his owne ripe judgement digest fully, and prevaile for the home prosecution of it, in this Honorable Court of Parliament."[2] Josiah Child wrote in a supplement to *A Discourse About Trade* that, "The fore-going Discourse I wrote in the Sickness-Summer at my Country-Habitation, not then intending to publish it, but only to communicate it to some Honourable and Ingenious friends of the present Parliament, who were pleased to take Copies of this for their own deliberate consideration and digestions."[3] Nicholas Barbon published *A Discourse Concerning Coining the New Money Lighter* in order to rebut John Locke's works because of the "the Reception they seem to have had from great Personages."[4] Daniel Defoe wrote of his object to counter popular opinion on taxes because "this vulgar Error has obtained so general a consent and approbation, that it needs not to be much inculcated. This the disaffected Part to the present Government are sufficiently sensible of, and therefore are not unactive in the establishment of an untruth."[5]

Many works were addressed to the Lords and Commons in Parliament assembled. *Reasons for Preserving the Publick Market of Blackwell-Hall* was "Humbly Offer'd to the Parliament."[6] *The Excise Rectify'd* was addressed to the "Honourable the Commons of England in Parliament assembled."[7] Joseph Trevers's *An Essay To the Restoring of our Decayed Trade* is addressed "To the Right Honourable Edward Seymour, Speaker of Right Honourable House of Commons; Treasurer of His Majesties Royal Navy, and one of His

2. Henry Robinson, *Englands Safety, in Trades Encrease. Most humbly presented to the High Court of Parliament* (London: Printed by E. P. for Nicholas Bourne, 1641), A2, Making of the Modern World.

3. Josiah Child, *A Discourse About Trade, Wherein the Reduction of Interest of Money to 4 l. per Centum, is Recommended* (London: A. Sowle, 1690), 30, Making of the Modern World.

4. Nicholas Barbon, *A Discourse Concerning Coining the New Money Lighter. In Answer to Mr. Lock's Considerations about raising the Value of Money* (London: Printed for Richard Chiswell, 1696), A2–A3, Making of the Modern World.

5. Daniel Defoe, *Taxes no Charge: in A Letter from a Gentleman, to A Person of Quality. Shewing The Nature, Use, and Benefit of Taxes in this Kingdom; and compared with the Impositions of Foreign States. Together with their Improvement of Trade in Time of War* (London: Printed for R. Chiswell, 1690), A2, Making of the Modern World.

6. *Reasons for Preserving the Publick Market of Blackwell-Hall, and restraining the Levant Company of Merchants from deferring their Shipping as long as they please. Humbly Offer'd to the Parliament* ([London, 1696?]), 1, Making of the Modern World.

7. John Farthing, *The Excise Rectify'd: Or, a Plain Demonstration, That The Revenue now raised thereby, is capable of being Improved at least Four or Five Hundred Thousand Pounds per Annum, which is now paid by the Subject, but diverted from its proper Chanel into private Hands* (London, 1695/6), A2, Making of the Modern World.

Majesties most Honourable Privy Councel."[8] These examples do not in any way exhaust the numerous instances.

Thomas Violet went on at perhaps the greatest length to outline in detail the motivations behind his published work. He first addressed *The Advancement of Merchandize* to John Bradshaw, the Lord President of the Council of State. One can infer why Violet turned to print from his opening statement: "My Lord! When first I attended your Lordship, about preparing of an *Act, against the Transporting of Gold*, your Lordship was pleased to take no notice of mee."[9] He then went on to say:

> Now my request is to all the worthie Merchants of this Nation, that som of them would bee pleased to take this argument into their hands, and what I have said undigestedly, and without a method, they with a more learned pen would perfect for the service of the Nation in general. Most of these Papers are transmitted down to the Honorable Council of Trade, by an order of the Council of State, and referred to their judicious consideration. And the true reason of my printing of them is, that som more learned pen might finish what I have roughly begun; and whosoever doth it, would do a great service to the Common-wealth.[10]

Violet published his works when lobbying had failed and with the further idea of inspiring other merchants and authors to improve his theory of commerce, so as to provide an even more convincing rationale to persuade the state to follow his recommendations.

LEVERS OF POWER

Merchants were clearly interested in influencing the government's trade policy. This undertaking could be complex as the fledgling English imperial nation-state was a variegated patchwork of interlocking parts, the whole

8. Joseph Trevers, *An Essay To the Restoring of our Decayed Trade. Wherein is Described, the Smuglers, Lawyers, and Officers Frauds, &c.* (London: Printed for Gilew Widdowes, 1675), 2, Making of the Modern World.

9. Thomas Violet, *The Advancement of Merchandize: or, Certain Propositions For the Improvment of the Trade of this Common-wealth, humbly presented to the Right Honorable the Council of State* (London: W. DuGard, Printer to the Council of State, 1651), A2, Making of the Modern World.

10. Violet, *The Advancement of Merchandize*, C2.

of which experienced a dramatic transformation that has been characterized as the birth of the modern state. Not only were different elements of
the state important to merchants and their concerns, but the elements and
their functions also changed over time.

The general contours of state transformation are well known. The
monarchies of the Tudors and Stuarts came under increasing financial
and sectarian pressures as the seventeenth century progressed. In 1640,
Charles I called Parliament into session. That Parliament refused to dis-
solve and became a locus of militarized political resistance to the King.
In 1642, civil war broke out. After a series of battles, through which
the Parliamentarians gained the upper hand, Charles I was executed
in January 1649. The Commonwealth was enacted on May 19, 1649;
however, Royalist support had simply shifted from Charles I to his
son, Charles II. It was not until Charles II fled Parliamentarian forces
and hid among the branches of the Royal Oak that the war was finally
halted in 1651.

The Parliamentarians had won the war, and on December 16, 1653, Oliver Cromwell was made Lord Protector. After a brief period of stability,
Cromwell died in 1658, leaving behind a political vacuum. In 1660, the
monarchy was restored under Charles II. Once again, a fragile peace was
unable to withstand succession dynamics. Charles II died in 1685 and was
succeeded by James II, who was much less effective at quelling the political unrest that continued to agitate the nation. In 1688, William of Orange
crossed the English Channel with Parliamentarian support to contest the
rule of James II. James II found few supporters and deserted the country for France in December of that year. William and Mary ascended
the throne under a new constitutional arrangement that increased the
powers of Parliament. Hostilities and conflict persisted through 1691, but
England had finally found its footing and had entered an extremely long
period of domestic political stability, economic growth, and international
political ascendancy.

These political events punctuated other processes of long-term transformation. The reign of the Tudor monarch Queen Elizabeth I (r. 1558–1603)
was highly personalistic, whereas the Georgian king George I (r. 1714–1727)
presided within a bureaucratized constitutional monarchy. In the first half
of the seventeenth century, the state only partially penetrated to local levels:
important officeholders were not well differentiated from constituents and

tended to represent community expectations rather than state priorities.[11] By the 1690s, partisanship and national politics had reached all levels of governance. The Court of the King's Bench played an increasingly important role in adjudicating local disputes, increasing the power of the centralized state.[12] The state had become a modernizing force that was intent on introducing new modes of economic activity to the countryside and capable of sustained military action overseas.[13] As England's political reach stretched to the Americas and Asia, the concerns of governing an expanding global empire became increasingly pressing. These momentous transformations naturally affected the paths through which the merchants interacted with and attempted to influence commercial policy. As a rule, the status of merchants was rising in the seventeenth century, which changed their level of access, and powerful merchants became increasingly intertwined with the political elite, through familial, economic, and political ties.[14] This rise in social status did not immediately translate into greater formal influence.

The sections of the state most important to commerce and commercial policy were the Crown, the Privy Council, the Parliament, the Court of the King's Bench, the incorporated boroughs, and the various trade committees and councils formed over the course of the century. Needless to say, merchants were excluded from the Crown. They were also absent from the aristocratic ranks of the Privy Council. More direct representation was possible in Parliament, though a majority position was never achieved. Merchants had the most influence in the local boroughs.

With the exception of the Interregnum, the Crown was an important source of privileges—such as monopoly charters—and susceptible to commercial and financial influences because of its difficult pecuniary situation. Parliament controlled tax revenues, and the Crown found itself chronically low on funds, particularly when trying to support military offensives.[15] In granting charters, the Crown stood to gain both direct payments or loans

11. Michael Braddick, "The Early Modern English State and the Question of Differentiation, from 1550 to 1700," *Comparative Studies in Society and History* 38, no. 1 (January 1996): 92–111.

12. Paul D. Halliday, *Dismembering the Body Politic: Partisan Politics in England's Towns, 1650–1730* (Cambridge: Cambridge University Press, 2003).

13. Steve Pincus, *1688: The First Modern Revolution* (New Haven, CT: Yale University Press, 2009).

14. Pincus, *1688: The First Modern Revolution.*

15. This situation changed with the formation of the Bank of England and the institution of the system of public debt in 1694, alleviating some of the financial pressure.

from the incorporated merchants and the possibility of increases in state revenue, which was generated in large part through taxes on overseas trade.[16] Queen Elizabeth I in particular was the subject of intense parliamentary criticism for selling an extraordinary number of special monopoly rights in order to raise funds.[17] It was this practice, however, that served as the basis on which large chartered firms began to dominate overseas commerce in the early seventeenth century. It was Queen Elizabeth I, for example, who chartered the English East India Company on the last day of 1600.

The chartering process turned out to be an important point of ongoing coordination and negotiation between merchants and the Crown. The charters were granted on a limited basis, so companies would have to appeal to the Crown for extension of their charters. This reapplication process often involved the extension of new loans or grants of money to the Crown. The government also drew upon the companies for political assistance in interactions with foreign powers. The Eastland Traders negotiated international relations with Sweden,[18] the East India Company brought the embassy of Sir Thomas Roe to the Mughal emperor Jahangir, and the Levant Company was crucial in maintaining smooth relations with the Ottomans.

Despite these instances of cooperation and delegation, the Crown was an unreliable partner for the chartered companies. It was not uncommon for the Crown to take money from one company for exclusive rights to trade, then simultaneously grant the same exclusive rights to a different organization. Charles I, for example, chartered the East India Company, became unhappy with its performance, and turned around and chartered the Courteen Company as a direct challenge to the East India Company and the monopoly rights he had granted to them.

---

16. S. R. H. Jones and Simon P. Ville, "Efficient Transactors or Rent-Seeking Monopolists? The Rationale for Early Chartered Trading Companies," *Journal of Economic History* 56, no. 4 (December 1996): 898–915.

17. As Christopher Hill memorably put it, a seventeenth-century English citizen "slept on monopoly feathers, did his hair with monopoly brushes and monopoly combs. He washed himself with monopoly soap, his clothes in monopoly starch. He dressed in monopoly lace, monopoly linen, monopoly leather, monopoly gold thread. His hat was of monopoly beaver, with a monopoly band. His clothes were held up by monopoly belts, monopoly buttons, monopoly pins. They were dyed with monopoly dyes. He ate monopoly butter . . . monopoly lobsters. His food was seasoned with monopoly salt." Christopher Hill, *The Century of Revolution, 1603–1714*, 2nd ed. (New York: W. W. Norton, 1961), 31.

18. R. W. K. Hinton, *The Eastland Trade and the Common Weal in the Seventeenth Century* (Cambridge: At the University Press, 1959), 66–70.

There was an element missing from the relationship between the Crown and the companies that is so commonsense today that we might take its existence for granted. Despite patchy support for companies, the Crown showed little intrinsic or sustained interest in the development of trade itself. This was the case until at least the 1660s.[19] The relationship appears to have been much more along the lines of a quid pro quo. Nevertheless, maintaining good relations with the Crown was understandably a priority for the companies, explaining in part why many took the Royalist side in the Civil War. Their decision did not pay off for long. Royal charters continue to exist to this day, but much of the power to assign monopolies and incorporate organized bodies passed first into the hands of the Commonwealth, and ultimately into the hands of Parliament.

The Crown was advised by the Privy Council, which was a small board composed of elite members of Parliament. The Privy Council considered and issued advice on many matters related to trade, such as the granting of charters, support of trade, and allowances on specie export. The Privy Council was a direct path to the power of the Crown and handled much of the more mundane business on its own. Thus, it was a central object of merchant's lobbying efforts. The Merchant Adventurers, for example, petitioned the Privy Council in 1598, hoping to restrict sales of cloth to Middelburg. Their influence was blocked, however, by another contingent of merchants, clothiers, and clothworkers who pushed the council to maintain current export levels.[20] Much later, in 1614, William Cockayne and his associates devised a scheme to export dyed and dressed cloth from England. They turned to the Privy Council for help realizing their project. The Privy Council supported the project by suspending the charter of the Merchant Adventurers and forbidding the export of white (i.e., undyed) cloth.[21] These actions stirred up protest by clothiers, clothworkers, and the Merchant Adventures. The Merchant Adventurers lobbied the council to reverse its decision. In cases such as these, similar instances of which reoccurred throughout the seventeenth century, merchant organizations both

19. Perry Gauci, *Politics of Trade: The Overseas Merchant in State and Society, 1660–1720* (Oxford: Oxford University Press, 2001), 10.

20. Barry E. Supple, *Commercial Crisis and Change in England, 1600–1642: A Study in the Instability of a Mercantile Economy* (Cambridge: Cambridge University Press, 1959), 24.

21. Supple, *Commercial Crisis and Change*, 34.

lobbied the council themselves and paid elite representatives to speak persuasively on their behalf.[22]

The Privy Council had deep ties to the Crown and tended to side with the royally backed chartered companies against other merchants, but it was also an independent voice. Whereas the Crown's actions were often transparently venal, the Privy Council espoused the philosophy of regulated corporate governance.[23] Corporate governance was aimed at producing an ordered and harmonious trade—not necessarily a dynamic and growing trade. This ideological position contributed to more consistent support for the chartered companies than had been offered by the Crown. The existence of an ideological position does not, however, mean that the Privy Council was immune to other forms of influence. Bribery was a common path to influence in that era. There should be little doubt that the members of the council accepted many fine gifts from merchants during their terms of service. After the Civil War and the Glorious Revolution, the Privy Council's influence over commercial affairs waned in parallel to the fortunes of the Crown.

While Parliament had clearly gained in power at the conclusion of the seventeenth century, it was not an unimportant player even in the sixteenth. At this point in time, England's Parliament was not a regularly meeting body. Sessions often lasted two or three months, and it was not unusual for two sessions to occur in one year. In many years, Parliament did not meet. Each time Parliament was called to session, there was a new election for parliamentary representatives. And it was the Crown that decided when Parliament should be called into being. This occurred when the sitting queen or king deemed it necessary to handle matters of business, such as the passing of financial bills. Thus, the powers of Parliament in the early seventeenth century were limited and exercised at the discretion of the Crown; yet Parliament had dominion over many financial issues. One the one hand, the Parliament of 1559 pleaded unsuccessfully with Queen Elizabeth I on the issue of her marital status. On the other hand, they passed several different acts that encouraged the shipping industry and regulated different

22. Ian Archer, "The London Lobbies in the Later Sixteenth Century," *Historical Journal* 31, no. 1 (March 1988): 17–44.

23. Barry E. Supple, "Thomas Mun and the Commercial Crisis, 1623," *Bulletin of the Institute of Historical Research* 27, no. 75 (May 1954): 91–94, https://doi.org/10.1111/j.1468-2281.1954.tb01014.x, 122; and Supple, *Commercial Crisis and Change*.

aspects of the leather trade, linen manufacturing, and the iron industry.[24] Parliament was an important vehicle for the determination of national trade policy through its control over the imposition of tariffs and duties.

Parliament also exercised its power elsewhere and increasingly over the decades. While it was the royal prerogative to grant monopolies, Parliament was often in the business of trying to revoke those privileges. The geographic basis of parliamentary elections translated into heavier representation of outport merchant interests than City (i.e., London) merchants. This tilt meant that chartered companies—which were mainly based in London—were not favored. Resistance to the chartered companies in Parliament frequently took the form of criticism of the idea of monopoly rights. Figures such as Walter Raleigh (who held a tin monopoly) and Francis Bacon engaged in heated debates over monopoly privileges in Parliament in the earliest years of the seventeenth century.

The way in which this issue was first raised in Parliament was tied to the practices of the monarch. As noted earlier, Queen Elizabeth I had generated considerable funds by selectively granting special monopoly privileges in return for monetary support (this was how Raleigh had obtained his tin monopoly). Many members of Parliament objected to this practice. Theirs was less a moral argument and more a commonwealth argument: they noted the broader negative impact of exclusionary practices on the trade and the prosperity of all. Queen Elizabeth I accepted the grounds upon which objections were raised, but testified that she had been deceived by individuals who "pretended to me that all my subjects should have publicke benefit and profit, as well as they should have private gain."[25] The narrative of the public benefit had already been established as an important litmus test for economic concerns within the halls of government.

Despite conceding to the logic of her critics, Queen Elizabeth I did not give up the practice of offering charters and patents—nor did later monarchs. Debates over monopoly privileges continued. One of the first actions of the revolutionary Long Parliament was to penalize monopolists and their close cousin, projectors. Projectors were individuals granted special rights by the state to collect customs and excise duties. In an internally divisive

24. P. W. Hasler, ed., *The House of Commons, 1558–1603*, 3 vols. (London: Published for the History of Parliament Trust by Her Majesty's Stationery Office, 1981).

25. Hasler, *House of Commons.*

purge, Parliament excluded projectors and monopolists from its ranks. It further constituted a committee to identify monopolists and projectors in Parliament and encouraged sitting members to denounce each other on those grounds. Fifty parliamentarians had been ejected by the spring of 1641.[26] Chartered companies were not automatically considered monopolies, and several prominent company merchants continued to serve in the Long Parliament, including Thomas Soame, Isaac Penington, Matthew Cradock, and John Venn. Collectively they represented ties to the Grocer's Company, the Levant Company, the East India Company, the Fishmonger's Company, the Massachusetts Bay Company, and the Merchant Taylor's Company.[27] Most of these men, however, did not survive Pride's Purge, another round of ejections that took place in 1648.

Over the same time period, merchants—both those company men and independents—were elected to Parliament at a declining rate. In 1572, there were eighty merchants in Parliament; in 1687, there were thirty-seven. The number of members of Parliament varied, but the total number of MPs increased over time while the number of merchant MPs fell. The percentage decreased from 15.8 percent in the 1580s to a low of 11 percent in the mid to late seventeenth century. Most of Parliament was composed of landed elites and lawyers. The aristocrats and professionals began to crowd out the merchants as Parliament became an increasingly well-trodden path to national recognition, advancement, and power. As a result, merchants never came close to gaining a sizable minority in Parliament. In part because they remained largely on the outskirts and in part because they were a diverse body with many different and often competing interests, merchants had recourse to methods other than direct participation in their attempts to influence Parliament. They used strategies similar to those used with the Privy Council. They engaged in direct lobbying efforts, hired councilors to argue their case, found ways to pay aristocrats and other MPs to speak on their behalf, held lavish dinners, and distributed gifts.[28] Some things do not seem to change.

The judicature played an important role in the regulation and management of trade. Merchants were also part of this process as they brought

26. Douglas Brunton and Donald H. Pennington, *Members of the Long Parliament* (London: Allen & Unwin, 1954), 56–57.

27. Brunton and Pennington, *Members of the Long Parliament*, 58.

28. Chris R. Kyle, "Parliament and the Politics of Carting in Early Stuart London," *London Journal* 27, no. 2 (2002): 6.

trials to court on a regular basis. Particularly after the Restoration, the newly empowered Court of the King's Bench oversaw the fate of several chartered companies. One important case was *East India Company v. Thomas Sandys* (1685).[29] Thomas Sandys was an interloper charged by the company for infringing on their Crown-granted privileges to exclusive trade in the East. Such a case would have been straightforward in the past, but this suit became a referendum on the legality of the Crown's right to grant privileges. Ultimately, the court found for the East India Company, effectively securing the continuation of the right of the Crown to enforce monopoly privileges.[30]

This understanding was to last only a few years. After 1688, the antimonopolist Whigs came to power, and a new court case, *Nightingale and others v. Bridges*, representing a dispute between the Royal African Company and an interloper, was brought to trial. This time the court found in favor of the interlopers, effectively ruling that parliamentary and common law took precedence over the right of the Crown to grant special trade privileges.[31] In 1692, Gilbert Heathcote challenged the right of the Privy Council to restrict trade and was able to pass a nonstatutory resolution in the House of Commons that reserved the right to restrict trade to an explicit act of Parliament.[32] In 1720, an act was passed that discouraged the creation of new joint-stock organizations by further restricting their formation to instances of special parliamentary acts or royal charter.[33]

There was one other locus of centralized state power relevant to the economic issues. In the seventeenth century, trade councils and committees first began to appear, formed to pursue specific inquiries and issues. The first of these committees appears to have been a poorly documented 1600

29. Thomas Sandys and England and Wales, Court of King's Bench, East India Company v. Thomas Sandys, 1683–1685, HLS MS 1268, Harvard Law School Library.

30. James Bohun, "Protecting Prerogative: William III and the East India Trade Debate, 1689–1698," *Past Imperfect* 2 (1993): 63–68, https://doi.org/10.21971/P74S3M; Pincus, *1688: The First Modern Revolution*, 376; and William Letwin, *Sir Josiah Child: Merchant Economist*, Kress Library of Business and Economics 14 (Boston: Baker Library; Harvard Graduate School of Business Administration, 1959), 221.

31. W. Darrell Stump, "An Economic Consequence of 1688," *Albion: A Quarterly Journal Concerned with British Studies* 6, no. 1 (Spring 1974): 26–35, https://doi.org/10.2307/4048209.

32. William A. Pettigrew, *Freedom's Debt: The Royal African Company and the Politics of the Atlantic Slave Trade, 1672–1752* (Williamsburg, VA: Omohundro Institute of Early American History and Culture; Chapel Hill: University of North Carolina Press, 2013), 43.

33. Ron Harris, "The Bubble Act: Its Passage and Its Effects on Business Organization," *Journal of Economic History* 54, no. 3 (1994): 623.

commission appointed by Queen Elizabeth I to investigate a shortage of coin. Gerard de Malynes is known to have been a part of this commission, but little information is available about its other members or activities. Special committees and councils to address the concerns of merchants had a scattered trajectory over the course of the seventeenth century. The next recorded committee was not formed until 1623.

The conditions surrounding the 1623 committee were economic and political turmoil. In 1622, England was two years into a significant trade depression. King James I might have turned to Parliament for a discussion of these difficulties, but his relations with that political body were troubled. He appears to have avoided calling Parliament to order unless absolutely no other alternative was possible. Public debate and outrage were high, however, and James I ordered a special committee of experts to report to the Privy Council on the causes of economic distress. The committee, convened in 1623, included three Crown officers and three merchants. One of the merchants was the author Thomas Mun.[34] Although the names of the other two merchants are not recorded, the act calling the committee into being indicates that the other two merchant representatives were a member of the Merchant Adventurers and a clothier.[35] As noted earlier, this committee became an important source of influential economic works.

The important work of the committee seems to have been recognized by state actors as useful. A semipermanent council of trade, composed of Privy Councilors and Crown officers, was instituted in 1630 and lasted until 1640.[36] In the turmoil of that decade, the institutional stability broke down; through the 1640s, various other councils were intermittently appointed. These mainly concerned themselves with the affairs of the American colonies. Eventually another permanent group was created, the Lords of Trade

---

34. Carlos Eduardo Suprinyak, "Trade, Money, and the Grievances of the Commonwealth: Economic Debates in the English Public Sphere During the Commercial Crisis of the Early 1620's," Texto para discussão 427, Centro de Desenvolvimento e Planejamento Regional (CEDEPLAR) da UFMG, Belo Horizonte, Brazil, June 2011, http://www.cedeplar.ufmg.br/pesquisas/td/TD%20427 .pdf.

35. A. W. Fitzroy, W. L. Grant, J. Munro, and Great Britain, *Acts of the Privy Council of England*, vol. 33, *1613–1614* (Burlington, ON: TannerRitchie, 2010; first published 1921 by His Majesty's Stationery Office), 190–91.

36. Charles M. Andrews, *British Committees, Commissions, and Councils of Trade and Plantations, 1622–1675* (Baltimore: Johns Hopkins Press, 1908), 13, http://archive.org/details/british committeooandrgoog.

and Plantations. In May 1696, this group was renamed the Board of Trade and Plantations, which gradually came to be known as the Board of Trade. In 1697, William Culliford became the first inspector-general of imports and exports. The second inspector-general was the author of economic tracts Charles Davenant.[37]

Although this institutional platform could be penetrated by merchants, even here they did not find themselves entirely welcome. According to Perry Gauci, "Stuart governors viewed the prospect of a large assembly of trading representatives as an inefficient and potentially disorderly body, and thus relegated merchants and traders to a subsidiary role, as informants and petitioners."[38] Merchants were intermittently placed in these committees but were never considered the sole authority on trade. The 1651 standing committee on trade called on merchants to offer testimony but solicited advice from judges, lawyers, and specialists in other areas as well. By 1655, two merchants, Martin Noell (member of the East India Company) and Thomas Povey, were proposing a new committee of trade in order to increase the influence of merchants in the governance of commerce. A new committee was formed, but contrary to their hopes, merchants once again formed only a small proportion of a large roster of members.[39]

Even the small amount of influence merchants had been able to carve out within these councils and committees came under attack after the Interregnum. The councils were undercut during the Restoration because royalists openly suspected the councils of attempting to undermine the power of the king through financial means.[40] The disputes among merchants over company privileges further limited what influence they had. The Council of 1668 was torn apart by a dispute between the East India Company and Levant Company representatives, William Love and Josiah Child, respectively. The Love-Child debate was particularly destructive and delegitimized the council and many of its members as contemporaries came to believe their arguments were motivated purely by material self-interest.[41]

37. William Deringer, *Calculated Values: Finance, Politics, and the Quantitative Age* (Cambridge, MA: Harvard University Press, 2018), 122.

38. Gauci, *Politics of Trade*, 181.

39. Andrews, *British Committees*.

40. Letwin, *Sir Josiah Child*, 13.

41. Letwin, *Sir Josiah Child*, 15.

Merchants did not consider these committees adequate to represent their concerns or communicate their valuable expertise in commercial affairs to the politicians running the state. Several, including Lewes Roberts and Thomas Roe, made public calls for the formation for a council of merchants to advise the state on economic matters.[42] This refrain was to be repeated many times over the course of the seventeenth century and beyond. As late as 1698, the otherwise powerful Charles Davenant noted that the presence of merchants in the offices of the Dutch state was crucial to the great commercial success of that country, bemoaned the lack of merchant representation in England, and advocated that increases were necessary for England to achieve comparable levels of economic development.[43]

Outside of the centralized state, there were other important areas of local influence. Urban centers, of which there were many, were governed by corporations.[44] We tend now to associate the corporate form with commerce and industry, but then corporations were more commonly understood to be groups or councils of elected officials bound together by rules and procedures into a governing body. These local governing corporations regulated local commercial activity while also providing local services and managing property.[45] Unlike central state offices, borough-level polities were dominated by merchants. Gauci reports that in the late seventeenth century, "more than half of civic office-holders also held posts within the City's trading and livery companies."[46] In London and elsewhere, it was beneficial to a merchant's stature to hold some kind of civic position, and thus those positions were sought after. Still, merchants attempted to minimize both the potential political fallout in an era of increasing partisanship and the hours away from their business concerns by seeking out less important positions.[47]

---

42. Lewes Roberts, *The Treasure of Traffike, or A Discourse of Forraigne Trade* (London: Printed by E. P. for Nicholas Bourne, 1641), Making of the Modern World; and Thomas Roe, *Sir Thomas Roe his Speech in Parliament. Wherein He sheweth the cause of the decay of Coyne and Trade in this Land, especially of Merchants Trade. [. . .]* (n.p., 1641), 10, Making of the Modern World.

43. Charles Davenant, *Discourses on the Publick Revenues, and on the Trade of England. In Two Parts* (London: Printed for James Knapton, 1698), Making of the Modern World.

44. Phil Withington, *The Politics of Commonwealth: Citizens and Freemen in Early Modern England* (Cambridge: Cambridge University Press, 2005).

45. Halliday, *Dismembering the Body Politic*, 101.

46. Gauci, *Politics of Trade*, 85.

47. Gauci, *Politics of Trade*, 87.

These local arenas gave some power to merchants, but not enough to satisfy them. Many of the issues dearest to the most powerful merchants were national and could not be handled at the borough level. The chartered companies were one such issue. The minority position of merchants within the halls of government closed off internal avenues for discussion. Merchants' limited access to the parliamentary floor and the councils and committees of state reduced the space available to them for instituting favorable policies and resolving disputes. This situation created a strong incentive to make public appeals in order to build support and constituencies outside of the state as part of the process of lobbying for the privileges they felt were necessary to the successful pursuit of trade. Ultimately, it was the marginalization of merchants in government that created a context in which they required different platforms to make their voices heard. A natural alternative was to publish works in the public sphere, appealing to the intended audience of the Crown, Privy Council, Parliament, and others with power and influence.

ORGANIZED CONTROVERSY

Marginalization was the context that led merchants and their advocates into the public sphere to make their opinions heard. Context, however, does not necessarily supply motivation. Motivation is where the chartered companies enter the picture. Not all the important work on economics in this era was exclusively about the companies. Yet the companies appear to have served as crucial stimuli—powerful enough to encourage more debates, more books, and a newly popular nationalist rhetorical framework for works. Chartered companies repeatedly lay at the center of the most significant economic debates of the century, but it may not be immediately obvious why.

One very straightforward answer is that many of the authors published at the behest of the companies for which they worked. Books and pamphlets were funded by companies and their adversaries as part of their lobbying efforts, which were designed to improve their bottom line or protect their existing interests. Independent slave traders launched an extremely successful pamphlet war against the Royal African Company.[48] John Cary's works

---

48. Pettigrew, *Freedom's Debt*, 40–44.

were paid for by the Bristol Society of Merchant Venturers. The East India Company court of directors debated whether to reprint Thomas Mun's *A Discovrse of Trade*.[49] The Royal Fishery employed John Collins as an accountant and author. Collins published at least two pamphlets for the company: *A Plea For the bringing in of Irish cattel, And keeping out of Fish Caught by Foreigners* (1680) and *Salt and Fishery, A Discourse thereof Insisting on the following Heads* (1682).[50] Robert Ferguson, likely author of *The East-India-Trade a most Profitable Trade to the Kingdom* (1677),[51] was recruited as an author by Thomas Papillon, member and director of the East India Company. The company records show that Ferguson was paid twenty guineas for writing a pamphlet. In all likelihood, he produced other publications for the company as well. Other favorable pamphlets appear to have been produced by different committees of East India Company principals.[52] These are some of the cases in which these informal practices have been documented and recorded. Many more instances of formal and informal patronage have doubtless slipped by without an observable trace. The companies clearly believed they could gain materially from guiding state policy and found publishing to be an effective strategy through which to pursue that goal.

The mechanisms driving debate were, however, more extensive and broader than calculated corporate strategy alone. Debates within companies also spilled over into the public realm. In 1638, the contentious chartering of the Vintners Guild produced a burst of published works.[53] In this case,

49. Richard Grassby, *The Business Community of Seventeenth-Century England* (Cambridge: Cambridge University Press, 2002).

50. John Collins, *A Plea For the bringing in of Irish cattel, And keeping out of Fish Caught by Foreigners* (London: A. Godbid and J. Playford, 1680), Making of the Modern World; and John Collins, *Salt and Fishery, A Discourse thereof Insisting on the following Heads* (London: A. Godbid and J. Playford, 1682), Making of the Modern World.

51. [Robert Ferguson], *The East-India-Trade a most Profitable Trade to the Kingdom. And Best Secured and Improved in a Company, and a Joint-Stock* (London, 1677), Making of the Modern World.

52. William Letwin has produced much of the evidence about the authorship of tracts by Ferguson, Papillon, and Child. I rely on his work but give final word on decisions of authorship to D. P. O'Brien and A. C. Darnell. See O'Brien and Darnell, *Authorship Puzzles in the History of Economics: A Statistical Approach* (London: Macmillan, 1982), https://doi.org/10.1007/978-1-349-05697-2, chap. 2; and William Letwin, *The Origins of Scientific Economics: English Economic Thought, 1660–1776* (London: Methuen, 1963), chap. 1.

53. Phil Withington, "Public Discourse, Corporate Citizenship, and State Formation in Early Modern England," *American Historical Review* 112, no. 4 (October 2006): 1016–38; and Anne Crawford, *A History of the Vintners' Company* (London: Constable, 1977), 118–20.

a central complaint of the membership was that William Abell, master of the company, had purposefully tamped down open discussion of the issue under contention, thereby restricting the ability of merchants to debate the decision in company meetings. These merchants were no longer allowed to exercise the rights of free speech within the company meetings of the Vintners, so they turned to the public sphere. Thomas Johnson's dispute with his former employer, the Eastland Company, resulted in the pamphlet *A Plea for Free-Mens Liberties* (1646).[54] Other instances of a similar nature illustrate that the public discussion of trade and commerce was not merely a two-sided dialogue between merchants and the state. It was a multipolar conversation among different parties with different interests at stake.

One reason the companies stirred up such immense controversy was their novelty. Most trade for most of human history and across most of the world had been conducted by individual traders—or peddlers, as JC Van Leur and Clifford Geertz referred to them—family firms, and partnerships. Chartered companies were much larger and had a more complex, legally defined internal structure. The difference can be helpfully illuminated by the contrast between a contract and charter: a contract defines the terms of an exchange; a charter defines a durable internal governance structure for a social body. The chartered companies of England's early modern era can be defined by three crucial characteristics: chartering, incorporation, and monopoly privilege.

These characteristics together were extremely uncommon before the early modern era, and they remained rare outside of England for at least another century. The Netherlands, France, Sweden, and Denmark did produce a smaller number of similar companies.[55] The rest of Europe produced very few. In Prussia, only five joint-stocks existed prior to 1800.[56] Spain did not adopt chartered companies until the eighteenth century.[57] The idea and

---

54. Thomas Johnson, *A Plea for Free-Mens Liberties: or The Monopoly of the Eastland Marchants anatomized by divers arguments (wch will also serve to set forth the unjustnesse of the Marchant-Adventurers Monopoly,)* [. . .] (n.p., 1646), Making of the Modern World (Gale Document Number U0100144924). On the link, see Hinton, *Eastland Trade*, 82–83.

55. Hanna Hodacs, "Chartered Companies," in *The Encyclopedia of Empire*, ed. John M. MacKenzie (n.p.: John Wiley & Sons, 2016).

56. Julian Franks, Colin Mayer, and Hannes F. Wagner, "The Origins of the German Corporation—Finance, Ownership and Control," *Review of Finance* 10, no. 4 (2006): 537–85.

57. Roland D. Hussey, "Antecedents of the Spanish Monopolistic Overseas Trading Companies (1624–1728)," *Hispanic American Historical Review* 9, no. 1 (February 1929): 1–30, https://doi.org/10.2307/2506638.

process of incorporation was completely foreign to the Islamic and Asian commercial worlds until the mid-nineteenth century.[58]

Among the earliest corporate forms were the tax-farming collectives, *societas publicanorum*, of the Roman Empire. It has been argued that these organizations were similar to the chartered companies of the seventeenth century in the sense that they had tradable shares, but most recent evaluations have concluded that this is highly unlikely.[59] These corporations seem to have disappeared from the economy after the fall of the Republic, so no clear line of commercial evolution links ancient Rome with early modern England.[60]

Carlo Taviani has made a compelling case that the earliest chartered company was the *Casa di San Giorgio*.[61] Genoese state debt had been funded by a variety of creditors, whose officers were formally recognized by the state. In 1407, the Genoese state created the *Casa di San Giorgio* to reduce the administrative burden of holding many different loan arrangements and to strengthen the rights of creditors, thereby reducing the cost of debt for the state.[62] The *Casa* became a private commercial association that was granted special privileges by the state with the intent of serving public interests. In this sense, it was very similar to the chartered companies of England. It survived almost four hundred years, serving as a central bank and managing the public debts of the city. By the time of its dissolution in 1805, it had come, much like other early modern chartered companies, to exercise territorial power as well. The *Casa* was, however, a *rara avis* for hundreds of years after its establishment.

In England and across Europe there were other organized commercial bodies, distinct from partnerships and family networks. These were guilds—semipublic spaces in which men, and even occasionally women,

58. Timur Kuran, "The Absence of the Corporation in Islamic Law: Origins and Persistence," *American Journal of Comparative Law* 53, no. 4 (Fall 2005): 785–834.

59. Geoffrey Poitras and Frederick Willeboordse, "The *Societas Publicanorum* and Corporate Personality in Roman Private Law," *Business History*, 2019, https://doi.org/10.1080/00076791.2019.1656719.

60. Moses I. Finley, *The Ancient Economy* (Berkeley: University of California Press, 1973), 144.

61. Carlo Taviani, "An Ancient Scheme: The Mississippi Company, Machiavelli, and the Casa Di San Giorgio (1407–1720)," in *Chartering Capitalism: Organizing Markets, States, and Publics*, ed. Emily Erikson (Bingley, UK: Emerald Group, 2015), 239–56.

62. Michele Fratianni, "Government Debt, Reputation and Creditors' Protections: The Tale of San Giorgio," *Review of Finance* 10, no. 4 (2006): 487–506, https://doi.org/10.1007/s10679-006-9006-7.

associated with one another in some sort of joint pursuit. Guilds were life-time associations characterized by strong social and moral bonds organized around the principle of fraternity. As a general rule, guilds were based on the principle of regulated membership and the monopolization of skill and labor. English guilds were usually formed around crafts, which could be very finely divided into specific types of expertise. In London, there was a guild of white bakers and a guild of brown bakers. The first had rights to white bread and the second to brown, and they appear to have frequently clashed over which breads were white and which were brown.[63] (Rye must have been problematic.) These guilds were mostly locally bounded monopolies that extended only to their immediate municipality.[64]

Ron Harris has recently argued that the reason the business corporation emerged in the seventeenth century in Europe—and not elsewhere—was that Europe offered a unique setting in which religious authority, the Catholic Church, was uncoupled from state political power. This uncoupling created a culture in which nonpolitical corporate bodies—such as guilds, universities, and town corporations—were able to proliferate.[65] Eventually, these bodies evolved into the business corporation.

In England, some of the largest and most powerful guilds transitioned into chartered companies. The first transitions were gradual and unfolded over centuries. As a result, the line distinguishing chartered guilds from chartered companies can be fuzzy, and debates about exactly which company was truly the first of its kind are ongoing. For example, Harris argues that the English East India Company was the first of its kind.[66] In many ways, it was. Nevertheless, it is also possible to agree that the Merchant Adventurers were the first chartered company in England, using "chartered company" as a slightly more encompassing term than "business corporation," which also requires joint-stock organization.

---

63. Archer, "London Lobbies," 26. These two guilds were known for long-standing tensions that stemmed from the possibility of categorizing different breads as brown and white. Hostilities were so intense between the two guilds, and the need for bread so fundamental, that the City of London intervened and forced a union of the two factions in 1569. The new guild was named the Worshipful Company of Bakers.

64. Ian Anders Gadd and Patrick Wallis, "Reaching Beyond the City Wall: London Guilds and National Regulation, 1500–1700," in *Guilds, Innovation, and the European Economy, 1400–1800*, ed. S. R. Epstein and Maarten Prak, 288–316 (Cambridge: Cambridge University Press, 2008).

65. Ron Harris, *Going the Distance: Eurasian Trade and the Rise of the Business Corporation, 1400–1700* (Princeton, NJ: Princeton University Press, 2020).

66. Harris, *Going the Distance*, 260–61.

The Merchant Adventurers were formed as a guild sometime in the medieval era. The term "adventurer" did not then mean someone who undertook wild exploits in a search for excitement, novelty, or gain, but instead had a much more mundane connotation of someone who bore risk. The term was commonly used to refer to merchants who risked large amounts of capital on the fate of overseas ventures. The recorded history of the guild begins in the thirteenth century, when it first appeared in documents described as an association of merchants trading to the Netherlands who had obtained overseas charters from foreign powers supporting their control of the cloth trade.[67] Though the guild held foreign charters, it did not then hold a royal charter within England. Royal charters were— and still are—granted by the Crown with the advice of the Privy Council. Charters were granted to universities, colleges, schools, and hospitals as well as to manufacturing and livery companies—and, ultimately, overseas trading companies.

Most guilds never sought to obtain royal charters. It was an expensive endeavor as charters were essentially bought from the Crown, and chartering invited Crown involvement in the activities of the guild. The benefit of a royal charter was the preservation or extension of exclusive privileges to certain areas of trade. For the Merchant Adventurers, the royal charter presumably helped them shore up their control over the export of cloth, particularly white broadcloth, from England to the Low Countries. After receiving a royal charter, the organization could rely on the state to help them enforce their monopoly. When they sought their charter, cloth was England's largest export, and the Merchant Adventurers were a correspondingly powerful force in overseas trade and the English national economy. Their wealth and power made the pursuit of a royal charter possible. By the early fifteenth century, royal charters confirming the trade privileges of the Merchant Adventurers begin to appear in archival sources.[68] Not until it was formally incorporated in 1564, however, did it became a chartered company.

By the late sixteenth century, the Merchant Adventurers had evolved into something new in the commercial landscape. They were formally

---

67. E. M. Carus-Wilson, "The Origins and Early Development of the Merchant Adventurers' Organization in London as Shown in Their Own Mediaeval Records," *Economic History Review* 4, no. 2 (April 1933): 148.

68. Carus-Wilson, "Origins and Early Development," 154.

incorporated and had Crown-granted rights to a national monopoly over a defined branch of trade or industry. The organization was much larger than any partnership, and the participating merchants were not related by family ties. The company was also different from existing commercial guilds. Whereas guilds were closer in style to labor unions, chartered companies were more similar to modern multinationals. These characteristics made the organization novel. But the Merchant Adventurers were not novel for long. Soon other, similar chartered organizations were formed. Commercial organization in sixteenth-century England experienced a "wave of corporateness."[69] In 1550, the capital possessed by these formally constituted and legally privileged companies stood at roughly 0.013 percent of the national total; by the end of the seventeenth century, it was 1.3 percent. This indicates not only the growth but also the large significance of chartered companies. Roughly 90 percent of national wealth was accounted for by land, households, and cattle;[70] thus, 1.3 percent can be very roughly estimated to account for 13 percent of all commercial capital.

These companies included two different types: the regulated company and the joint-stock company. Regulated companies were groups of merchants who operated and financed their ventures independently but collectively agreed to abide by a set of common rules. These rules defined a specific conduct, such as buying only from one designated entrepôt. Membership was not always lifelong or inheritable, differing in this way from membership in guilds, but more similarly, new members were subject to the approval of the group. Many of the earliest chartered companies were regulated companies. They include the Merchant Adventurers, the Levant Company, the Eastland Company, the Muscovy Company, and later the Royal African Company. Unlike the Merchant Adventurers, the Levant, Eastland, Muscovy, and Royal African companies were created to pursue new areas of commerce—meaning they were not simply recognized and chartered after having already established control of some branch of trade. The Eastland Company, created in 1579, was formed to expand England's trade in the Baltic and granted exclusive privileges in

69. Jelle C. Riemersma, "Oceanic Expansion: Government Influence on Company Organization in Holland and England, 1550–1650," *Journal of Economic History* 10, supplement (1950): 33.

70. William Robert Scott, *The Constitution and Finance of English, Scottish and Irish Joint-Stock Companies to 1720*, (Cambridge: At the University Press, 1912), 1: 439.

order to pursue that goal. The Levant Company was established in 1581 to develop trade with the Ottoman Empire, and again granted exclusive privileges to that end. The Muscovy Company was intended to increase trade with Russia, and the Royal African was expanding the fledging slave trade on the west coast of Africa.

The second type of company, which became more prevalent later in the seventeenth century—and which most would consider to be the more sophisticated or modern organizational form—was the joint-stock. Joint-stocks are different from regulated companies in that they have pooled capital and centralized administration, and they allow for the sale of transferable shares of stock. Many early works of scholarship on the chartered companies treat joint-stock organization as the central defining feature of the chartered companies and discount the importance of regulated companies because of their similarity to guilds. However, my focus is on the state-merchant relationship, and the relationship of the regulated companies to the state was very similar to that of the joint-stocks, leading to a similar role in the stimulation of debate over economic policy. Therefore, for my question, it is appropriate to consider both as one group.

The first enduring joint-stocks in England were adaptations to existing regulated companies that were responding to the exigencies of long-distance trade. The English East India Company, for example, began as a regulated company but centralized the administration and began to pool capital after realizing that infrastructural investment would greatly increase profit. The principals saw that warehouses, then called factories, could smooth demand in overseas ports highly responsive to the arrival of large foreign ships. To support the construction and maintenance of overseas factories, the East India Company owners created a store of permanent capital by selling transferable shares in the company. The transformation of the company was an immediate and recognizable success and likely served as an impetus behind the diffusion of the joint-stock form over the course of the seventeenth century.[71]

71. Interestingly, however, there were several occasions on which joint-stock companies became regulated companies. The Muscovy, also called the Russia Company, created in 1555, and the Guinea or Royal African Company, created in 1588, were initially created as joint-stocks, but divested themselves of their centralized features and became regulated companies after experiencing financial and commercial difficulties.

Not long after, the Virginia Company was founded for the colonization of North America. It was followed by the Plymouth Company, the Guiana Company, and the Company of the New River—all created before 1610. By 1700, more than 160 companies had been chartered. The seventeenth-century boom in the creation of companies came to an end with the 1720 Bubble Act, which required that the creation of all joint-stock companies had to be approved through a parliamentary vote. Companies continued to exist, but the model of the large-scale monopolistic company embodied in the great chartered companies began to wane. Over time, the remaining chartered companies began to appear like relics of a past age.[72]

The question remains: why would the novelty of the companies have translated into new publications and new ways of thinking about economics? One possibility is that the companies stimulated economic thought because they were engines of economic growth. Economic growth has long been assumed to have been related to increasing knowledge of economic matters. If companies increased prosperity, perhaps they were simply an intervening variable—a medium through which growth stimulated thought.

Whether the adoption of joint-stock forms and chartering actually stimulated economic growth, however, remains an open question. The companies were an organizational innovation, and a straightforward interpretation lends itself to the idea that they therefore spurred growth—much as the profitability of modern multinationals are now seen as central to the economic health of nations. As joint-stocks became more common, the transferability of the shares enabled innovations in public and private finance. Permanent capital allowed for larger companies and more complex administrative structures. The new business format also affected the nature of merchant associations by loosening the communal lifetime commitment of guild membership, as well the committed membership characteristic of regulated companies, and creating a new commercial, profit-based, and potentially transitory mode of commercial engagement based on shareholding. Ann Carlos and Stephen Nicholas have shown that the companies' experiments with new financial techniques and modes of internal governance offered

---

72. For a recent, comprehensive overview of the companies and their role in the development of capitalism, see Emily Erikson, ed., *Chartering Capitalism: Organizing Markets, States, and Publics* (Bingley, UK: Emerald Group, 2015).

new and effective ways to solve the complex logistical, informational, and trust problems that had plagued early modern overseas trade.[73]

This view, however, has been challenged by many scholars, who argue instead that companies hindered what would otherwise have been a larger trade expansion spurred on by other factors. George Unwin argued, for example, that the regulations and language of the company charters actually restricted entry to trade, implying that they would have had a dampening rather than an invigorating impact.[74] S. R. Epstein and Maarten Prak have convincingly maintained that guilds were already conducive to innovation and economic growth and that chartered companies did not constitute a significant improvement in that regard.[75] Stephen Jones and Simon Ville argued that the chartered companies were inefficient rent-seekers.[76] And Sheilagh Ogilvie took the position that chartered companies had a stifling effect on economic growth.[77]

These recent debates are actually a continuation of the public controversies that have dogged the companies from their inception. The chartered companies are still encouraging productive dialogues and insightful economic research. Now, as in the seventeenth century, much of the contention arises because of the exclusionary nature of the companies. It was the restrictions imposed upon large areas of trade that led Ogilvie, Jones, Ville, Epstein, Prak, and Unwin to doubt the companies' beneficial impact. The same was true for merchants and thinkers of the past.

The very nature of companies leads to differentiation because companies are defined by membership—some are in the company, some are out.

73. Ann M. Carlos and Stephen Nicholas, "Agency Problems in Early Chartered Companies: The Case of the Hudson's Bay Company," *Journal of Economic History* 50, no. 4 (December 1990): 853–75, https://doi.org/10.1017/S0022050700037852; Ann M. Carlos and Stephen Nicholas, "Managing the Manager: An Application of the Principal Agent Model to the Hudson's Bay Company," *Oxford Economic Papers* 45, no. 2 (April 1993): 243–56; and Ann M. Carlos and Stephen Nicholas, "Theory and History: Seventeenth-Century Joint-Stock Chartered Trading Companies," *Journal of Economic History* 56, no. 4 (December 1996): 916–24.

74. George Unwin, "The Merchant Adventurers' Company in the Reign of Elizabeth," *Economic History Review* 1, no. 1 (January 1927): 35–64.

75. S. R. Epstein and Maarten Prak, eds., *Guilds, Innovation, and the European Economy, 1400–1800* (Cambridge: Cambridge University Press, 2008).

76. Jones and Ville, "Efficient Transactors"; and S. R. H. Jones and Simon P. Ville, "Theory and Evidence: Understanding Chartered Trading Companies," *Journal of Economic History* 56, no. 4 (December 1996): 925–26.

77. Sheilagh Ogilvie, *Institutions and European Trade: Merchant Guilds, 1000–1800* (Cambridge: Cambridge University Press, 2011).

The early companies of the seventeenth century were particularly divisive because they were founded as monopolies and given exclusionary rights to different areas of trade. As companies became increasingly common in the seventeenth century, they segmented economic life by creating organizational boundaries that placed merchants into different areas of trade and created a class-wide rift between independent merchants and company merchants.

Conflicts over the high stakes of company operations arose at all levels. As happened in the Vintners, internal debates ended up making their way into the public sphere. The companies contributed to this process in more ways than one. They not only fomented controversy, but they also provided a space for argumentation and fostered a culture of public engagement. Phil Withington's work has established the centrality of corporate citizenship to the development of public discourse in the early modern period.[78] While the town corporations played an important role in this process, commercial incorporations (i.e., the companies) were also crucial. The large chartered companies created a semipublic space for debate and democratic governance within their board rooms and meeting halls. Companies were often described by contemporaries as mini-commonwealths. While the walls of the company created controversy between merchants, the merchants within those walls were engaged in a nearly constant and largely egalitarian process of negotiation, debate, and cooperation. Stock owners could expect to have a voice in company debates, conflicts were settled by votes, and company merchants had to learn to "politick" in order to influence company policy. The tradition of corporate citizenship within the companies was one of debate, discussion, and argumentation. In this sense, the companies contributed to creating the culture of debate that was essential to the emergence of a healthy public sphere. The internal space of dialogue and debate created within the companies was one of the driving forces in the expansion and transformation of that public sphere.[79]

Organizational activists did not fight only with themselves. Companies fought with other companies—the long-running rivalry between the Levant and East India Company being perhaps the best example. The Levant Company had the rights to the overland trade to the Mideast, and the East India

78. Withington, "Public Discourse."
79. Withington, "Public Discourse."

Company had rights to the sea route. How this was negotiated at the center was a subject of long-standing contestation. But the biggest fracture was between company merchants and independent merchants.

Company merchants espoused a philosophy of corporate governance that held that trade was dangerous unruly if left to itself and needed to be disciplined by a large and powerful organization. Independent merchants held that corporate privileges infringed upon basic freedoms as enshrined in the Magna Carta. For example, the Suffolk clothiers wrote at the onset of the 1621 trade depression to complain that "the merchants being incorporated and settled into companies, do by constitutions among themselves so cross the ancient and accustomed course of their trade concerning the free selling and buying of their cloth . . . that they hold it to be one chief cause [of the depression]."[80] As Barry Supple notes, this sentiment was typical of the time, but one that was repeatedly contested by the companies themselves.

Often the conflict between company and independent merchants was not about whether privileges should exist, but to whom those privileges should be granted. Independent merchants like William Cockayne and William Courteen did not contest the practice of chartering trade privileges; they just wanted to be the ones holding those privileges. But the company-independent division was particularly incendiary because it mapped onto other important tensions. As noted earlier, chartering was an expensive process made easier by significant political connections. Those situated in the capital city of London were much more likely to have the connections and capital to make the effort. The wealthier guilds and organizations—those that could bear the expense and had the right contacts with the Crown—tended to be based in London.[81] But the privileges of the chartered companies were not limited to London; they were national, not local. The clustering of special national privileges around London merchants aggravated outport merchants, who both wanted monopoly rights of their own and resented the exclusions that monopolies imposed upon them.

Perhaps most significant of all, the company-independent merchant division aligned with the emerging political conflict that by midcentury was to erupt into civil war. As extensively documented by Robert Brenner, the companies in the early part of the century relied upon royal charters for

---

80. Supple, *Commercial Crisis and Change*, 63.
81. Gadd and Wallis, "Reaching Beyond," 293.

their lucrative privileges. Their loyalties in the conflict tended to be with the royalists. The independent merchants instead found champions in the anti-monopoly tendencies of Parliament, and their loyalties often followed suit.[82]

In sum, the money and resources the companies provided and the high stakes of the debates over their areas of privilege provided motivation to merchants within and without their organizational boundaries to put pen to paper. The newness of the company form constituted a challenge to traditional norms that might otherwise have tamped down conflict. And the fault lines created by their exclusionary monopolies added fuel to old fires within the merchant/commercial class.

THE SPACE BETWEEN THEM

These unfamiliar objects were magnets for controversy that spilled out into the public realm and there took on a life of its own. What made the public engagement truly inevitable was the political setting. This moment in English history was one in which the state and the commercial world were sending out tentative feelers toward each other. The chartered companies were one of the means through which these two spheres were increasing their interactions. Despite this movement toward greater coordination and integration, there was still a significant gulf between the centralized state of the Crown and Parliament and merchant activity. Because the advantages of state-granted privileges and favorable policies were so great, and because merchants' internal routes of influence in the state were limited, it made sense for company merchants to advocate for themselves and their organizations by making reasoned appeals to the public in an attempt to obtain new or continued privileges from the state.

Why indeed would anyone take a private issue and attempt to involve other parties by disseminating information about it publicly? In 1975, E. E. Schattschneider observed: "Nothing attracts a crowd so quickly as a fight. Nothing is so contagious as a fight."[83] He understood the process behind that contagion to depend on attempts to unsettle the outcome. Each new

82. Robert Brenner, *Merchants and Revolution: Commercial Change, Political Conflict, and London's Overseas Traders, 1550–1653* (London: Verso, 2003).

83. Elmer Schattschneider, *The Semi-Sovereign People: A Realist's View of Democracy in America* (Boston: Wadsworth, 1975), 1.

participant drawn into a fight changes the balance of force. For someone who is losing a fight, the best strategy may be to get more people involved. In the economic debates of the seventeenth century, a company or individual who could not get traction with the Crown, Privy Council, or Parliament turned to publication. The idea was to bring more people into the conversation and upset the balance of power working against them. Appealing to the reading public was a way of gaining leverage in negotiations with the state. This debate would likely not have been conducted within the public sphere if seventeenth-century merchants had been given more direct influence over state commercial policy.

The public sphere is sometimes spoken of as if it were a new or comparatively recent historical phenomenon, associating its emergence with seventeenth-century England and the rise of parliamentary politics, coffeehouses, and circulars. This understanding does some damage to work on the public sphere. Jürgen Habermas, for example, did not write about the creation of the public sphere; he wrote about the transformation of the public sphere. Hannah Arendt's conceptualization of the public realm is based on the polis of antiquity. Nevertheless, something was in the air in seventeenth-century Europe. Printing presses were turning out materials at an unprecedented rate. Literacy was on the rise. Urbanization was increasing. Scientific discourse gained traction, Francis Bacon espoused a new philosophy of empiricism, and the Royal Society was founded in 1660. Across northern Europe, important conversations about politics, philosophy, and ethics were taking place in print. These conversations seem to have stimulated, echoed, or replicated conversations people were having in the new coffeehouses and public houses that dotted the landscape.[84] Democratic governance and political representation were already firmly established in the Netherlands and had gained a strong foothold in England by the beginning of the century. The possibility of political representation pulled more people into the process of political discourse in both places.

Habermas described this process as the construction of the bourgeois public sphere—the realm of political and public discourse that we still

---

84. Steve Pincus, "'Coffee Politicians Does Create': Coffeehouses and Restoration Political Culture," *Journal of Modern History* 67, no. 4 (December 1995): 807–34; and Phil Withington, "Intoxicants and Society in Early Modern England," *Historical Journal* 54, no. 3 (September 2011): 631–57, https://doi.org/10.1017/S0018246X11000197.

experience today—in which public opinion has political force, and where pundits and politicians exert themselves to sway that opinion one way or the other. Habermas emphasized the importance of the early-modern-era shift from manor to home in this transformation. In the medieval era, productive effort was largely contained within the feudal structure of the fief. In the manor, serfs or peasants produced goods and resources by laboring on the land owned by their lord. Production was encapsulated by a paternalistic system of authority in which economic relations reproduced power relations and the economic and the political were merged in one system. In this world, representative politics—i.e., public activity—was confined to a small group of elite actors. Habermas argued that in the seventeenth century, production moved off the manor as industry and trade expanded. Most important, production began to take place outside the domain of the lord, and economic relationships no longer echoed and reproduced the political hierarchy. Instead, economic life began to operate and expand in a separate sphere—the private sphere. Political authority withdrew from the manor and became increasingly centralized in the nation-state. Most interestingly, Habermas pointed out that the two now distinct spheres, one of political authority and the other of private economy, still needed to coordinate and communicate with each other. Thus, a new sphere of communicative action emerged to fill this need: the public sphere.[85]

At its most abstract, this process—or structural response—was at work in the generation of the new economic literature of the seventeenth century. Merchants were not well integrated or represented in the government. The state's shortsighted interventions into commercial affairs, such as the granting of patents and privileges, caused unrest and dissension both among merchants and between merchants and the state. The merchants felt the need to communicate their preferences to the state. One path was lobbying the state or speaking to Parliament. They tried these options. But they also pursued another path, publishing works for all to read, in order to convince the largest possible constituency of their arguments and gain support and influence.

---

85. Jürgen Habermas, *The Structural Transformation of the Public Sphere: An Inquiry Into a Category of Bourgeois Society*, trans. Thomas Burger with the assistance of Frederick Lawrence (Cambridge, MA: MIT Press, 1991; originally published as *Strukturwandel der Öffentlichkeit* [Darmstadt and Neuwied: Hermann Luchterhand Verlag, 1962]).

Public appeals could function in more than one way. They provided another avenue through which to influence elites. Any MP who missed parliamentary testimony might pick up the argument if it were circulated as a popular pamphlet. Published works could also persuade a larger constituency that might echo their authors concerns—again with the hope of ultimately influencing powerful actors. And finally, they could lend additional legitimacy to an argument. If published arguments were considered reasonable and compelling by the reading public, elite political actors would have more reason to give them fair consideration.

This dynamic suggests a modification of the Habermasian conceptualization of the bourgeois public sphere. Habermas essentially had two spheres interacting: the state and the household. But multiple actors contributed and fought across the public arena. A more accurate representation is a network of interacting agents. Margaret Somers defined the public sphere as "a contested participatory site in which actors with overlapping identities as legal subjects, citizens, economic actors, and family and community members, form a public body and engage in negotiations and contestations over political and social life."[86] Or as Jeffrey Alexander writes, the public sphere is constructed out of a series of "performances and counter-performances" made up of written and spoken communicative acts between many parties.[87]

The public sphere in this sense is a zone of potential influence. In the public sphere, the public can try to influence the state, the state can try to influence the public, and the public can try to influence the public—often with the intent of indirectly influencing the state. Appealing to the public has historically been about building constituencies by means of reasoned discourse or compelling narratives. But just as the state is not a unified actor, neither is the public. And the public sphere is not a physical location or a region. Coffeehouses, open plazas, public houses, classrooms, and bowling alleys may all contribute to the development of the public sphere; the public sphere arises anywhere that collective needs, desires, aims, or goals are negotiated or debated.

86. Margaret R. Somers, "Citizenship and the Place of the Public Sphere: Law, Community, and Political Culture in the Transition to Democracy," *American Sociological Review* 58, no. 5 (October 1993): 587–620, https://doi.org/10.2307/2096277, 589.

87. Jeffrey C. Alexander, "The Societalization of Social Problems: Church Pedophilia, Phone Hacking, and the Financial Crisis," *American Sociological Review* 83, no. 6 (December 2018): 1066, https://doi.org/10.1177/0003122418803376.

Harrison White's conceptualization of the public is perhaps closest to accommodating this complex and messy set of interactions, dialogues, spectacles, and showboats that links both interlocutors and audiences. Ann Mische and White defined publics as "interstitial social spaces characterized by short-term co-presences, as well as by intersections between multiple network domains."[88] Publics are social arenas—not physical spaces—in which people from different spheres of life interact. They might occupy the floor of the Royal Exchange, the steps of the Castle Church, or a Twitter thread. They can be constituted by actors from the commercial world interacting with state elites—as theorized by Habermas. But they are not limited to state-merchant interactions. The size of the public will be determined by the number of interactions between actors from different domains and walks of life. Publics can also be comprised of members of the Levant Company arguing with members of the Eastland Company, pastors preaching to their flock, or actors portraying fictionalized court intrigues for large audiences. Indeed, the great majority of published works in the seventeenth century had nothing to do with economics. But an increasingly large proportion did. And this expanding segment of the public sphere was built largely out of the debates and controversies that surrounded the monopoly privileges accorded to the new corporate form of the chartered company.

The theory of the public provided by Harrison White gives insight into the character of the discourse that might emerge in such a space. White's conception emphasizes that publics are a distinct social space because they require code-switching, in which individuals from different locations learn to speak a common cultural dialect.[89] Different populations, speaking slightly different languages with slightly different logics underpinning their rhetorical strategies, have to find a common set of understandings and expressions. Many different researchers have found that similar

---

88. Ann Mische and Harrison White, "Between Conversation and Situation: Public Switching Dynamics Across Network Domains," *Social Research* 65, no. 3 (Fall 1998): 695–724.

89. Harrison C. White, "Network Switchings and Bayesian Forks: Reconstructing the Social and Behavioral Sciences," *Social Research* 62, no. 4 (Winter 1995): 1035–63; and Eiko Ikegami, "A Sociological Theory of Publics: Identity and Culture as Emergent Properties in Networks," *Social Research* 67, no. 4 (Winter 2000): 989–1029.

situations create new kinds of discourse.[90] A nonacademic entering into a disciplinary conference for the first time might experience the strange dislocation that occurs when you travel across these informal cultural boundaries. Everyone is speaking English, but no one is making much sense. The theory here suggests that there is the possibility for something new to arise in bridging attempts to link otherwise disconnected but established fields. So, for example, we might expect a new language and style of inquiry to evolve around the expanding field of computational social sciences, which draws on the disparate fields of computer science, statistics, political science, sociology, and economics. For the seventeenth-century gulf between the state and a fractured merchant class, it suggests that a new rhetorical mode or discursive style was needed for individuals in these spheres to communicate and coordinate with one another.

THE NEW DISCURSIVE MODE

The defining features of the new economics literature were nationalist sentiments, empiricism, and abstraction. These replaced the religious sentiments, scholasticism, local specificity, and individual-level focus that permeated medieval works on economic matters. The argument outlined above has at least one implication for the content and style of the new discourse. The new level of abstraction found in the arguments had a structural component to it related to the need to bridge spheres. Publishing in the public sphere is an act intended to address and persuade the largest possible audience. The larger your audience is, the more likely it is that it will contain people outside of your immediate situation. The new authors were likely to reach a higher level of abstraction than had previous, more localized conversations—exactly because they needed to appeal to a broader group.

90. Mark A. Pachucki and Ronald L. Breiger, "Cultural Holes: Beyond Relationality in Social Networks and Culture," *Annual Review of Sociology* 36 (2010): 205–24, https://doi.org/10.1146 /annurev.soc.012809.102615; Roger Friedland, "The Endless Fields of Pierre Bourdieu," *Organization* 16, no. 6 (November 2009): 887–917, https://doi.org/10.1177/135050840934111; Jennifer C. Lena and Mark C. Pachucki, "The Sincerest Form of Flattery: Innovation, Repetition, and Status in an Art Movement," *Poetics* 41, no. 3 (June 2013): 236–64, https://doi.org/10.1016/j.poetic.2013.02.002; Harrison C. White and Frédéric Godart, "Stories from Identity and Control," *Sociologica* 1, no. 3 (November–December 2007): 1–17, https://www.rivisteweb.it/doi/10.2383/25960, 2; and Mohr and White, "How to Model and Institution."

It was also this way for the emerging factionalized political discourse that was springing up across the England in the seventeenth century. Peter Bearman showed that nationalized political discourse had its roots in the expansion of the conversation about religious loyalties from the local parish to the crosscutting political alliances of elites increasingly tied to the court.[91] The expansion of the audience from the local to the national level necessitated a shift from local concerns to a broader, more abstract discourse about beliefs and ideologies. These supplanted the former complaints about rivals, regional land disputes, and irritating neighbors. The disjuncture between the commercial and political spheres would also have helped drive the increasingly abstract nature of the economic literature as it grew and developed in an expanding set of conversations that began to take on a life of their own, to cohere into what Daniel Defoe called the literature of "universal commerce."[92]

The characteristics of the actors in conversation and the relative balance of power between them can also illuminate the specific shift in the changing contents and frames of the new economic literature. If the literature grew largely out of merchants' debates, the habits of mind and social standing of the merchant authors should go a fair way toward explaining some of these characteristics. Theories have already been offered that the low standing of merchants led them to try to bolster their arguments with facts and statistics.[93] Merchants would also have unparalleled access to the details of trade and commerce, so it would be natural for them to draw on this information. Increased empiricism would be a spontaneous result of merchant authorship.

Explaining the adoption of a nationalist rhetorical mode requires a slightly more complex argument. As with the larger argument of this book, there are two components: the negotiation, or distance, between the state and merchants, represented most clearly by the merchants' marginal political representation, and the importance of the chartered companies. Not only the gulf, but also the direction of the argument and the power balance between disputants, drove the adoption of the nationalist rhetorical mode. In this case, it is important to think not just about the gulf between actors,

91. Peter S. Bearman, *Relations Into Rhetorics: Local Elite Social Structure in Norfolk, England, 1540–1640*, Arnold and Caroline Rose Monograph Series of the American Sociological Association (New Brunswick, NJ: Rutgers University Press, 1993).

92. Deringer, *Calculated Values*, 132.

93. Letwin, *Origins of Scientific Economics*.

but who those actors were. Merchants were trying to influence state actors. The best and clearest way to do so was to consider arguments from the perspective of the state. What is best for the nation? The merchants were imagining the concerns of the Crown, the Privy Council, and Parliament and trying to appeal to those concerns. This encouraged the widespread adoption of nationalist frames and tropes about wealth and prosperity, as well as the focus on national economic development. Targeting this audience naturally led to a rhetorical engagement with the interests of state. The nation, the commonwealth, the safety of England, all became primary points of reference and the standpoint from which to evaluate trade policy, company regulations, lending practices, currency restrictions, excise taxes, and all other economic behaviors and practices.

A central fact about the companies further increased the relevance of nationalist framing. As pointed out by Philip Stern, the companies existed in an ambiguous space between public and private that lent itself to attempts to debate about the common good.[94] The state extended monopoly privileges to companies that were of great material benefit. In return, two things were asked of the companies. The first was money. The second was less concrete. There was an expectation established that the companies should act for the public good by organizing trade. At that time, commerce had a bad reputation. Merchants were seen as greedy and corrupt. If left to their own devices, it was thought, they were likely to defraud the public or destroy branches of trade through uncontrolled competition. The companies were expected to discipline the merchants' behavior to produce better outcomes. Companies, for example, were expected by the state to promote the public good by upholding moral standards and behavior consistent with civility, citizenship, and a healthy commonwealth.[95] They were also emissaries of the state. This idea was part of the philosophy of the corporate governance of trade.[96] The state used charters to delegate the governance of trade to organizations with

---

94. Philip J. Stern, "Companies: Monopoly, Sovereignty, and the East Indies," in *Mercantilism Reimagined: Political Economy in Early Modern Britain and Its Empire*, ed. Philip J. Stern and Carl Wennerlind (New York: Oxford University Press, 2013), 177–95.

95. Withington, *Politics of Commonwealth*; and Thomas Leng, "Interlopers and Disorderly Brethren at the Stade Mart: Commercial Regulations and Practices Amongst the Merchant Adventurers of England in the Late Elizabethan Period," *Economic History Review* 69, no. 3 (August 2016): 823–43.

96. David Pennington, "Beyond the Moral Economy: Economic Change, Ideology and the 1621 House of Commons," *Parliamentary History* 25, pt. 2 (2006): 214–31.

which they had a direct relationship and that were to some extent beholden to the government, and therefore under its direct influence.

The unique relationship the chartered companies had to the state and their purported role in commercial governance put the companies in a strange area floating somewhere between public and private. The quasi-public nature of companies stirred debate over their essential character. Companies were seen alternately as miniature commonwealths fostering community and brotherhood or as sites of exclusion, privilege, and collusion. The legal status and moral expectations of companies fostered confusion. The privileges granted to the chartered companies were for the private gain of the members—but were granted under the premise that those private gains would have public benefits. The extent to which the companies were true monopolies—because their privileges were distributed across a group—was a seemingly endless source of contemporary debate. The chartered companies thus confused the concepts of public and private good in their practice, providing ample complexity to fuel continuing debate.

CONCLUSION

It is difficult to fully understand the impact of merchant-state relations in early modern England without historical knowledge of the institutions through which they interacted. People do not seem to change much over time, but institutions change dramatically. Companies, governance, and commerce were all very different in the seventeenth century than they are now. In the seventeenth century, merchants did not entirely lack political power and influence, but their control over the actions of the state was limited. Because of low rates of representation in the state, merchants had to fight their battles in part by proxy, by influencing council members and MPs. Sometimes this was accomplished through council participation, parliamentary testimony, or petitioning, but merchants also turned to public appeals and reasoned arguments to amplify their lobbying efforts.

Although they lay outside the formal state apparatus, chartered companies were a key institutional device modulating the relationship between the state and merchants. A couple of key pieces of information emerge from the history. One is that the era of the chartered companies ran from the late sixteenth century to 1720, the same era in which economic thought experienced the important transformation described in chapters 1 and 2.

Additionally, the introduction of chartered companies stoked controversy. They were unusual organizations and were granted unusual privileges. They incited the resentment of nonelite merchants, outport merchants, manufacturers, and workers—as well as the representatives of those interests in Parliament. And they provided material and institutional resources that encouraged public debate. No doubt many lively conversations echoed through the coffeehouses and bars, but books and pamphlets became central vehicles for advancing economic interests by way of argument and analysis because of the marginally powerful position of the merchants. And while these debates were undertaken in order to advance the interests of those involved, they also, perhaps incidentally, developed new lines of inquiry into the relationship among trade, privileges, monopoly, and national prosperity that would prove extremely generative over the long term.

A theoretical framework centered on Harrison White's conceptualization of "publics" that also draws from other theorists of the public sphere can help make sense of this historical detail. The theory proposes that the gaps between different arenas of life can lead to new styles of discourse emerging from the attempt to bridge those gaps. If correct, it suggests that, in this case, the distance between the world of the merchants and the world of the state led merchants to reframe their thought in a nationalist language in order to bridge that discursive gulf. The new abstract nature of the debate can be explained by the large number of disputants dispersed throughout England. The empiricism can be explained by the habits of mind of the merchants who authored the texts. And the nationalist framing can be understood as a rhetorical move intended to persuade an audience of state elites that was further encouraged by the public/private nature of companies. The next three chapters use different methods of analysis to test the accuracy of this explanation.

Chapter Four

AUTHORS AND THEIR NETWORKS

The economic thought of the medieval era is fascinating and rich, if also different in kind from classical and modern economics. One of the most renowned economic thinkers from the British Isles was John Duns Scotus, a Franciscan monk beatified by Pope John Paul II. Thomas Aquinas was from the Lazio region of present-day Italy. The Salamanca school of Spanish theologians included Francisco de Vitoria, Luís Saravia de la Calle, Domingo de Soto, Tomas de Mercado, Francisco García, Martín González de Cellorigo, Luís de Molina, Pedro de Valencia, and Navarrus, also known as Martín de Azpilcueta. The Piedmontese priest Giovanni Botero produced notable works. And Jean Bodin, the French statesman, also made important conceptual contributions. This list, though not comprehensive, at least indicates the broader trend that economic discourse in the medieval era took place mainly outside of England and did not include merchants.

In England, things were different. It was not only the important authors—or those authors who came to be celebrated over time—who were drawn from the commercial class. Much of the growth of the literature as a whole can be attributed to the entrance of merchants into the publication process. Priests and moral philosophers did not stop contributing to economic thought, but their voices seem to have been drowned out by a new chorus of practical and pragmatic men of the world trying to reach the ears of the state.

BIOGRAPHICAL DATA ON AUTHORS

In this second half of the book, I turn to evaluating the theory that the representation of companies and merchants was a key factor in the seventeenth-century transformation of economic thought. In this chapter, I focus on the authors, their social position, and their social-structural position. For the explanation I have offered to be true, it must also be the case that merchants—and even more specifically, but not exclusively, company merchants—were actively writing and publishing economic texts. And because the companies were central loci of the communicative interaction between the state and merchants, structurally we should expect authors (as compared to nonauthors) to be well positioned in the world of companies. Additionally, if the marginality of political representation plays a role, we should expect to see merchants less well positioned than nonmerchants in the political world of the councils and committees of trade. Using authorship, investment, committee membership, and biographical data, I evaluate these hypotheses.

It is true that English merchants authored a greater and greater number of economic texts over the course of the seventeenth century. For more clarity on how the authorship rates changed, I turned to the texts themselves. Publishing anonymously or behind a pseudonym was a common practice of the time, making the process of documenting authorial trends more difficult than it might otherwise have been; however, 3,259 of the nearly 7,000 authored economic texts in England from 1580 to 1720 were written by individuals who either identified themselves or, in a smaller number of cases, were later identified by historians. Combined data from the *Oxford Dictionary of National Biography*, *Palgrave's Dictionary of Political Economy*, the *History of Parliament Project*, and Wikipedia provided some biographical detail for 723 separate authors of those texts.[1] In many cases, but not all, the information included birth and death years, class standing, occupational status, parents' profession, educational history, nationality,

---

1. *Oxford Dictionary of National Biography* (Oxford: Oxford University Press, 2004; online ed., 2008), https://www.oxforddnb.com/; Robert Harry Inglis Palgrave, *Palgrave's Dictionary of Political Economy*, new ed. (London: Macmillan, 1925); The History of Parliament: British Political, Social & Local History, https://www.historyofparliamentonline.org/; and Wikipedia, https://www.wikipedia.org. Wikipedia was used as a source for additional references and a cross-check for other possible individuals, not as a confirmatory source.

affiliations with and positions held within companies, dates positions were held, and the dates and offices of both elected and appointment government positions. Because it is an important marker of status, even whether or not an individual was included in the *Oxford Dictionary of National Biography* provides valuable information and was noted. There are also cases in which anonymous authors listed their class/occupational category.

In table 4.1, the publication data are broken down by the class/occupational background of the author. This typology has seven categories: clergy, gentry, noble, merchant, military, professional, and yeoman. These categories could be inferred from the biographical data and generally capture the relevant class and professional attributes that could be expected to shape different types of contributions.

Nobility was and continues to be an important way of classifying individuals and was generally explicitly noted in biographical entries. This category includes lords, viscounts, barons, dukes, earls, and marquesses. Gentry is another ascriptive elite status that does not quite reach the rank of nobility; it includes sirs, baronets, knights, and others individuals of high social standing. In this category, I also included authors who self-identified or who used the honorific Esquire or gentleman. Authors were identified as belonging to the clergy when they were described as occupying positions within the church, when it was noted that they acted as ministers or preachers, or when their names included titles indicating church affiliation, such as reverend or bishop. Authors with positions in the army or whose names included titles such as captain were coded as military. Yeoman captures farmers and peasants, who did contribute a small number of agricultural texts to the corpus. No honorific indicated merchant occupational status, so only those explicitly noted as merchants or as participating in some sort of trade are categorized as merchants. Professional is a little bit of a catch-all. It captures individuals who could not be identified as elites (nobles or gentry), were not a part of the church, were not in the military, and were

TABLE 4.1

Publications by class/occupational category of author

Noble	Gentry	Clergy	Military	Professional	Merchant	Yeoman	Total
247	279	294	74	718	587	47	2,246
(11%)	(12%)	(13%)	(3%)	(32%)	(26%)	(2%)	

not merchants; it includes lawyers, writers, physicians, poets, playwrights, academics, and other individuals holding less common occupations—such as George Shelley, a once celebrated calligrapher.

While the majority of known authors wrote only one article, in keeping with Pareto's law, a small minority were unusually prolific. The astoundingly productive Daniel Defoe contributed 142 separate publications to the corpus. He is the farthest outlier of the group—by quite a way. There were also a number of cases in which anonymous authors provided information in the text or on the title page that could be used to identify their class or occupational category. The most frequent designation was gentleman— often a gentleman residing abroad in some location about which he had written. Twenty-seven of these pseudonymous authors identified as gentleman or used initials followed by "gent." Four more texts styled themselves as authored by English gentlemen abroad, and another two texts by a "country gentleman." Twenty-seven different anonymous authors identified themselves as merchants. Using such identifiers, I was able to identify the class/occupational background of 2,246 publications. Table 4.1 breaks down the publications by class category.

As can be seen in table 4.1, merchants make up the second most common type of contributor over the entire period. What is not captured is the number of professionals who were hired by merchants to write on economic matters. This practice was a known strategy, though largely undocumented, as the merchants took this step in an attempt to hide their role in the debates. For these and other reasons, there is good reason to believe that these figures undercount the number of merchant-authored publications.

Pseudonyms are one way of uncovering the hidden patterns driving anonymity. Many pseudonyms were both colorful and revealing. There were several self-identified "person of honour," somewhat fewer "persons of quality," one "person of honour lately deceased," and one "person of whatever quality you please." "Well-wishers" were common, as were "lovers of king, country, truth and commerce," along with one "lover of the good old cause." Medley's footman authored a text, as did the mysterious Monsieur M, Jenny Distaff, and Robert Tell-Truth. There are also several more individuals trying to convince readers of their lack of personal bias: a "person uninterested," the "impartial pen of an eye-witness," and "an unworthy member of the said citie." These authors wanted most of all to be seen as dispassionate and therefore reliable experts.

Their protestations of objectivity were almost certainly linked to the common understanding of the time that merchants could not be trusted to advance disinterested arguments. Contemporaries often assumed (with ample reason) that merchants publishing on trade were making self-interested arguments in order to improve their own bottom line.[2] Nicholas Barbon, for example, went so far as to suggest—slightly tongue in cheek—that the entire balance-of-trade theory was "invented by some merchants, on purpose to mislead Mens Reasons about Trade."[3] If adopting the pseudonym a "sober stander-by, who is wholy unconcern'd in the ministry, or the funds" does not quite ring true, another method was simply to write anonymously. Others reached further into the past. Child used the pen name Philopatris to evoke patriotism, but that was also the title of a work now known to have been falsely attributed to the Assyrian satirist, Lucian of Samosata, which is a little ironic given Child's penchant for misrepresentation.

The general distrust of merchants was symptomatic of their role in the social hierarchy, which also had implications for patterns of anonymity. Merchants were low status.[4] Because society put a lesser value on their activities, they were individually less likely to enter the historical record, and the activities that they engaged in were also less likely to be documented. The nobility and even lesser gentry were considered worthy of documentation by virtue of their social position. The military and clergy were attached to extensive bureaucracies that recorded the service of individuals for organizational purposes—and often left those records to posterity. Merchants who were not affiliated with companies had no extensive bureaucracies to record their activities and positions, and the chroniclers of the great events of the time paid them little attention. One result is that many merchants who did identify themselves probably cannot be associated with bibliographic information because their lives did not enter into the historical record. They did not have entries in *Palgrave's* or the *Oxford Dictionary*. Further, the low social status of merchants would have discouraged authors from identifying themselves as merchants. Why signal your status as an untrustworthy

---

2. Perry Gauci, *Politics of Trade: The Overseas Merchant in State and Society, 1660–1720* (Oxford: Oxford University Press, 2001.

3. Nicholas Barbon, *A Discourse Concerning Coining the New Money Lighter. In Answer to Mr. Lock's Considerations about raising the Value of Money* (London: Printed for Richard Chiswell, 1696), 52, Making of the Modern World.

4. Gauci, *Politics of Trade.*

member of the self-interested class? The implication is that both anony-mous authors and those using a pseudonym were more likely to have been merchants than aristocrats, military officers, or ecclesiastics.

If we expect that merchants were more likely to publish on matters of trade, the breakdown of anonymous authors by subject supports the idea that more anonymous authors were merchants. Table 4.2 presents a cross-tabulation of the data reporting the number of anonymous and named authors who did or did not write on the topic of trade. The total number of units is represented in the lower, right-hand cell: 6,916. This count is the number of publications. Authors are associated with the articles they wrote; thus, the same authors can be counted as many times as they published or reprinted a text.

In table 4.2, the counts are represented in the main body of the cells with column percentages, rounded to the nearest whole, in parentheses. The table gives a sense of the distribution of anonymity across the subject of trade. The split across the topic of trade is not even. As noted previously, just slightly more than half of the authors were anonymous, but roughly 62 percent of the documents about trade were written by anonymous authors and only 38 percent by named individuals. For those interested, a simple chi-square test shows that the factors are significantly different than expected by chance, as reported in the note below the table.

Merchants were also among the least likely to be included in the *Oxford Dictionary of National Biography*. Table 4.3 categorizes the authors with class or status information by class/occupational category and whether or not they were included in the dictionary. This table uses the author—not the article—as the unit of analysis.

TABLE 4.2
Cross-tabulation of anonymous texts on trade

Anonymous	No trade	Trade	Totals
No	2,566 (50%)	694 (38%)	3,260
Yes	2,539 (50%)	1,117 (62%)	3,656
Totals	5,105 (100%)	1,811 (100%)	6,916

*Chisq = 76.042, df = 1, p-value < 0.0001

TABLE 4.3
Class/occupational category by inclusion in the *Oxford Dictionary of National Biography*

	Noble	Gentry	Clergy	Military	Professional	Merchant	Yeoman
Included	89	85	152	11	224	89	22
	(85%)	(83%)	(96%)	(65%)	(95%)	(65%)	(92%)
Excluded	16	17	6	6	14	49	2
	(15%)	(17%)	(4%)	(35%)	(5%)	(35%)	(8%)
Total	105	102	158	17	238	138	24

Merchants and military have the highest rates of undocumented lives with respect to the *Oxford Dictionary*. This breakdown indicates that contributions by those with military experience may be undercounted in the data, but much more significantly, given the higher volume of contributions, the lives of merchant authors are also likely to have escaped the net of biographical history at higher rates than other categories. The lives of nobility and gentry are fairly well represented, although the 15 and 17 percent exclusion rates indicate the possibility that a number of authors who laid claim to an elevated status may not have been completely truthful— given that we would expect most elites to have been captured by the dictionary. Yeomen are well documented, perhaps because published contributions by such individuals were an uncommon and therefore notable event. The highest levels of representation in the dictionary are accorded to the clergy and professionals; the latter made it into the dictionary 95 percent of the time, indicating that a much smaller number of professionals than merchants are undocumented in the data. While we might expect that the number of documented professionals who authored economic texts is a good indicator of the actual population of professional authors, there is evidence that the number of documented merchants is lower than the actual number of merchant contributors.

Two additional trends indicate that merchant contributions are being undercounted. As the century progressed—and the literature became increasingly dominated by trade, companies, and finance—anonymity grew. Rates peaked from 1660 to 1679, but were consistently higher in the second half of the century than the first. Table 4.4 shows rates of publication for anonymous versus named authors, by text, over twenty-year periods from 1580 to 1720.

TABLE 4.4
Anonymous authors

	1580–1599	1600–1619	1620–1639	1640–1659	1660–1679	1680–1699	1700–1720
Named	45	106	121	453	417	808	1,310
	(80%)	(54%)	(57%)	(45%)	(41%)	(46%)	(49%)
Anonymous	11	91	91	546	606	952	1,359
	(20%)	(46%)	(43%)	(55%)	(59%)	(54%)	(51%)
Totals	56	197	212	999	1,023	1,760	2,669

TABLE 4.5
Publications with authors in the *Oxford Dictionary of National Biography*

	1580–1599	1600–1619	1620–1639	1640–1659	1660–1679	1680–1699	1700–1720
Yes	43	104	117	447	405	776	1,248
	(77%)	(53%)	(55%)	(45%)	(40%)	(44%)	(47%)
No	13	93	95	552	618	984	1,421
	(23%)	(47%)	(45%)	(55%)	(60%)	(56%)	(53%)
Totals	56	197	212	999	1,023	1,760	2,669

Surprisingly, even the coverage of authors in the *Oxford Dictionary of National Biography* goes down slightly over time. Table 4.5 shows the representation of publications by authors in or out of the dictionary over the same twenty-year periods.

The decline is steep over the transition to the seventeenth century and continues a slight but steady downward trend over the first half of the century, plateauing in the second half. This pattern is notable given that historical records usually improve over time. The trend suggests that as the literature on economics became more abstract, more theoretical, and more clearly focused on a smaller set of well-defined problems—such as value, rent, growth factors, and specie flow—the number of texts published by unknown authors increased. There is little to explain this trend other than that the contributions made by merchant authors increased at pace with their desire for anonymity.

As noted in table 4.1, the percentage of texts authored by individuals who can be verified to have worked as merchants in this pivotal period for economic thought is already high relative to other groups, at 26 percent. It is also evident that merchant contributions increased over the period of interest.

TABLE 4.6
Articles by class/occupational status

	Noble	Gentry	Clergy	Military	Professional	Merchant	Yeoman
1580–1599	0	2 (7%)	2 (7%)	0	23 (77%)	1 (3%)	2 (7%)
1600–1619	5 (6%)	9 (11%)	17 (21%)	3 (4%)	37 (46%)	8 (10%)	2 (3%)
1620–1639	6 (7%)	6 (7%)	16 (17%)	17 (19%)	27 (29%)	20 (22%)	0
1640–1659	19 (6%)	59 (18%)	43 (13%)	21 (6%)	111 (34%)	67 (20%)	8 (3%)
1660–1679	35 (12%)	42 (14%)	30 (10%)	16 (5%)	108 (36%)	54 (18%)	14 (5%)
1680–1699	67 (12%)	72 (13%)	65 (12%)	9 (2%)	152 (28%)	162 (30%)	13 (2%)
1700–1720	115 (13%)	89 (10%)	121 (14%)	8 (1%)	260 (30%)	275 (31%)	8 (1%)
Totals	247	279	294	74	718	587	47

Table 4.6 shows the counts and percentages of publications by class over the twenty-year periods from 1580 to 1720. The percentages are row percentages so that the relative contributions of the different class/occupational statuses may be compared. This table presents a number of interesting facts. Military contributions peaked in the period during which the Civil War occurred. Merchant contributions jumped in the period that captures the 1620s and again in the period that captures the 1690s, right when we see the most dramatic changes in the economic literature: the period when the balance-of-trade doctrine took shape and the period in the 1690s when that doctrine was challenged by nascent free-trade arguments. Gentry contributions peaked from 1630 to 1650 and declined thereafter. The small number of texts contributed by yeomen peaked from 1650 to 1670. Clergy contributions peaked from 1610 to 1630. Even excluding the small-number inflation of the first two decades, professionals clearly made a declining contribution to the economic literature over time. The drop is relatively steady. In contrast, merchant contributions show a steady increase. There is one slight dip in merchant authorship from 1640 to 1680, but it does not fall below the levels of any but the immediately previous two-decade period. Indeed, by the 1690s, merchants were contributing more than any

other group, including professionals, whose high numbers date entirely to the earlier decades of the period.

The tables are based on the count of known merchants. If we generalize from the known sample of authors in the *Oxford Dictionary*, it is possible to estimate the number of merchant contributions for the entire set of publications. Calculating across the second row of table 4.3 shows that 45 percent of the authors that were not included in the dictionary but for which we do have biographical information on their class/occupational status were merchants. We can use those percentages to roughly estimate what number of the 3,776 publications not documented by the dictionary were by merchants. This estimate assumes a one-to-one correspondence between authorship and text, which is conservative in this instance since professionals were more likely to write more than one text. The total of undocumented merchant-authored texts would come to 1,669. Similarly, we might estimate that since professionals wrote only 5 percent of the publications where we have class information but authors were not included in the dictionary, 5 percent of 3,776 additional publications authored by professionals are likely to exist in the data set. This fraction comes to 189. Adding these figures to the original count results in an estimated 2,256 total merchant publications and 907 total professional publications—33 percent and 13 percent, respectively, of the total set of publications. These estimates push merchants well beyond the other categories to the highest percentage of authorship out of all the occupational/class categories on a publication-by-publication basis. Whether one uses the known or estimated count, the merchant contribution to the total set of publications was substantial, and their contribution to the theoretically and empirically innovative literature on trade was even greater.

The innovative works that had a long-lasting conceptual impact on the development of economics were in the subareas of trade and finance. Of publications with known authors, 42 percent of tracts on finance were authored by merchants, the highest category. Professional authors were responsible for 31 percent of these texts. Merchants also contributed the most to the discourse on trade, authoring 45 percent of the publications on trade. The second largest category was again professionals, with 30 percent. The remaining categories of authors contributed between 5 and 10 percent. Given the documented pattern of anonymity and obscurity, it is likely that the already large contribution of merchants to the literature was even larger than we are able to observe. With respect to the chartered companies in all of this, 69 percent of texts authored by an identifiable merchant were authored by merchants known to have held significant positions within a chartered company.

NETWORK POSITION AND DISCOURSE

Merchants were contributing a larger and larger proportion of the works on economic topics over the seventeenth century, and company merchants made up the largest component of these merchant authors. It is possible to see, further, that the merchants who authored texts were embedded in the world of corporate ownership. The members of the state's committees and councils of trade who authored economic texts were better connected and more deeply embedded in this trade policy domain than nonauthors. But merchants as a group were structurally more disadvantaged in these councils and committees than other types of individuals. This supports the larger theory that these economic writings were a mechanism for coordination across the worlds of the state and commerce because these were the two main sites through which merchants and states interacted.

In the commercial world of the companies, we might expect that the positive social support created by being deeply embedded within the investment community would increase the likelihood that these merchants would put forth the effort to produce and publish a text in support of the community. A densely linked commercial world may have provided them with the social support they needed for publication, while also increasing their commitment to that world and thus giving them reason to publicly defend it. Interaction ritual theory suggests that positive, clustered interactions increase the energy and creative forces upon which such creative production relies.[5] Individuals in a densely linked investment space might also have a kind of vision advantage, in that they are linked to many other people and therefore exposed to many different sources of information about economic processes. This exposure to different individuals with different business practices, for example, may be crucial to generating insights about trade.

5. Randall Collins, *Interaction Ritual Chains* (Princeton, NJ: Princeton University Press, 2005).

Such a theory does not necessarily imply, however, that ties to all individuals will provide equal information. Mark Granovetter's weak tie theory (1973) and Ronald Burt's structural holes theory (1995) suggest that ties to individuals who lie outside of a tightly connected group of interconnected friends can provide new information with greater ultimate value.[6] These theories differ from embeddedness theory in that there is a greater emphasis on emotional valence and moral support in embeddedness theory and a stricter focus on information flow in weak ties and structural holes. For example, in a market where you just need to know the price of a good, the strength of the tie through which you get that information may not matter much. Such settings and needs are more appropriately described by structural holes theory. If, instead, you are making a decision about whether to go on a group vacation and you care more about how much you like the other people intending to go and the extent to which those other people like each other, embeddedness theory is more appropriate. Structural holes theory, in contrast to embeddedness theory, suggests that lower levels of embeddedness are more beneficial to actors because if they are not in a deeply embedded, densely knit cluster, they are more likely to have access to different sources and therefore nonredundant information. Thus, there are theoretical reasons to expect that authors may also possess ties that span outside of dense clusters. The two possibilities are not mutually exclusive. Both can be assessed with network analysis.

Figure 4.1 represents the affiliations between chartered companies and authors of economic texts as captured in the biographical data. These affiliations are representations of share ownership or company service. Dark nodes represent companies, and light nodes represent authors. Labels are centered directly above the node they represent and identify a few of the larger, more recognizable companies (too many labels quickly overwhelm the image and obscure the network). The size of the node varies based on degree, where larger nodes have a higher degree and degree is the number of ties a node has to other nodes. A cursory glance, for example, indicates that the East India Company has the most ties to authors in the data. It may also be possible to see that light nodes have ties only to dark node and dark

---

6. Mark S. Granovetter, "The Strength of Weak Ties," *American Journal of Sociology* 78, no. 6 (May 1973): 1360–80; and Ronald S. Burt, *Structural Holes* (Cambridge, MA: Harvard University Press, 1995).

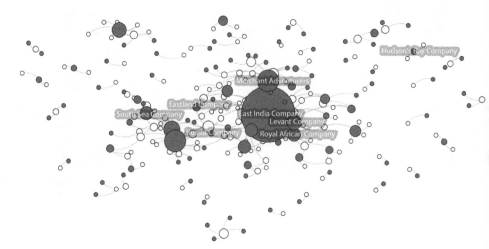

FIGURE 4.1. Network of authors and companies

nodes have ties only to light nodes—indicating that companies have direct ties only to authors, not to other companies. That is because this is a bipartite network that represents only company-author ties. Companies may be tied only indirectly through shared affiliations with the same author. The image reveals something about the relationship between companies. Companies with ties to the same author are drawn closer together by the algorithm that places the nodes in space. As is evident, the network has a large, dense component at the center that captures most of the nodes. These are companies drawn together because of one or more shared ties to authors. The closest companies—for example, the Levant, the East India Company, the Royal African Company, and the Merchant Adventurers—all had more than one individual who had experience investing in or working for more than one of these companies and also authored economic tracts. In total, the network is composed of 249 nodes and 240 edges.

OWNERSHIP AND AUTHORSHIP DATA

The ties in figure 4.1 represent only a subset of the larger universe of ownership ties in the world of chartered company investment. Many individuals who did not author public texts also held shares in the companies. A full history of investment data for the time period, from 1550 to 1720, is not available; however, there are data from 1600 to 1640, which was a crucial generative phase for the economic literature of the seventeenth century.[7] The data capture investors in all of the major trading and colonial ventures from 1603 through the 1630s.

This ownership data set is the basis for a more complete representation of the investment world of the early seventeenth century: an investor-by-company matrix of affiliations consisting of 6,149 separate investors and thirty-five companies. Merging the ownership data with the authorship data provides a means to gauge the structural position of merchant authors within the world of company investment.

The names of investors and authors were matched across the two data sets. Duplicate names were identified using a fuzzy matching process that pulled out the closest name and scored the Levenshtein distance between the names drawn from both the authors' biographical data and the investor data.[8] This process eliminated highly unlikely pairs from consideration. All matches that scored over ninety (out of one hundred) were then checked manually. This last pass was particularly important for identifying instances in which more than one individual with the same name invested in the same or a different company, which was not unusual for common names such as John Allen. In these cases, I used additional biographical information, such as birth and death dates and patterns of ownership, to identify the correct person. When a positive means of disambiguating identities was not available in the historical record, none of the names were marked as authors. A positive sign of the validity of the data is that the number of authors identified as affiliated with the companies in the biographical data is only twenty people different from the number identified in the investor data. Cases in which disambiguation was not possible account for most of these discrepancies. There are 155 authors associated with companies in total, which is 21 percent of the authors for whom we have any detailed information. Because the companies were an object of contention, this number does not represent independent merchants unaffiliated with companies who nevertheless wrote, often critically, about those companies.

---

7. These data were generously shared with the author by Henning Hillmann, from his work on the economic and social determinants of elite mobilization in the English Civil War. Henning Hillmann, "Mediation in Multiple Networks: Elite Mobilization Before the English Civil War," *American Sociological Review* 73, no. 3 (June 2008): 426–54.

8. The Levenshtein distance is a measure of the number of deletions, insertions, and substitutions required to transform one string into another.

THE OWNER-AUTHOR NETWORK

While the details of the data can be mundane, the end result is an image of a complex and deeply embedded world of connections among companies. Figure 4.2 represents the bipartite network of investor-company ties. Nodes are both companies and individuals, and ties exist only between individuals and companies—there are no company-to-company ties nor individual-to-individual ties. Labels are not included to preserve legibility. Dark nodes again represent chartered companies. White nodes represent other

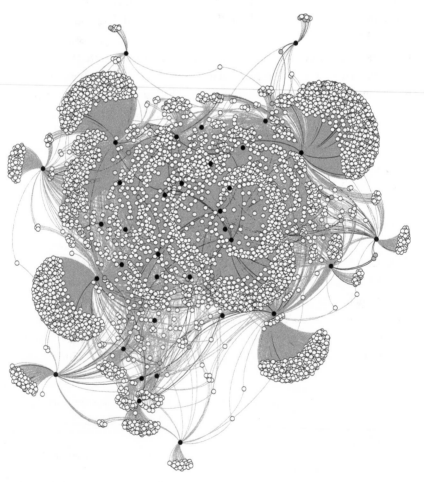

FIGURE 4.2. Investor-company network

individuals invested in the companies, and gray nodes represent the authors who were invested in the companies. Ties represent share ownership.

In this network, too, the East India Company, Merchant Adventurers, Levant Company, and Muscovy Company are located in the dense core of interconnections, where many of the most renowned authors also lie, including Thomas Mun and Edward Misselden. Those of lesser fame, who were yet of early importance to the emergence of the genre of this style of economic writings, are also positioned within this dense core, including Dudley Digges, Lewes Roberts, and John Wheeler. These were well-connected and powerful merchants, deeply embedded in the elite merchant networks of the time. Other names you might expect to see here, such as Josiah Child or Thomas Papillon, are excluded from this time period—as is the Royal African Company, which was not founded until 1660.

In order to conduct an analysis of this network and the social-structural position of authors in the company world, I collapsed the bipartite network represented in figure 4.2 into a person-by-person projection of the affiliation data. This conversion does a better job representing the structure of the community around and between the authors of the texts. In the person-to-person network, common membership in a company is converted into a tie between individuals; for example, if John Arundell and Nicholas Bennett are both invested in the Merchant Adventurers, they will be represented in this network as having a direct tie between them. Because many companies had a large number of investors, this person-to-person network is markedly denser than the company-to-investor network, with 3,925,081 ties between investors. Visualizations are extremely messy and largely uninformative for a network of this size and density. They are much less legible than the investor-company network shown in figure 4.2, which is why the two-mode network is shown rather than its one-mode projection used in the analysis.

Projections of two-mode data hold special problems for analysis.[9] The conversion creates increased density and clustering that can throw off

9. Anke Piepenbrink and Ajai S. Gaur, "Methodological Advances in the Analysis of Bipartite Networks: An Illustration Using Board Interlocks in Indian Firms," *Organizational Research Methods* 16, no. 3 (July 2013): 474–96, https://doi.org/10.1177/1094428113478838; and Zachary Neal, "The Backbone of Bipartite Projections: Inferring Relationships from Co-Authorship, Co-Sponsorship, Co-Attendance and Other Co-Behaviors." *Social Networks* 39 (October 1, 2014): 84–97. https://doi.org/10.1016/j.socnet.2014.06.001.

network measures. Creating ties between all individuals associated with a group can also build in false equivalences. Comembership in a group of two hundred is, for example, likely to create a different type of relationship between individuals than comembership in a group of ten. Following Newman, I use a weighted tie inversely proportional to group size to account for these differences.[10]

Comparing across owner-authors and owners who did not author texts can give us a sense of the structural position of authors in the larger corporate network. The most straightforward measure of node-level structural characteristics is degree. In an unweighted network, degree is a count of the number of ties a node possesses—in a social network, this value is the number of people to whom a person is connected. In a two-mode network of companies and owners, it is the number of companies a person is invested in—or, from the other perspective, the number of people who have bought shares in a company. Converting the network into a one-mode projection changes the interpretation slightly. In an owner-to-owner network, degree would measure the number of individuals with whom an actor coinvests.

At this point it is worth considering how meaningful it was to own stock in a company. I used to own stock in Apple. Inferring a personal connection between myself and all the other individuals who held stock in Apple in the early 2000s would be misguided because stockholding is now overwhelmingly mediated by the market. Stock ownership in the early seventeenth century was a different matter.[11] Stock ownership was a new phenomenon that was still confined to a small population of wealthier individuals. Most of them probably spent their afternoons together in the small coffeehouses of Exchange Alley in London. Stock holding of any significant size entailed oversight of the affairs of the firm and voting privileges in the board meetings. By most accounts, company meetings were raucous, democratic affairs with much back and forth and widespread participation.[12] The bond of coinvesting in a company had a meaning that has been largely lost over time.

10. M. E. J. Newman, "Scientific Collaboration Networks: I. Network Construction and Fundamental Results," *Physical Review E* 64, no. 1 (July 2001): 016131, https://doi.org/10.1103/PhysRevE .64.016131.

11. Anne L. Murphy, *The Origins of English Financial Markets: Investment and Speculation Before the South Sea Bubble* (Cambridge: Cambridge University Press, 2009).

12. Phil Withington, "Public Discourse, Corporate Citizenship, and State Formation in Early Modern England," *American Historical Review* 112, no. 4 (October 2006): 1016–38.

It may be, however, that co-ownership would have less meaning in a very large company than in a small company even then. This consideration led me to weight the network, using a weighted degree measure as a simple approximation of prominence in the company world. Figure 4.3 presents the distribution of values for weighted degree for company owners divided into two populations: authors and nonauthors. The solid line represents authors. The stippled line represents nonauthors. The two vertical solid and stippled lines represent the mean values for these populations. The higher average weighted degree of authors is an indicator that authors were not often marginal figures in the commercial world.

This figure is not a frequency distribution but instead a kernel density distribution, essentially a smoothed line representing the frequency

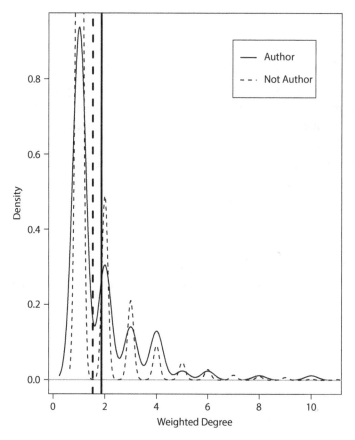

FIGURE 4.3. Weighted degree distributions of authorship, owner-to-owner company network

of values at each level. The x-axis represents the weighted degree of the nodes and the y-axis, the density function, which is higher when there is a greater number of occurrences of the corresponding x-axis value. Thus, for example, we can see that the highest rate of occurrence for nonauthors is at a value of one degree: most nonauthors have a low weighted degree.

There are many more nonauthors than authors, but authors have a higher degree than nonauthors. The number of identified authors in the data set is small enough that the difference is not statistically significant at the 95 percent level with bootstrapped estimates. Confidence intervals are presented in table 4.7, which shows the intervals for all the different measures presented in this section of the chapter. The difference is not tremendous, but is noticeable. The higher degree of authors is a tempered indication that they occupied, on average, a more prominent and well-connected position in the commercial universe than their less literary colleagues.

Another way to think structurally about community position is embeddedness. Nodes with higher degree are more likely to be deeply embedded in the network through their many associations, but this does not necessarily have to be the case. Whereas degree is an ego-level count, embeddedness is more about the position of the node within the larger network. It is a theoretical concept that addresses whether the individuals occupy more or less dense portions of the larger network.[13]

Operationalizing embeddedness has proven to be difficult. To date, the most effective measure has employed k-cores, which are an iteratively calculated measure of how many ties collectively bind together different layers of group membership in a network.[14] The unusual structural features

TABLE 4.7
Confidence intervals for company network measures, authorship

	Weighted degree	Topological overlap	Weighted transitivity
Author	3.38705	0.00956	0.73565
	(3.13494–3.63206)	(0.00912–0.01050)	(0.70860–0.77132)
Nonauthor	3.18030	0.00881	0.75423
	(3.07577–3.25144)	(0.00840–0.00943)	(0.74363–0.76633)

13. Mark S. Granovetter, "The Strength of Weak Ties," *American Journal of Sociology* 78, no. 6 (May 1973): 1360–80.

14. James Moody and Douglas R. White, "Structural Cohesion and Embeddedness: A Hierarchical Concept of Social Groups," *American Sociological Review* 68, no. 1 (February 2003): 103–27, https://doi.org/10.2307/3088904.

of bipartite networks pose a problem for k-cores as the nesting properties are different from regular social networks. In addition, there is no
way to incorporate weighted ties into the measure as it is currently conceived. These features make applying k-cores to these data inadequate and
potentially misleading. Instead, I use a measure developed first in genetic
research called topological overlap.[15] Though it lacks the theoretical link
to social embeddedness provided by k-cores, the advantage is that is a
measure of interconnectivity that can incorporate the information given
in weighted ties,[16] which are so crucial to understanding the nature of this
ownership network.

Topological overlap is easiest to conceptualize at the dyad level. If
two nodes share all their neighbors, their overlap is one. If they share no
neighbors, their overlap is zero. The measure at the level of the node is
the average of the overlap over all dyads—i.e., the average overlap with all
of the other nodes in the network. If nodes are in richly interconnected
groups, they will have many of the same ties. Topological overlap captures whether individuals are highly interconnected with their neighbors.
It does not capture anything about the size of the neighborhood. A small
but highly interconnected subgraph of the larger network could score the
same as a larger and similarly interconnected subgraph. What it can capture is a sense of whether the authors are embedded within densely interconnected communities.

Figure 4.4 represents a density plot of the distribution of topological
overlap across nonauthors and authors within the person-to-person projection of the company-investor network. Authors are represented by the
solid line and nonauthors by the stippled line. In this plot, the mean values
are again represented by the vertical lines.

Authors have higher topological overlap than nonauthors. As can be
seen from the distribution, this difference seems to stem mainly from the
fact that authors are less likely to have extremely low values of topological overlap, as evidenced in the size of the peak of the density function at
the lower, left-hand values of topological overlap. The difference indicates

---

15. Steve Horvath, *Weighted Network Analysis: Applications in Genomics and Systems Biology*
(New York: Springer, 2011); and Ai Li and Steve Horvath, "Network Module Detection: Affinity
Search Technique with the Multi-Node Topological Overlap Measure," *BMC Research Notes* 2, no.
1 (July 2009): 142, https://doi.org/10.1186/1756-0500-2-142.

16. Horvath, *Weighted Network Analysis*; and Li and Horvath, "Network Module Detection."

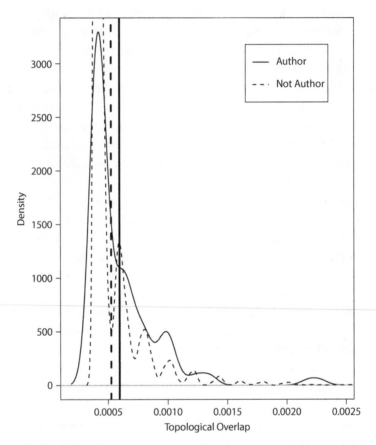

FIGURE 4.4. Topological overlap distribution of authorship, owner-to-owner company network

that authors are more likely to occupy densely interconnected areas of the ownership-corporate community network.

One further measure of community structure is transitivity, or the clustering coefficient.[17] The clustering coefficient is another node-level measure of community density. Instead of looking at whether two nodes have ties to the same other nodes, the clustering coefficient measures the density of ties among all of the nodes in a given neighborhood. In an acquaintance network, if everyone you know also knows one another, you

17. Duncan J. Watts and Steven H. Strogatz, "Collective Dynamics of 'Small-World' Networks," *Nature* 393 (June 4, 1998): 440–42.

would have the highest possible value for your clustering coefficient: a value of one. Though conceptually similar, there is an important difference between topological overlap and the clustering coefficient. High values of topological overlap are produced when nodes have ties to the same people. It does not capture whether those people also have ties to each other. This latter feature is what is measured by the clustering coefficient and transitivity. As first conceived by Watts and Strogatz, the clustering coefficient does not adjust for weighted values, so I use a closely related weighted transitivity measure.[18]

A slightly different pattern emerges in figure 4.5. In this case, authors have lower transitivity than their nonauthor peers. Again, this is because of a lack of extreme values at one end of the measure. Whereas nonauthors are very likely to have extremely high levels of weighted transitivity, authors are only marginally more likely to have such high levels.

Transitivity is a measure of community clustering, but is often associated with negative impacts that can follow from too much density. In order to have the beneficial effects that flow from community support, there has to be some density of ties. Through these ties, resources, information, and emotional support can flow. Groups use dense ties to build up regular patterns of activity, and they appear to be a source of norms and institutions that help coordinate activity and encourage social flourishing and development.[19] But if ties are too dense, individual autonomy might be suffocated, norms can become too restrictive, and information flow becomes redundant and unhelpful. Individual autonomy can suffer in the closed net of restrictively dense and overlapping relationships. The distribution of transitivity across the two populations indicates that authors tended to escape this fate.

From the perspective of structural holes theory, there is a brokerage advantage to having lower transitivity. The authors structurally had an advantage by linking disconnected actors within the more densely connected subsets of the network. In combination with the topological overlap measure, it can be inferred that authors were situated in dense areas of the network. However, even within these highly cohesive areas, there were individuals with

18. A. Barrat, M. Barthélemy, R. Pastor-Satorras, and A. Vespignani, "The Architecture of Complex Weighted Networks," *Proceedings of the National Academy of Sciences of the United States of America* 101, no. 11 (March 16, 2004): 3747–52, https://doi.org/10.1073/pnas.0400087101.

19. Damon Centola, "The Social Origins of Networks and Diffusion," *American Journal of Sociology* 120, no. 5 (March 2015): 1295–1338, https://doi.org/10.1086/681275.

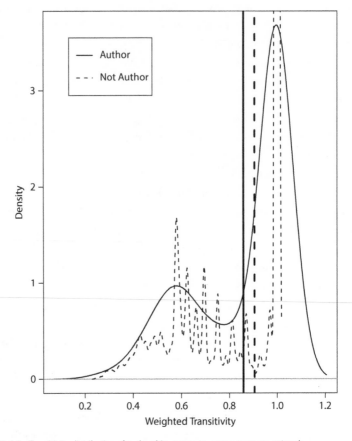

FIGURE 4.5. Transitivity distribution of authorship, owner-to-owner company network

many friends in common but no direct ties to each other. These investors inhabited proximate parts of the network, often in the densely connected regions, but were not invested in the same company. The advantage of linking these types of individuals is that it combines the benefits of local network diversity with those of belonging to a connected community.

Together the two figures suggest that authors may indeed have been acting as local brokers in the sparser areas of the more densely embedded communities of ownership. Economic authors seem to have inhabited areas of the network that combined two beneficial aspects of network structure: having brokerage connections between disconnected individuals and occupying densely connected communities. They appear to have been

better-connected individuals occupying a structurally advantageous position within the larger company network. They were not significantly different from other company figures, but they also were not at any structural
disadvantage in this world.

The confidence intervals for all these measures are again noted in
table 4.7. The confidence intervals are presented in parentheses and constructed by bootstrapping.

COUNCILS OF STATE

The second interactional locus for the new dialogue on economics was the
state. The areas of the state most closely connected to commercial policy
were the councils and committees of trade—the precursors to the modern
Board of Trade. State committees and councils were important forums for
the development of economic arguments.[20] Several important works were
initially prepared for presentation to the various iterations of the boards
of trade that appeared over the course of the seventeenth century. Antago-
nisms that arose in councils fostered engagement and public debate, such
as the intense rivalry between Mun and Malynes.[21] There are even some
instances of supportive interlocutors finding each other and furthering
their own development as economic thinkers through positive dialogue, as
appears to have occurred, for example, between John Locke and John Cary.
In this stage of the analysis, I evaluate the structural position of authors
versus nonauthors in these councils and committees using the same measures as in the previous analysis of the company network.

The committee data used to construct the network have been gathered from
two sources. In 1908, Charles Andrews published *British Committees, Commissions, and Councils of Trade and Plantations, 1622–1675*, which described
all committees occurring in those years and includes detailed membership
information.[22] *Office-Holders in Modern Britain: Volume 3, Officials of the
Boards of Trade 1660–1870* (1974) has membership rosters for all Councils

20. Paul Slack, "The Politics of English Political Economy in the 1620s," in *Popular Culture and
Political Agency in Early Modern England and Ireland: Essays in Honour of John Walter*, ed. Michael
J. Braddick and Phil Withington (Woodbridge, UK: Boydell Press, 2017), 55–72.

21. Slack, "English Political Economy."

22. Charles M. Andrews, *British Committees, Commissions, and Councils of Trade and Plantations, 1622–1675* (Baltimore: Johns Hopkins Press, 1908).

and Committees of Trade from 1660 to 1870.[23] Both data sources were used to compile a complete list of members for all trade committees, commissions, and councils from 1622 to 1720. The Andrews publication is less systematic then the later volume, but it does consistently list committee members. For the analysis of council networks, I again merged the data collected from these two sources with the authorship information for economic texts.

The data on the membership in the councils and committees of trade posed its own unique problems. Nobles were identified variously by name or by title across different councils. Different individuals, often descendants, held the same title, and individuals held different titles over the course of a lifetime. For example, the title Earl of Nottingham could have been used to refer to Charles Howard the First, Charles Howard the Second, or Charles Howard the Third Earl of Nottingham and Baron Howard of Effingham. It may have also referred to Daniel Finch, the Eighth Earl of Winchelsea and Second Earl of Nottingham. (I know this means there are two different Second Earls of Nottingham; I don't understand it either.) The first Charles Howard dates out of the relevant councils, and the second Charles Howard seems to have accomplished little worthy of record. The third Charles Howard, the Third Earl of Nottingham and Baron Howard of Effingham, lived from 1610 to 1681, but has gone down in the historical record as having ruined his prospects by marrying for love. Daniel Finch, on the other hand, was both a privy councilor and secretary of state during the appropriate period. He is the one.

To match authors to council members, I converted titles to names, disambiguating between those holding the same title using dates of the councils and biographical information, such as birth and death years, years of service in Parliament, and any other helpful details I could cull from the historical record—including, as occurred in some cases, a history of madness, which I took (perhaps wrongly) to preclude important government service. After this process, names were matched across the data sets again using a fuzzy matching process that picked the most similar name and assigned it a score. Unfortunately, many of the individuals serving on the councils and committees of state were identified only by their last name and first initial. I considered the resulting matches with scores above 90 on a case-by-case basis, while also attempting to resolve cases in which the last name appeared alone. If the first initial and last name matched across

23. John Christopher Sainty, *Office-Holders in Modern Britain: III, Officials of the Boards of Trade, 1660–1870* (London: Athlone Press, 1974).

cases, I assumed a match even without additional identifying information, because of the greater likelihood that a council member would be both capable and likely to publish on economic issues. In a small number of cases, individuals were identified as offices, and the identification of the individual in question was not possible. This occurred with the first Commission of Trade, in which three individuals were identified only as Crown officers and two others only as city merchants. It was not necessary to be a member of Parliament to serve on a council or committee. Many of these individuals were appointed in an advisory capacity. Committees were usually a mixture of titled MPs and untitled appointees.

The networks of council and committee members that encompasses these authors is another bipartite or two-mode network, with 343 nodes, 304 of which are individuals who served on at least one of the thirty-nine councils spanning period from 1622 to 1720. Trade councils before 1622 were very uncommon. Queen Elizabeth I convened one council in which Malynes participated in the first years of the seventeenth century, but details of its constitution or members are scant. I converted the 343-node council-person network into a person-to-person network of 304-by-303 possible ties. The council network is considerably less dense than the ownership network, as the average number of individuals serving on councils or committees was lower than the number of people invested in one of the large chartered companies. This makes a visualization of the person-to-person network much easier on the eye. Figure 4.6 presents this person-to-person network of government representation. Nodes are colored according to whether individuals authored an economic publication: authors are dark gray; nonauthors are white. Again, ties are weighted in inverse proportion to the size of the council or committee on which individuals were seated.

The size of the nodes and their labels in the image are determined by degree, where larger nodes and labels have more connections. A few of the more prominent authors are labeled. Readers will by now be familiar with the names Thomas Mun, Gerard de Malynes, Josiah Child, and John Locke. Denzil Holles, a famous statesman and the first Baron of Holles, published a version of his January 31, 1642, remarks to Parliament "concerning the poor trademens petition."[24] Bulstrode Whitelocke, another

---

24. Denzil Holles, *Mr. Hollis, His Speech in Parliament: On Munday the 31th of January, Vpon the delivery of a Message from the House of Commons, concerning the poore Tradesmens Petition* (London: J. Hammond, 1642), Making of the Modern World (Gale Document Number U0109132611).

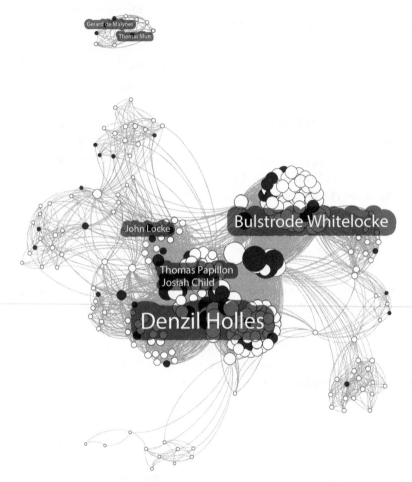

FIGURE 4.6. Person-to-council network of membership for trade councils

colorful aristocrat, was elected to Parliament in 1626. His contribution to the economic literature was a posthumous publication, *Memorials of the English Affairs* (1682).[25] Thomas Papillon was an English merchant and a director of the East India Company. His 1677 tract was titled *The East-India-trade a most profitable trade to the kingdom.*[26]

25. Bulstrode Whitelocke, *Memorials of the English Affairs: or, an Historical Account of What passed from the beginning of the Reign of King Charles the First, to King Charles the Second His Happy Restauration* (London: Printed for Nathaniel Ponder, 1682), Making of the Modern World.

26. Thomas Papillon, *The East-India-Trade a most Profitable Trade to the Kingdom. And Best Secured and Improved in a Company, and a Joint-Stock. Represented In a Letter written upon the Occasion of two Letters lately published, insinuating the Contrary* (London, 1677), Making of the Modern World.

Using the same methods of analysis as in the previous section, it turns out that authors were more likely than nonauthors to be prominent, embedded, and structurally autonomous members of the state councils and committees of trade. Being deeply engaged in this policy universe appears to have stimulated public engagement.

Figure 4.7 represents the weighted degree distribution across authors and nonauthors in the trade committee world. The solid line represents authors and the stippled line nonauthors. Once again, the vertical lines represent mean values. In this case, the difference is significant. Confidence intervals are presented in table 4.8.

On average, authors have more ties to other committee members than nonauthors. They are more prominent figures. Authors average at a degree of 4.7, whereas nonauthors average 3.89.

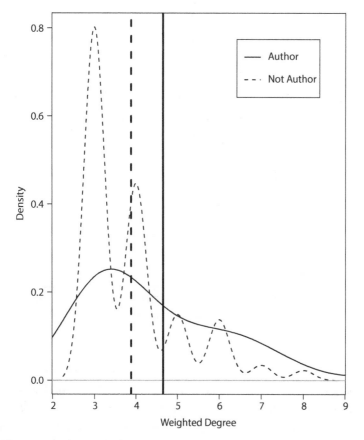

FIGURE 4.7. Weighted degree distribution of authorship, councils and committees

TABLE 4.8
Confidence intervals for committees and councils network, authorship

	Weighted degree	**Topological overlap**	**Weighted transitivity**
Author	4.65385	0.01539	0.66770
	(4.12692–5.04471)	(0.01384–0.01612)	(0.62876–0.71072)
Nonauthor	3.88489	0.01224	0.72893
	(3.73885–3.95360)	(0.01175–0.01306)	(0.70481–0.74632)

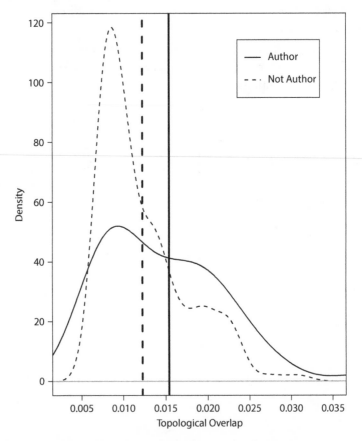

FIGURE 4.8. Topological overlap distribution of authorship, councils and committees

Topological overlap tells a similar story. Figure 4.8 presents the distributions and mean values for authors and nonauthors. Solid is authors; stippled is nonauthors. The mean value for authors is 0.02, and the mean value for nonauthors is 0.01. This difference is statistically significant at

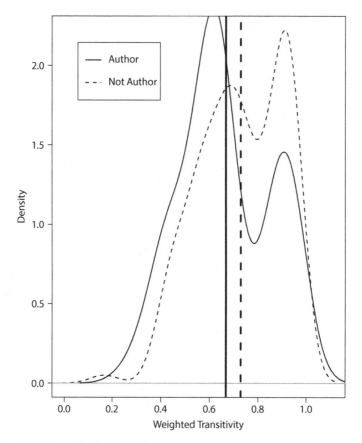

FIGURE 4.9. Transitivity distribution of authorship, councils and committees

the 95th percent level. Fewer authors have extremely low overlap, and the distribution is shifted right, so there is also a larger number of authors at the higher values.

It is interesting to note that transitivity is also lower for authors than for nonauthors, although this difference does not reach statistical significance. Figure 4.9 presents the weighted transitivity scores for authors (solid) and nonauthors (stippled), with vertical lines indicating mean values.

Fewer authors reach the extreme lower values of transitivity. Authors were more prominent, better connected, and more deeply embedded in the trade policy network than nonauthors. Engagement in both the company and trade council worlds appears to stimulate the publication of economic texts, helping to underscore the importance of the state and the company in this significant shift in discourse and expansion of the public sphere.

Table 4.8 again presents the bootstrapped 95 percent confidence intervals for all measures' mean values.

MARGINALIZATION OF MERCHANTS

There is one additional structural story to be noted in the committee and council data. The committees, councils, and boards of trade were the most important dedicated institutional vehicle through which the centralized state addressed matters of commerce. The last question to be addressed is the extent to which merchants were more or less deeply embedded within this institution of commercial governance. The network image shown a few pages ago in figure 4.6 provides some initial clues.

Two of the most renowned contributors to the development of economic theory, Mun and Malynes, belong to a cluster that has no ties to the main component. This cluster is the famous Committee of 1623 from which the balance-of-trade concept emerged with such forceful clarity in the arguments between the two men. The structural disconnect is a result of the irregularity of such dedicated committees at the time and emblematic of the difficulties the emerging nation-state had in properly addressing fluctuating economic conditions.

Two of the most prominent authors are Denzil Holles and Bulstrode Whitelocke. A quick glance reveals that Holles and Whitelocke are better connected (i.e., have a higher number of connections to others in the network) than the four more famous merchants labeled in the council network (Malynes, Mun, Papillon, and Child). Holles and Whitelocke were landed aristocrats with significant political stature. Holles, in particular, was famous for his role in the Civil War and Restoration. However, his pamphlet has not gone down in history as a notable contribution to economic thought. Whitelocke, once Keeper of the Great Seal, was also known for an area of expertise other than economic matters. He was primarily a politician and lawyer. They participated in the conversation, but did not make deep contributions to economic thinking. Yet they were very prominent figures in the councils and committees network. Their central position is the result of the high value placed on aristocratic lineage and good family in state operations. Direct knowledge of commercial affairs was not

nearly as important as noble birth to placement on trade committees. This
preference for nobility over expertise kept merchants in a comparatively
marginal position on the trade committees.

Table 4.9 breaks down the number of authors belonging to each class/
occupational category, which gives a preview of things to come. The data
on the class background of the council and committee members come from
the *Oxford Dictionary of National Biography*; however, 112 of the 304 individuals could not be identified.

A skewed representational distribution is immediately apparent. Nobles
make up 45 percent of the serving members, while merchants make up
8 percent. The only lower proportion is clergy members, who make up 2
percent of the population. Even more interesting is the rate of publication
across the different groups. Among the nobles, gentry, clergy, and professionals, about one quarter of those serving publish some kind of economic
tract. The rate is even lower among the military. But among the merchants,
the rate is much higher, exceeding 50 percent. Even when serving on the
councils and committees of trade, merchants were apparently the most
likely to believe that their arguments needed to be publicly amplified.

This fact may be explained by the position the merchant authors held
relative to the other authors on the councils and committees. Merchants
certainly attempted to sway policy by serving, but they never achieved the
kind of representation in the councils of government that they desired.
They were peripheral relative to nobles, gentry, and professional council
members.

Figure 4.10 displays the weighted degree for the classes/occupational
categories of the authors that served in the councils or committees of trade
from 1600 to 1720. The vertical bars represent the mean values. The solid
line represents merchants, the nobles are dotted, gentry are short dashes,
professionals have a dash-dot-dash pattern, the one author form the clergy

TABLE 4.9
Class/occupational category, committees and councils

	Noble	Gentry	Clergy	Military	Professional	Merchant
Author	22	11	1	1	8	9
Nonauthor	65	29	3	14	22	7
	87	40	4	15	30	16
	(45%)	(21%)	(2%)	(8%)	(16%)	(8%)

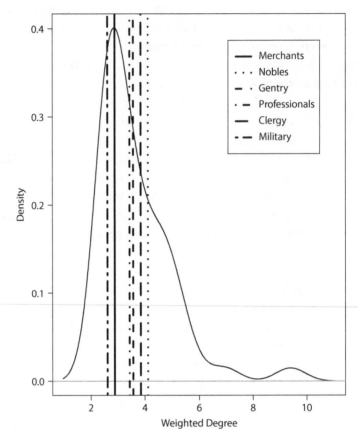

FIGURE 4.10. Average weighted degree by class/occupational status, councils and committees

has a long series of dashes, and the one military author has a long-short-long-short dashed line. The distribution of values for all forty-nine authors is given in the background for information. Thus, this figure differs from the previous ones in that there is no comparison set for the distribution—only the mean values. Nobles have the highest weighted degree. The military has the lowest, and merchants come in at the second lowest average weighted degree. Merchant authors appear to have been able to secure a spot on a council or committee here or there, but their connections within that world were limited.

Figure 4.11 shows the average topological overlap values for each class. Somewhat surprisingly, the sole clergy member author appears to occupy

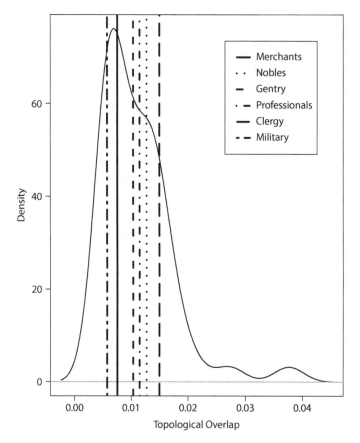

FIGURE 4.11. Average values of topological overlap by class/occupational status, councils and committees

the most densely interconnected area of the network. This honor goes to J Cockburn.[27] J Cockburn appears to have been John Cockburn, a parish clergyman who began his career at the King's College in Aberdeen. He was a prolific author, although only one of his publications, *A Short History of the Revolution in Scotland* (1712), touched on economic matters significantly enough to be included in the economics titles data set.[28]

27. I cannot be absolutely certain that J Cockburn the clergyman and author is also the council member, but given his proximity to the Crown and biographical details, it seems very likely.

28. John Cockburn, *A Short History of the Revolution in Scotland. In a Letter from a Scotch Gentleman in Amsterdam to his Friend in London* (London: Printed by the Booksellers of London and Westminster, 1712), Making of the Modern World.

In 1714, the queen designated him a bishop of the American colonies. The appointment, however, never came to fruition.[29] Instead it appears that he served on three separate committees, the Council of Trade and Plantations of 1715, 1716, and 1718, which were all fairly small and in which most members rotated off after one year. Colonel Thomason, who served on the 1651 Standing Committee of the Council of Trade on Trade, is more fully shrouded in the mists of history. Without these two outliers, a clear pattern emerges. Nobility is at the top of the structural ladder, and merchants are at the bottom. Merchants were significantly less well integrated into the community than nobles, gentry, and professionals.

Interestingly, the pattern found for investors with regard to local density is reversed for merchant authors within the network of trade committees. Figure 4.12 presents the distribution of the weighted transitivity measures for nodes across the class groupings.

Again, with the exception of the sole clergy member, the figure shows that merchant authors have the highest values, meaning they are more likely than other subpopulations to have densely interconnected ego networks. Most of the people they are linked to are also linked to each other. Merchants' average weighted transitivity rounds to a high of 0.8. Nobles are more likely to have low clustering coefficients. Their average value is 0.57, indicating they are more likely to be linked to individuals who are not linked to each other. In terms of the bipartite network, this means that nobles are more likely to have served on different committees, and merchants less so. Table 4.10 presents the confidence intervals for nobles and merchants. As can be seen from the table, the structural disadvantage of the merchants relative to the nobles is statistically significant as there is no overlap in the confidence intervals.

In this policy world, merchants occupied a marginal and structurally disadvantaged position. Not many merchants were granted privileged positions within trade councils in the first place, and those who were did not often serve on more than one committee. Merchants were not well represented in this important branch of the government, and thus were more likely to have to marshal external support to make their voice heard.

29. Alexander Gordon, "Cockburn, John," in *Dictionary of National Biography, 1885–1900*, ed. Leslie Stephen, vol. 11 (London: Smith, Elder, 1887), http://www.archive.org/details/dictionary ofnati11stepuoft.

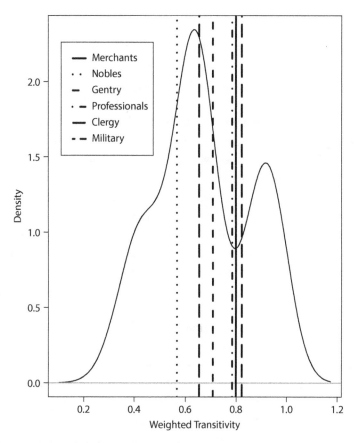

FIGURE 4.12. Average values of weighted transitivity by class/occupational status, councils and committees

TABLE 4.10
Bootstrapped confidence intervals for committees and council network, class

	Weighted degree	Topological overlap	Weighted transitivity
Noble	4.156479	0.01292293	0.565259
	(3.723643	(0.0113047	(0.5045452
	−4.556968)	−0.01436108)	−0.6186677)
Merchant	2.889976	0.007357408	0.7988256
	(2.616137	(0.005722055	(0.7293896
	−3.095355)	−0.00869072)	−0.8824924)

CONCLUSION

The lives of two prominent merchants illustrate the personal impact of distance from the state and company membership. Thomas Gresham (c.1519–1579) was a wealthy merchant and financier responsible for some of the great financial developments in early modern English history, and John Wheeler (1553–1611) was a prominent merchant and author of an important text on the Merchant Adventurers. Both were company men.

Gresham began his career with the Mercers' Company while receiving a degree at Cambridge and over time became a prominent member of the Company of Merchant Adventurers. In 1565, he founded the Royal Exchange. A man of many accomplishments, Gresham rose to prominence as an adviser to King Edward VI, Queen Mary I, and Queen Elizabeth I. Some readers may know Gresham from the law of economics named after him, which refers to the principle that bad money drives out good. More specifically, Gresham described the tendency of people to offload debased coinage whenever possible and to hoard properly valued coins, and the logical consequence of those actions, which is an increase the amount of debased coinage in circulation.

It was not Gresham but Henry Dunning Macleod, the Scottish economist, who coined Gresham's law posthumously in 1860. Gresham did not publish his thoughts on economics. He was not participating in an attempt to build collective knowledge about economic matters; he was providing advice to his monarchs. His contributions to economics, and the observations to which Macleod referred in naming the law, were extracted from formal correspondence and state papers. Gresham was not an author; he was an adviser and policy maker. He did not publish his economic theories in the public realm. His proximity to and influence over the Crown meant that there was little need for him to advocate in the public sphere for his ideas. He had a much more direct route through which to implement policy change. Gresham demonstrated significant insight into economic matters for the time, but his location in the institutional structures of early modern England made the process of making that knowledge public superfluous or even perhaps contrary to his interests.

Similar political influence was not granted to John Wheeler. Whereas Thomas Gresham was born the son of a Lord Mayor of London and educated at Cambridge before entering the world of commerce, John Wheeler was of more humble origins.[30] Wheeler was nevertheless able to amass a considerable fortune in his lifetime and became an esteemed officer of the Company of Merchant Adventurers. He was elected to the position of company secretary in 1601. John Wheeler was not entirely without access to the state, but it was significantly more limited than Sir Thomas Gresham's. Some of this may have been Wheeler's fault. He reputedly turned down an offer of a position in the service of the Queen.[31] Perhaps if he had accepted he might have cultivated greater influence, but as it turned out, he had little direct contact with Queen Elizabeth I and, as her negative treatment of the Adventurers in the 1590s conclusively establishes, he had little sway over her commercial policies. Several times throughout the later years of her reign—and after the death of Gresham—she passed decrees or issued licenses that favored competing merchants and directly threatened the continued existence of the company.

As it was, Wheeler was forced into a defensive position. The Merchant Adventurers attempted to lobby the Queen and Privy Council for support, but failing to achieve their objective, Wheeler took to a new medium. In 1601, he published a long defense of the company, its privileges, and its practices. *A Treatise of Commerce* touched upon ideas about the operations of the commercial world and trade, including the role of special privileges in trade, and provided one of the first detailed descriptions of company organization.[32] While it is mainly useful now as a historical record of the Merchant Adventurers, in the seventeenth century it was an early assay in the incipient debate over how best to manage trade to national advantage.

The weak structural position occupied by Wheeler was common among merchants of the seventeenth century. Even though they had more knowledge about trade and commerce, merchants occupied a subordinate position to nobles and gentry in the network of councils and committees of trade. They were less deeply embedded in the network, had fewer connections, and occupied fewer autonomous structural positions—all of which should have given them ample motivation to seek other avenues of influence. The

---

30. George Burton Hotchkiss, introduction to *A Treatise of Commerce*, by John Wheeler (Clark, NJ: Lawbook Exchange, 2004), 4.

31. Hotchkiss, introduction.

32. Wheeler, *A Treatise of Commerce*.

public sphere—a context that could amplify their arguments in the ears of the Parliament, Privy Council, and Crown—was a natural alternative.

The councils and committees acted as sites that encouraged authorship. More deeply embedded and connected individuals in these worlds had higher rates of authorship. This effect seems to have been stronger for merchants, who published at higher rates than other committee members. The companies were also an important locus of publication. Authors of economic texts tended to be slightly more embedded and interconnected, though the association was weaker in this context.

The weaker effect here may be due to the fact that merchants fighting both for and against chartered companies were a crucial stimulus to productive economic debate, implying that some but not all of the merchants contributing economic texts would be strongly embedded in the company-owner affiliation network. Other merchants outside of the company ownership network also undoubtedly participated in the debates.

Ultimately, one of the most compelling reasons to believe that merchants' positions relative to the state drove the development of a new economic discourse is that merchants were authoring economic texts at an increasing rate. The introduction of a new population into an existing setting is a well-theorized mechanism of institutional change.[33] Merchants took up authorship to promote their own agenda, which had the additional effect of driving the literature in the direction of trade and finance. Merchants brought their own habits of mind to the attempt to penetrate the inner workings of commerce, price levels, and specie flow—habits that sent them searching through tallies and account books rather than biblical or philosophical texts. And since they were trying to bridge that structural distance between states politics and the world of commerce, they were careful to link their interests to the idea of national prosperity.

33. John W. Mohr and Harrison C. White, "How to Model an Institution," *Theory and Society* 37, no. 5 (October 2008): 485–512, https://doi.org/10.1007/s11186-008-9066-0.

Chapter Five

REPRESENTATION, COMPANIES, AND PUBLICATIONS

The structural analysis of chapter 4 provides support for an explanation based in the particularities of state-merchant interactions in England. However, structural analysis alone cannot rule out alternative explanations. It does not provide a basis for adjudication between competing hypotheses. Such adjudication is important, as there have been many theories developed over time as to why economic thought underwent such a significant quantitative and qualitative transition in England in the seventeenth century.

The early modern era was a time of significant change along many different dimensions. England, along with many European states, experienced several transitions that have been thought potentially consequential for the development of economic theory. Existing theories have been focused largely on five external factors. One influential theory has been that the expansion of seventeenth-century English economic thought can be attributed to the emergence of the public sphere.[1] Many other historians of economic thought have posited that the increasing complexity of economics caused by the development process translated directly into increasingly

---

1. Joyce Oldham Appleby, *Economic Thought and Ideology in Seventeenth-Century England* (Los Angeles: Figueroa Press, 1978); Andrea Finkelstein, *Harmony and the Balance: An Intellectual History of Seventeenth-Century English Economic Thought* (Ann Arbor: University of Michigan Press, 2009); and Peter Lake and Steve Pincus, "Rethinking the Public Sphere in Early Modern England," *Journal of British Studies* 45, no. 2 (April 2006): 270–92.

sophisticated attempts to explain economic phenomena.[2] Some authors hypothesized that the particularly difficult logistical complexities of overseas trade were an important trigger for more complex economic thinking.[3] Still others have argued that the emergence of nation-states stimulated the development of new ideas in the nation's attempts to control and amass economic resources through the consolidation of domestic power and imperial expansion.[4] Most recently in this vein, Erik Reinert, Sophus Reinert, and Pernille Røge have emphasized the role of international competition between nations in stimulating early modern economic discourse.[5] More generally, a significant body of work has demonstrated a relationship between proximate economic disruptions and new developments in economic thought, including the strides made in the seventeenth century.[6]

2. E. Ray Canterbery, *A Brief History of Economics: Artful Approaches to the Dismal Science* (Singapore: World Scientific, 2011), 32–33; Maurice Dobb, *Theories of Value and Distribution Since Adam Smith: Ideology and Economic Theory* (Cambridge: Cambridge University Press, 1975), 20; Ronald Meek, *Economics and Ideology and Other Essays: Studies in the Development of Economic Thought* (London: Chapman and Hall, 1967), 203; and Eric Roll, *A History of Economic Thought* (London: Faber and Faber, 1992), 12–13.

3. Parakunnel Joseph Thomas, *Mercantilism and the East India Trade: An Early Phase of the Protection v. Free Trade Controversy* (1926; reprint, Mansfield Center, CT: Martino Publishing, 2009); William J. Barber, *British Economic Thought and India, 1600–1858: A Study in the History of Development Economics* (Oxford: Clarendon Press, 1975); Lynn Zastoupil, *John Stuart Mill and India* (Stanford, CA: Stanford University Press, 1994); Sophus A. Reinert and Pernille Røge, eds., *The Political Economy of Empire in the Early Modern World* (Basingstoke, UK: Palgrave Macmillan, 2013); and Emily Erikson, "The Influence of Trade with Asia on British Economic Theory and Practice," in *Global Historical Sociology*, ed. Julian Go and George Lawson (Cambridge: Cambridge University Press, 2017), 182–98.

4. Joseph A. Schumpeter, *History of Economic Analysis: With a New Introduction*, rev. ed. (New York: Oxford University Press, 1954), 143; John Kenneth Galbraith, *Economics in Perspective: A Critical History* (Boston: Houghton Mifflin, 1988); Douglas Irwin, *Against the Tide: An Intellectual History of Free Trade* (Princeton, NJ: Princeton University Press, 1996); and Jacob Viner, *Essays on the Intellectual History of Economics* (Princeton, NJ: Princeton University Press, 1991), 45–53.

5. Erik S. Reinert and Sophus A. Reinert, "Mercantilism and Economic Development: Schumpeterian Dynamics, Institution-Building and International Benchmarking," in *The Origins of Development Economics: How Schools of Economics Thought Have Addressed Development*, ed. Jomo K. S. and Erik S. Reinert (New Delhi: Tulika Books; London: Zed Books, 2005), 1–23; and Reinert and Røge, *Political Economy of Empire*.

6. Robert Eagly, *Events, Ideology, and Economic Theory: The Determinants of Progress in the Development of Economic Analysis* (Detroit, MI: Wayne State University Press, 1968); Mary O. Furner and Barry Supple, eds., *The State and Economic Knowledge: The American and British Experiences* (Cambridge: Cambridge University Press, 2002); J. D. Gould, "The Trade Crisis of the Early 1620's and English Economic Thought," *Journal of Economic History* 15, no. 2 (June 1955): 121–33; Jonathan Israel, "England's Mercantilist Response to Dutch World Trade Primacy, 1647–1674," in *State and Trade: Government and the Economy in Britain and the Netherlands Since the Middle Ages*, ed. Simon Groenveld and Michael Joseph Wintle (Zutphen: Walburg Pers, 1992), 50–61;

More recently, Paul Slack and Carl Wennerlind have argued that the seventeenth-century innovations in economic thought were rooted in the trade depression of the 1620s.[7]

In this chapter, I use times series methods to both asses my hypothesis and consider these alternative explanations. In total, the model includes eleven other time series that represent these alternative explanations for the noted transformation. This kind of assessment requires a statistical approach. Using a database constructed for this purpose, I use annual variation over time to analyze the relationship between the number of chartered companies, the number of merchants in Parliament, the publication rates of economic texts, and a number of possible confounding factors. The dependent variable, or the outcome of interest, is the number of publications of economic texts in England and Scotland calculated annually.[8] This is the same data set initially presented in chapter 1. It is made up of 6,585 economic titles compiled from the *Making of the Modern World* database and the *English Short Title Catalogue.*

Using a vector autoregression (VAR) time series framework, the model tests whether the number of chartered companies and levels of parliamentary representation are good predictors of increases in the publication rate of economic texts in the following year. In the VAR time series analysis, time is broken into discrete chunks—years—which are compared to each other in order to draw conclusions about the relationship between publication rates of economic texts and different factors that might have influenced publishing trends over the period of interest. Although the time series analysis can only consider the count of texts, and does not assess variation in what they discussed or changing moral frameworks, it provides a within-case analysis of differences over time—a central method for establishing causality within comparative historical inquiry.[9]

Lars Magnusson, *Mercantilism: The Shaping of an Economic Language* (London: Routledge, 1994), 60–62; Barry E. Supple, "Currency and Commerce in the Early Seventeenth Century," *Economic History Review* 10, no. 2 (1957): 239–55, https://doi.org/10.2307/2590860; and Barry E. Supple, *Commercial Crisis and Change in England, 1600–1642: A Study in the Instability of a Mercantile Economy* (Cambridge: Cambridge University Press, 1959).

7. Paul Slack, *The Invention of Improvement: Information and Material Progress in Seventeenth-Century England* (Oxford: Oxford University Press, 2015); and Carl Wennerlind, *Casualties of Credit: The English Financial Revolution, 1620–1720* (Cambridge, MA: Harvard University Press, 2011).

8. The number of texts published in Scotland is extremely low.

9. James Mahoney and Dietrich Rueschemeyer, eds., *Comparative Historical Analysis in the Social Sciences* (Cambridge: Cambridge University Press, 2003).

TIME SERIES ANALYSIS

The VAR model includes several time series stretching from 1550 to 1720. As noted earlier, 1720 marks the year in which the incorporation process was legally redefined, changing the nature of the chartering process, making before and after comparisons challenging. Times series analysis is subject to censoring issues, so I expanded the time frame to the mid-sixteenth century. The initial year of the data, 1550, is prior to the legal incorporation of the first chartered company in England, but does not represent a specific historical event that clearly demarcates the onset of the wave of incorporation. The transition from guilds and partnerships to companies was a gradual process.[10] The period from 1550 to 1720 saw a quantitative as well as a qualitative transition in economic thought. The number of publications increased nearly exponentially. At the same time, the number of chartered companies rose at a rapid pace, and merchant representation decreased for much of the century. Without a statistical model, it is hard to tell how tightly coupled these movements truly were.

Although statistical methods like time series analysis cannot take the place of textual or institutional analysis, one great advantage to deploying them for a full assessment of the causes and consequences of different historical actors and events is that they can control for other factors of possible importance. Overseas trade, for example, was expanding in the seventeenth century. It is plausible—and the argument has been made—that the increasing complexities of this early phase of globalization brought about the development of economic theory: the increasing interdependencies in trade made understanding the factors that affected economic growth and contraction less straightforward, and therefore economic theory was developed as a guide to action. This idea is clearly different from the argument I have put forward. Time series modeling can assess and control for the impact of overseas trade growth.

Another advantage of using VAR has to do with the way it can control for trends. Overseas trade, publishing rates, and the number of chartered companies were all on an upward trend from 1550 to 1720—as were many other factors. It was, after all, the early modern period—the era that led to the Industrial Revolution and the transformation into what we now call modernity.

---

10. The results are robust to later starting dates.

A straightforward linear regression might find an association between factors simply because they were on a similar upswing over the period of interest. It is unlikely, however, that all of these factors caused one another. Instead, common sense suggests that the ubiquitous upswing across factors was either a lucky happenstance for Europe or the result of some other climactic, demographic, or evolutionary pressure. Times series analysis controls for trends as well as the autocorrelation between years (i.e., the likelihood that things will be more similar the closer they are in time), thus increasing our confidence that the results reveal a true association rather than a coevolutionary pathway. This is because the VAR model does not assess the association between trend lines. Instead it assesses annual fluctuations around the trend.

These advantages give the statistical approach the powerful capacity to look beyond surface appearances to uncover hidden patterns. Authors often tried to obscure their company affiliations and aspirations because they did not want to be seen as nakedly promoting their own self-interest—mainly for fear of losing their audience. Indeed, the extremely common focus on the wealth and prosperity of the nation in seventeenth-century economic texts served both as a means of persuasion and as a cloak to disguise specific individual and organizational interests. This pretense has made uncovering the real relationship between company and merchant interests and the new language of economic discourse more difficult than it might have been. A systematic appraisal of the number of texts and the predictive power of the number of companies can reveal associations that would otherwise evade even close readings that focus narrowly on the explicit claims made in the texts themselves.

Explanatory Variables

The central argument I have made is that the contentiousness, organizational structure, and resources of chartered companies led individuals to publish economic arguments in order to challenge or support company privileges and practices in a context in which government influence was constricted. At minimum, a measure of the number of chartered companies and a measure of merchant political representation are necessary to assess this argument quantitatively. The first independent variable is, therefore, the cumulative number of chartered companies annually. Unfortunately, the dissolution of companies was rarely recorded, and when information is available, it often seems to have been a fuzzy, drawn out process without a clear end point, so there are no data on the life span of companies.

The count of chartered companies founded was compiled from two comprehensive catalogs of British companies: George Cawston and Augustus Henry Keane's *The Early Chartered Companies (A.D. 1296–1858)* (1896) and W. R. Scott's *The Constitution and Finance of English, Scottish and Irish Joint-Stock Companies* (1912).[11]

Figure 5.1 presents the cumulative number of chartered companies on an annual basis. The number of economic publications is also included as a stippled line for comparison, which is repeated for all the following time series. Since dissolution data are not present in the historical record, this is the count of all companies founded.[12] As is evident from the figure, there was a gradual increase in the number of companies over the early seventeenth century that plateaued briefly from 1640 to 1660. It is likely that the conflicts in and around the Civil War (1642–1651) affected founding rates in this period. After 1660, the rates resumed a steady upward trend, and in the 1690s, the numbers shot up during a moment of great enthusiasm for joint-stock companies. This increase was followed by relatively low rates of company incorporation, which can be explained by noting that these figures do not capture the formation of all companies or partnerships, but only those firms granted special privileges by national charter, a practice that declined as Britain transitioned into the modern period.

I have also argued that an important factor affecting publication rates was a low proportion of merchant representation in the state. Merchant representation is included in the analysis through parliamentary membership—specifically, the number of merchants serving in the House of Commons of the British Parliament. This count represents the extent to which merchants permeated the highest levels of government accessible to them, which should have affected the extent to which they had recourse to avenues of discussion within the government to influence policy decisions.

---

11. George Cawston and Augustus Henry Keane, *The Early Chartered Companies (A.D. 1296–1858)* (London: Edward Arnold, 1896); and William Robert Scott, *The Constitution and Finance of English, Scottish and Irish Joint-Stock Companies to 1720*, 3 vols. (Cambridge: At the University Press, 1912).

12. There were no formal mechanisms through which the dissolution of companies was recorded. Even when the history of a company was well documented, the dissolution was often a fuzzy process with no clear end point. In most cases, however, there is simply no information.

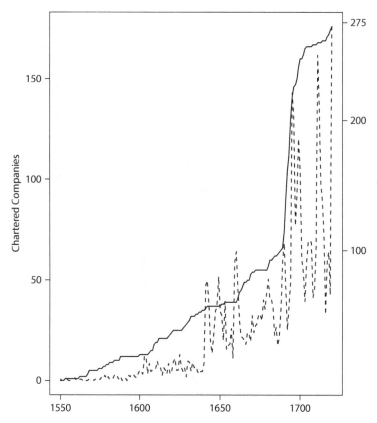

FIGURE 5.1. Chartered companies, cumulative

Figure 5.2 shows the number of merchants serving in the House of Commons from 1558—the first Parliament of the reign of Queen Elizabeth I—to 1720. The solid line represents the number of merchants in Parliament. As readers will quickly note, this series has an unusual stepwise appearance. This is because Parliament in the sixteenth and seventeenth centuries met sporadically and for irregular periods of time. Elections were held at the beginning of each session. Although Parliament was not in session all year, for the purposes of the figure I consider the term of elected members to last from their election at the beginning of a parliamentary session to the beginning of the next parliamentary session—at which time they may have been reelected or replaced.

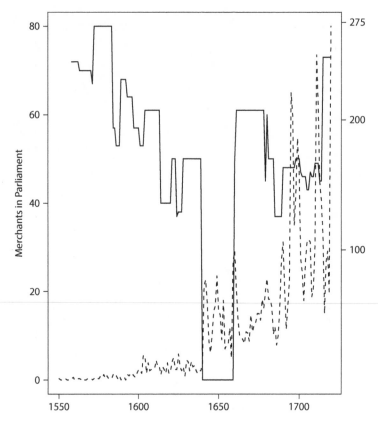

FIGURE 5.2. Merchant representation in Parliament

The data on merchant representation was gathered from the History of Parliament research project and *Members of the Long Parliament*.[13] Exact figures on the Long Parliament are not available and difficult to calculate because of the large numbers of deaths and dismissals that occurred during

13. Data from the History of Parliament research project were gathered from the following publications: David Hayton, Eveline Cruickshanks, and Stuart Handley, eds., *The House of Commons, 1690–1715*, 5 vols. (Cambridge: Published for the History of Parliament Trust by Cambridge University Press, 2002); P. W. Hasler, ed., *The House of Commons, 1558–1603*, 3 vols. (London: Published for the History of Parliament Trust by Her Majesty's Stationery Office, 1981); Basil Duke Henning, ed., *The House of Commons, 1660–1690* (London: Published for the History of Parliament Trust by Secker & Warburg, 1983); Romney Sedgwick, *The House of Commons, 1715–1754*, 2 vols. (London: Her Majesty's Stationery Office, 1970); and Andrew Thrush and John P. Ferris, eds., *The House of Commons, 1604–1629*, 6 vols. (Cambridge: Published for the History of Parliament Trust by Cambridge University Press, 2010). Members of the Long Parliament data were gathered from Douglas Brunton and Donald H. Pennington, *Members of the Long Parliament* (n.p.: Archon Books, 1954).

that contentious period and the recruitment process that was undertaken to replace missing persons. Missing values from the unusual session are imputed in the analysis using the median value. Unfortunately, no data were available from 1550 to 1557. The categorization scheme in the data also changed slightly from volume to volume, each covering different years of parliamentary history. From 1558 to 1603, the count of merchants picks up "merchants" and "tradesmen"; from 1604 to 1629 and 1660 to 1690, it includes only "merchants"; from 1690 to 1715, it includes "merchants" and "financiers." In the final 1715 Parliament (which was not followed by another parliament until 1722), it picks up only "merchants."

As the figure shows, merchant representation fell over the course of the seventeenth century, picking up some after the Civil War. Merchants were largely supplanted by an increase in lawyers over the sixteenth and early seventeenth centuries.[14] The majority of seats were held by gentry, though peers, nobles, yeoman, and military men were also elected at lower rates.[15]

ALTERNATIVE FACTORS

Civil Society and Cultural Influence

The development of a public sphere that supported the production and distribution of published works in both nations—as well the availability of relevant moral and philosophic discourses—was a potentially central factor to the development of innovative economic theory. It has been argued that the rise of economic thought in England at this time was due to the tremendous growth of civil society and public debate that resulted from the English Civil War (1642–1651) and the Glorious Revolution of 1688.[16] Joyce Appleby maintained that these events encouraged the development of a vigorous publishing community and a voracious reading public.[17] Thus, there is significant support for the idea that rise of civil society in England explains the rise in economic texts. The machinery was certainly in place to pump out a large body of writings on economics.

14. Hasler, *House of Commons, 1558–1603*.

15. Hayton, Cruickshanks, and Handley, *House of Commons, 1690–1715*; Hasler, *House of Commons, 1558–1603*; Henning, *House of Commons, 1660–1690*; Sedgwick, *House of Commons, 1715–1754*; and Thrush and Ferris, *House of Commons, 1604–1629*.

16. Steve Pincus, "Rethinking Mercantilism: Political Economy, the British Empire, and the Atlantic World in the Seventeenth and Eighteenth Centuries," *William and Mary Quarterly* 69, no. 1 (January 2012): 3–34, https://doi.org/10.5309/willmaryquar.69.1.0003.

17. Appleby, *Economic Thought and Ideology*, 4.

The publishing industry was growing across Europe in the seventeenth century, and large increases were apparent in the British Isles as well. Although the dramatic growth of publishing is not sufficient to explain the rise of political economy, particularly as it did not produce a similar increase in economic texts in other European nations, it nevertheless clearly remains an important component of the rise of political economy in England. If, for example, textual production had remained largely in the hands of monasteries, as was true of incunabula, then it is very likely that moral considerations would have continued to take priority in discussions of commerce, trade, and industry. Since a secular interpretation of commerce and trade is a defining feature of political economic texts in England in the seventeenth century, and very arguably a central reason for their lasting influence, the establishment of a commercially based print industry and culture clearly played a significant role.

It is possible that the rise in texts on trade, commerce, and industry was carried on the tide of a general increase in public discussion of all matters. Jan Luiten Van Zanden analyzed the factors driving textual production across Europe and found that the price of books, the index of real income, and the literate share of the population explain much of the variance in the production of texts from 1470 to 1580 and that urbanization rates and counts of universities and monasteries account for 60 percent of cross-national variation in textual production.[18] Because there was no change in the number of universities in England from 1550 to 1720, I do not include this time series. And because there were no new monasteries, I have no expectation that they would help explain the increase in economic publications. Moreover, whereas the universities were an important site for the production of moral philosophy and the monasteries participated in the medieval traditions of scholastic approaches to just price and usury, neither the university nor the monastery was a significant site for the new economic works of the seventeenth century.[19] Potentially more helpful would be time series on urbanization rates, book prices, literacy

18. Jan Luiten Van Zanden, "Common Workmen, Philosophers, and the Birth of the European Knowledge Economy: About the Price and the Production of Useful Knowledge in Europe, 1350–1800" (paper presented at the GEHN conference on Useful Knowledge, Leiden, Belgium, September 2004; revised October 12, 2004), https://www.researchgate.net/publication/254428476 _Common_workmen_philosophers_and_the_birth_of_the_European_knowledge_economy.

19. William Letwin, *Sir Josiah Child: Merchant Economist*, Kress Library of Business and Economics 14 (Boston: Baker Library; Harvard Graduate School of Business Administration, 1959).

rates, and the index of real income. These series are not available on an annual basis for the period of interest. Instead I include the annual rate of all books published, which these variables are meant to predict. These data are drawn from the *English Short Title Catalogue*. Although literacy rates, book prices, and the index of real income have been shown to affect publication rates and thus are likely to affect the number of economic texts produced through that pathway, the existence of an independent pathway through which they would affect the publication rates of economic texts is less tenable.

Figure 5.3 represents a plot of the number of all texts against the number of economic texts published each year. The count of all texts produced in England and Scotland or published in English is taken from the *English Short Title Catalogue*.

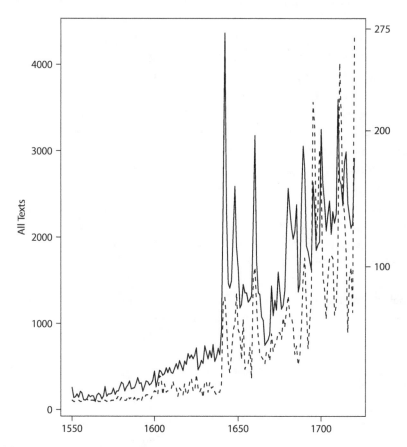

FIGURE 5.3. Texts published annually

Economic Development

Economic growth was one of the earlier factors considered relevant by theorists speculating on the structural conditions that encouraged the development of economics over time.[20] The mechanisms linking development to economic theory are not always explicitly identified, but the general idea is that increasing complexity in finance and commerce produced correspondingly more sophisticated and complex explanations, which formed the basis of the development of economic thought. In this view, economic thought is a kind of mirror for economic life. Economic growth is also an important control, as it is likely to be associated with other potentially important variables, such as the size of the reading public. To capture economic growth, I use gross domestic product (GDP) trends drawn from *British Economic Growth*, the most recent and authoritative work on estimating these measures in the early modern period.[21] The data are trends calculated with respect to the value of year 1700, which is set to 100.

As shown in figure 5.4, GDP rose significantly from 1550 to 1720. The increase was fairly steady, although there are dips and turns throughout the progression. A serious dip occurred in the 1590s, stagnation marked the 1630s and 1640s, a rapid increase was followed by a sudden crash in the 1650s, and a serious downturn in the first decade of the eighteenth century was followed by a sharp uptick.

Overseas commerce was an area of particularly high growth in this era and may have had an effect independent of total levels of economic development.[22] Independent effects may be related to the complex logistical problems associated with overseas trade or individuals' grappling with price fluctuations linked to overseas specie flow. The series tracking trends in overseas trade is also drawn from *British Economic Growth*.[23] As before, the index is set to 100 at 1700, and the series is calculated as differences from that center point. These estimates are displayed in figure 5.5.

20. Canterbery, *Brief History of Economics*, 32–33; Dobb, *Theories of Value*, 20; Meek, *Economics and Ideology*, 203; and Roll, *History of Economic Thought*, 12–13.

21. Stephen Broadberry et al., *British Economic Growth, 1270–1870* (Cambridge: Cambridge University Press, 2015).

22. Thomas, *Mercantilism*; Barber, *British Economic Thought*; Zastoupil, *John Stuart Mill*; Reinert and Røge, *Political Economy of Empire*; and Erikson, "Influence of Trade."

23. Broadberry et al., *British Economic Growth*.

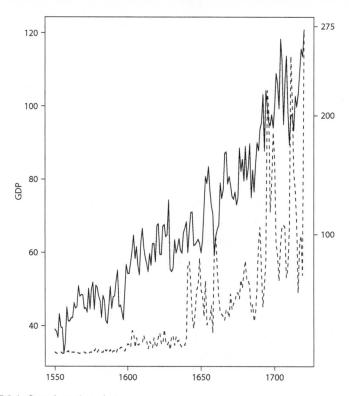

FIGURE 5.4. Gross domestic product

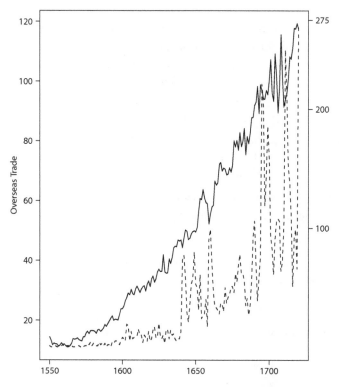

FIGURE 5.5. Rates of overseas commerce

Commerce shows the smoothest progress over the period, with very few marked discontinuities, but there is some evidence of increasing variability at the beginning of the eighteenth century.

State Capacity

The seventeenth century lies squarely in the era of mercantilism, which is known for the way early modern states intertwined economic and political interests through a double focus on power and plenty. The economic texts produced in this era are commonly known as mercantilist texts, and many prominent scholars have argued that the state was instrumental in stimulating their publication.[24] In this view, early economics can be seen as a tool of the state in its efforts to understand and control the chaos of the markets. It follows that an increasingly powerful state may have allocated greater resources to developing economic theory, thus spurring publication rates. From this perspective, economic texts can be understood as theories that allowed emerging nation-states to make sense of and control the markets. Such a perspective does seem to explain changes in economic thought in France and Germany—specifically, the development of Cameralism and Colbertism. Indirectly, the chartered companies depended upon state sponsorship and acted as a tool to increase state capacity; therefore, the increased the power of the state is a crucial background variable whether or not it has an independent effect. In including a time series that addresses state capacity, however, the goal is to measure the direct effect of increased state capacity on the production of economic texts.

State capacity has been intimately tied to the development of mercantilist economic theory, as the first modern work on mercantilism conceived of it as a form of state building.[25] Schmoller's approach emphasized mercantilist policy over mercantilist thought, and tied the development of mercantilist thought to the needs of the increasingly centralized and powerful emerging

24. Galbraith, *Economics in Perspective*; Irwin, *Against the Tide*; Reinert and Reinert, "Mercantilism and Economic Development"; Reinert and Røge, *Political Economy of Empire*; Schumpeter, *History of Economic Analysis*, 143; Viner, *Intellectual History of Economics*, 45–53.

25. Gustav von Schmoller, *The Mercantile System and Its Historical Significance: Illustrated Chiefly from Prussian History; Being a Chapter from the Studien ueber die wirthschaftliche politik Friedrichs des Grossen*, ed. and trans. William James Ashley (New York: Macmillan, 1897), Making of the Modern World.

nation-states of the early modern period. Whether mercantilism is conceived as a tool facilitating the expansion of state powers or an outgrowth
of increasing state capacity, one interpretation that has emerged from this
body of work is that mercantilist political economy was developed in order
to serve the needs of the emerging nation-state. The causal relationship
can be vague in these works, but the association is between the increase in
state power and the production of economic works—as, for example, when
Schumpeter refers to the relationship between mercantilist writers and the
"rising National State."[26]

State capacity is a multidimensional concept difficult to pin down in one
measure, particularly one recorded on an annual basis. Here I use tax revenue as a proxy for state capacity, as it both contributes to state capacity, by
providing a source of funds, and serves as an indication of the state's ability
to extract resources from the population. Tax revenues of the English state
are drawn from the European State Finance Database, English Revenues,
1485–1816, made available by the UK Data Archive.[27] Figure 5.6 plots these
revenues over the period of interest. The plot shows evidence of sharp discontinuities—notably, the absence of tax revenue for much of the 1640s as
a result of the English Civil War. The extreme variability in the following
years appears to be indicative of the ad hoc nature of tax collection prior to
the reformation of the system in the 1680s, after which a smoother upward
trajectory is evident.

It is also possible that the state had a different type of impact—namely,
that parliamentary activity stirred up controversies that were addressed in
the public sphere. To control for this possibility, the number of days parliament was in session each year is included. As described in greater detail in
chapter 4, the Crown and later Parliament also commissioned several trade
councils, committees, and commissions over the period of interest. Paul
Slack has argued that these councils—particularly the council of 1622—
were generative of the new literature on economics.[28] A dichotomous
variable in the data indicating whether a council was held in each year is
therefore also included.

26. Schumpeter, *History of Economic Analysis*, 143.

27. R. Bonney, European State Finance Database: English Revenues, 1485–1816 (UK Data Service [SN 3118], October 13, 1993), http://doi.org/10.5255/UKDA-SN-3118-1.

28. Slack, "English Political Economy."

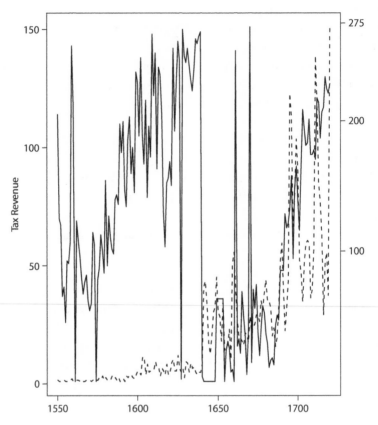

FIGURE 5.6. Estimates of tax revenue

Rechartering

Many of the larger companies were rechartered several times over the course of their history. The renewal of a charter served as an opportunity for the state to extract additional monies from the company. It also frequently stirred up controversy, as critics fought against and proponents fought for renewal. A count of the number of recharters of the largest companies annually is included as another time series. This count includes renewals of the charters of the East India Company, the Eastland Company, the Royal African Company, the Merchant Adventurers, and the Levant Company.

Political Upset

Two additional variables in the model are series of politically and commercially disruptive events. Political turmoil often leads to both actual and perceived opportunities to change the existing balance of power among merchant groups and elite actors—and certainly did so in early modern England.[29] The long-standing debate between Tory and Whig/Land and Labor was active in the seventeenth century, contributed to the upheaval of 1688, and was resolved in favor of manufacturers and Whigs with the creation of the Bank of England in 1694.[30] Thus, one reason to consider these political disruptions is that individuals had additional incentives to take action in order to seize the opportunity to institutionalize preferences and privileges for different economic sectors. While many emerging nation-states experienced significant political turmoil, this does not rule out the possibility that political disruptions spurred public contention over economic policies, thus contributing to the growth of political economy.

While all nations experience economic disruptions, changing social and economic conditions have clearly affected the contents of economic thought, particularly when economic thinkers confront severe economic disruptions in their work. Perhaps the most notable example of the profound effect of events on economic thought is the work of John Maynard Keynes in interpreting the causes of the Great Depression. Arguments as to what has driven the development of economic theory have been framed as based on two irreconcilable viewpoints, one emphasizing the internal logic of economic discourse and the other, the proximate influence of historical circumstance.[31] In the latter, the relevant events are economic in nature—for example, high inflation and trade depression. The underlying logic is that economic disruptions force individuals (and societies) to think through the causes of problems to attempt to resolve them. Economic disruptions are such a common feature of economic life that it is clear they

29. Robert Brenner, *Merchants and Revolution: Commercial Change, Political Conflict, and London's Overseas Traders, 1550–1653* (London: Verso, 2003); Bruce G. Carruthers, *City of Capital: Politics and Markets in the English Financial Revolution* (Princeton, NJ: Princeton University Press, 1999); Steve Pincus, *1688: The First Modern Revolution* (New Haven, CT: Yale University Press, 2009).

30. Pincus, *1688: The First Modern Revolution*, 366–99.

31. Joseph Spengler, "Exogenous and Endogenous Influences in the Formation of Post-1870 Economic Thought," in *Events, Ideology and Economic Theory: The Determinants of Progress in the Development of Economic Analysis*, ed. Robert V. Eagly (Detroit, MI: Wayne State University Press, 1968), 159–205.

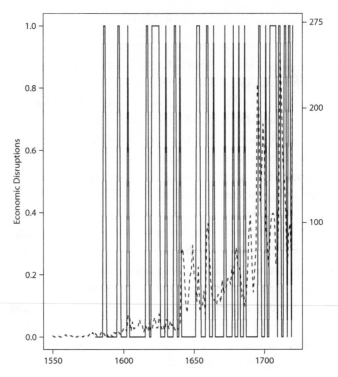

FIGURE 5.7. Economic disruptions

do not constitute a sufficient condition for the rise of political economy; however, there is certainly reason to suspect they may have had an effect.

W. R. Scott gathered data on the conditions of overseas trade and constructed a time series including disruptive events and general trade conditions. Events include items such as "Fears as to the succession, reported death of Anne, run on Bank of England," "Effect of crisis in cloth trade," and "Famine, tonnage dispute, plague."[32] Events are coded here as a dichotomous variable (1 if event, 0 if not). Scott includes the Civil War and the Glorious Revolution as disruptions in his series. I exclude them in this variable in order to construct a distinct variable for domestic political disruptions (again, 1 indicates the events listed and 0 their absence).

Figures 5.7 and 5.8 plot the relationship between trade disruptions and economic text production and domestic political events and economic text production, respectively.

32. William Robert Scott, *Constitution and Finance*, 1:465.

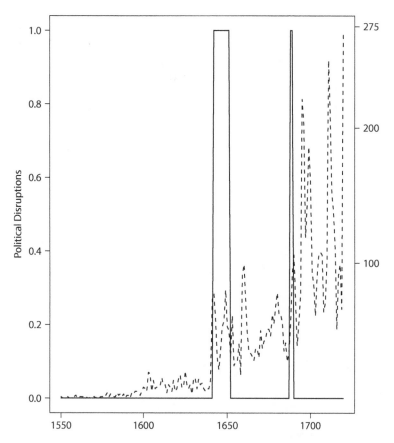

FIGURE 5.8. Major political disruptions

Population Growth and Year

Population growth could also have affected textual production rates through more than one path, including economic growth and the potential size of the reading public. Population rates are drawn from *British Economic Growth*, again the most recent authoritative presentation of these estimates. As is evident from figure 5.9, population growth was steep from 1560 to the late 1650s, dipped roughly from 1660 to 1690, then resumed its steady upward march. This trend is also set to 100 at 1700. Finally, as a double check for the possibility of a residual trend remaining after the differencing process, a dummy variable for year is also included.

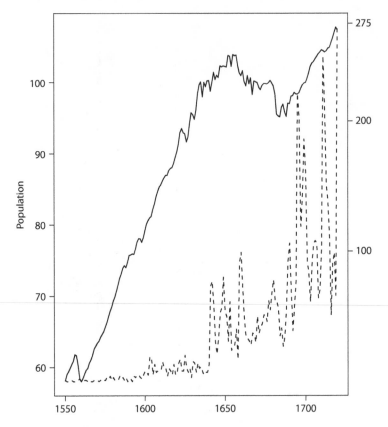

FIGURE 5.9. Annual population estimates

THE MODEL

Autoregression (AR) is a statistical technique used to model time series data. In the AR model, one assumes a data set that contains n real valued scalar observations of a process. The data set is assumed to be temporally ordered so that the first datum corresponds to time $t = 0$ and so on. AR assumes that the observations are generated by a linear dynamical system. In other words, an observation at time $t + 1$ is generated by applying a linear function (a function of the form $ax + b$ where x, $b \in R$) to the observation at time t and adding noise. AR fits a linear regression to the data set to determine these unknown coefficients in the linear function.

Vector auto regression (VAR) generalizes this process to a vector of observations at every time t. VAR tries to find a vector of coefficients that multiply the data observed at time t to approximate a dependent variable, which in this case is the number of economic texts at time $t + 1$. VAR uses multivariate linear regression to fit these coefficients. Less formally, VAR uses past data to predict future data under the assumption that the future data depend on the current data by a linear function. The assumption that the process is linear is a significant assumption, as linear functions are a small subset of all functions, but is helped by the multivariate Taylor expansion, which implies that linear functions can locally approximate continuously differentiable nonlinear functions. To be explicit about terminology, VAR often refers to using a vector of covariates to predict a scalar dependent variable, which is what this investigation focuses on. VAR can be generalized to the vector-to-vector case, but this is not the model employed in this work.

The first step in the analysis is the differencing of the data. Time series analysis is premised upon stationary or approximately stationary data, where the mean, variance, and autocorrelation are constant over time. Differencing, the procedure in which the value of Y is recalculated so that $Y = Y_t - Y_{t-1}$, is used to eliminate trends that cause data non-stationarity. In this case, for example, there was a general trend upward across many types of social and economic data in the early modern period that made differencing necessary to avoid spurious associations. The Boolean covariates are not differenced because the resulting column would contain only two non-zero values. Differencing the cumulative number of chartered companies founded over time results in the annual founding rate, which also shows an upward trend, so the founding rates are differenced as well. The resulting data pass the Johansen test, ensuring that it is cointegration-free with a p-value of less than .01 and ready for analysis.[33] The regression coefficients may be interpreted as how much the change in a variable from one year to the next affects the production of economic texts.

Missing values are imputed with the median of the respective column. Imputation allows utilization of all of the available data and prevents biases

33. Bernhard Pfaff, Eric Zivot, and Matthieu Stigler, Reference manual for Package 'urca' (Version 1.3-0): Unit Root and Cointegration Tests for Time Series Data, CRAN Repository, September 6, 2016, 1–2, https://cran.r-project.org/web/packages/urca/urca.pdf.

that can occur when incomplete rows are discarded. Only 0.6 percent of the data are missing, so this does not have a large effect on the final model. The columns are scaled to unit variance. Finally, the times series are lagged one year behind the dependent variable in order to account for the time involved in writing and publishing a text. This time line is consistent with the rate at which these texts were generally produced, as they were frequently written and published expeditiously in order to respond to specific circumstances or the publication of another text. For example, Thomas Mun and Edward Misselden published texts in 1621 in response to a trade depression that began in 1620. Gerard de Malynes very quickly published an attack on Misselden's work in 1621. Misselden responded to Malynes with another essay in 1622. It took some time to write and publish these works, but they were put into circulation on a comparatively shorter timetable than in contemporary book publishing, which is actually quite remarkable given the technological constraints of the period.

A supervised learning approach to estimation was employed, which reduces calculation time. The model is first trained on a subset of the data, then coefficients are calculated. The code used for this method is available online, along with the data for verification purposes.[34] Confidence intervals were generated using standard estimation methods.

Results and Interpretation

Tables 5.1 and 5.2 present descriptive statistics for all variables. Table 5.1 presents the original data; table 5.2 presents the processed version of the data, which has been differenced and scaled.

Figure 5.10 presents a visualization of the coefficient estimates. The bars represent coefficient estimates, and the center arrow represents the 95 percent confidence interval for the estimate. When the confidence interval overlaps zero, the coefficients are not significant.

---

34. Mark Hamilton, mhamilton723/tseries: Version 0.2.1 (filename: "mhamilton723/tseries-0.2.1.zip"), Zenodo, September 20, 2017, https://doi.org/10.5281/zenodo.897193; and Mark Hamilton and Emily Erikson, mhamilton723/sociology: Version 0.1 (filename: "mhamilton723/sociology-0.1.zip"), Zenodo, September 24, 2017, https://doi.org/10.5281/zenodo.995677. The code utilizes and contributes to the python package tseries (Hamilton 2017), which provides a simple API for creating time series models using *any* internal model that fits the API of the popular machine learning package sklearn.

TABLE 5.1
Descriptive statistics for unprocessed data

	Count	Mean	StDev	Min	Med	Max
Year	171	1635	49.51	1550	1635	1720
Companies	171	1.03	2.51	0	0	18
GDP	171	68.03	20.98	32.46	63.44	120.82
All texts	171	1108.49	932.12	95	684	4361
Population	171	88.5	15.35	58.03	95.73	107.72
Economic turmoil	171	0.3	0.46	0	0	1
Tax revenue	159	1675.04	1761.81	194	730	6508
Trade councils	171	0.45	0.5	0	0	1
Commerce	171	49.97	32.14	11.01	44.14	119.27
Domestic politics	171	0.07	0.26	0	0	1
Merchants in Parliament	163	50.2	21.98	0	50	80
Recharters	171	0.19	0.41	0	0	2
Days in Parliament	171	93.77	113.63	0	53	365
Economic texts	171	38.51	50.93	0	15	272
Text subset	171	15.65	29.56	0	4	198
Philosophical texts	171	2.9	3.22	0	2	17
Political texts	171	45.7	79.71	0	6	626

TABLE 5.2
Descriptive statistics for preprocessed data

	Count	Mean	StDev	Min	Med	Max
Year	170	1	0	1	1	1
Companies	170	0.01	1	−3.96	0	5.65
GDP	170	0.08	1	−3.09	0.06	3.1
All Texts	170	0.04	1	−4.94	0.02	4.34
Population	170	0.36	1	−3.5	0.52	2.99
Economic turmoil	170	0.66	1	0	0	2.17
Tax revenue	170	0.12	1	−4.55	0.03	4.16
Trade councils	170	0.02	1	−2.61	0	2.61
Commerce	170	0.16	1	−3.68	0.1	4.69
Domestic politics	170	0.28	1	0	0	3.9
Merchants in Parliament	170	0	1	−6.98	0	6.84
Recharters	170	0	1	−3.48	0	3.48
Days in Parliament	170	0.01	1	−3.3	0	3.5
Economic texts	170	0.06	1	−2.9	0	7.12
Text subset	170	0.05	1	−4.86	0	7.64
Philosophical texts	170	0.01	1	−3.34	0	5.56
Political texts	170	0	1	−6.24	0	5.39

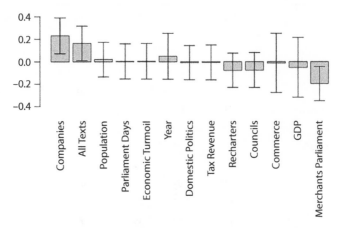

FIGURE 5.10. Coefficients with confidence intervals for economic texts

There are three significant variables for the publication of economic texts. The largest positive and significant coefficient is *Companies*. *All texts* has a smaller estimated effect, and the lower band of the confidence interval lies extremely close to zero. The only significant negative coefficient is the count of merchants represented in Parliament, *Merchants in Parliament*. All other variables have confidence intervals that overlap with zero. Table 5.3 presents the results of the time series analysis in table form.

While the time series analysis presents evidence that the increasing prevalence of chartered companies did encourage the production of economic texts and that merchant representation decreased publication rates, the possibility of unobserved factors influencing the association between variables remains. In order to consider whether unobserved confounding variables were producing the observed association between companies and economic texts, the same model was run on two different dependent variables. Publication rates from two closely related branches of literature that have no clear and plausible link to the formation of chartered companies were chosen as test cases: philosophical texts and political texts. The counts of these texts were extracted from the *English Short Title Catalogue*. The results of these models are presented in figures 5.11 and 5.12, for ease of interpretation, then again in table 5.4 for precise estimates.

TABLE 5.3
Model results

	Coefficient estimate	95% Confidence interval
Chartered companies	0.23	0.39/0.07
Merchants in Parliament	−0.2	−0.04/−0.35
Days in Parliament	0.00	0.16/−0.15
Trade councils	−0.08	0.08/−0.23
Recharters	−0.08	0.08/−0.23
Domestic politics	−0.01	0.14/−0.16
Economic turmoil	0.01	0.16/−0.15
Tax revenue	−0.01	0.15/−0.16
GDP	−0.05	0.22/−0.32
Commerce	−0.01	0.25/−0.28
Population	0.02	0.17/−0.13
All texts	0.16	0.32/0.01
Year	0.05	0.25/−0.16

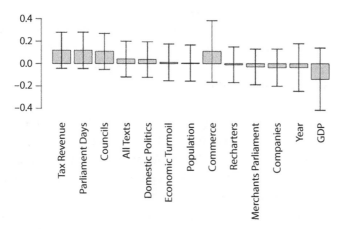

FIGURE 5.11. Coefficients with confidence intervals for philosophical texts

Figure 5.11 presents the results of the model fitted with philosophical texts as the dependent variable. Moral philosophy is closely related to economics and an important predecessor of economic thought. Philosophy in this era appears to unfold relatively independent of temporal concerns—or

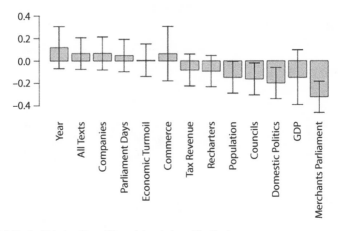

FIGURE 5.12. Coefficients with confidence intervals for political texts

at least to these specific temporal concerns. None of the estimates is significant, and they are all small relative to the estimates for economic and political texts. Note that the y-axis varies across figures, adjusted to the size of the confidence intervals estimated for each model. The fact that economic texts appear to respond differently than philosophic texts in the seventeenth century supports the idea that there was a significant divergence between these two fields at this time.

Political texts are, as should be expected, more responsive to earthly matters. The results of modeling political texts are presented in figure 5.12. *Chartered companies* is not significant. *Population, Political disruptions,* and *Merchant representation* are significant. All of these effects are negative. The negative impact of domestic political upheaval is not as surprising as it might appear on first glance, as publications often increase heading into period of contentious activity and then decline in the midst of the actual conflict. Given that there was a class element to the political conflicts of England's seventeenth century, the negative impact of merchant representation, which means that increases in merchant representation decreased publication rates of political texts, also makes substantive sense based on the logic that greater merchant representation would decrease the need for public articulations of merchant political grievances.

Table 5.4 presents the precise estimates. The two models indicate that the prevalence of chartered companies was not significantly associated

TABLE 5.4
Additional models

	Philosophy Coefficient	95% Interval	Politics Coefficient	95% Interval
Chartered companies	−0.04	0.13/−0.2	0.07	0.21/−0.08
Merchants in Parliament	−0.03	0.13/−0.19	−0.32	−0.18/−0.46
Days in Parliament	0.12	0.28/−0.05	0.05	0.19/−0.1
Trade councils	0.1	0.27/−0.05	−0.16	−0.02/−0.31
Recharters	−0.01	0.15/−0.17	−0.09	0.05/−0.23
Domestic politics	0.04	0.2/−0.12	−0.2	−0.06/−0.34
Economic turmoil	0.02	0.18/−0.15	0.01	0.15/−0.14
Tax revenue	0.12	0.28/−0.04	−0.08	0.06/−0.23
GDP	−0.14	0.14/−0.42	−0.15	0.1/−0.39
Commerce	0.11	0.38/−0.17	0.06	0.31/−0.18
Population	0.01	0.17/−0.16	−0.15	−0.01/−0.29
All texts	0.04	0.2/−0.12	0.07	0.21/−0.08
Year	−0.04	0.18/−0.25	0.12	0.31/−0.07

with the publication rates of philosophical texts or political texts, whereas they were significantly associated with the publication of economic texts. Thus, the additional models increase our confidence in the results and decrease the likelihood that unobserved factors are producing a spurious association. The findings also provide support for the importance of merchant representation in the state as a contributing factor encouraging public economic thought; however, the relationship between merchant representation and textual production appears as though it is tied into a larger process implicated in the expansion of the public sphere across both economic and political dimensions.

Goodness-of-fit statistics are presented for all models in table 5.5. The R-squared statistic is presented for the model evaluated in both the undifferenced and differenced data, where differencing is represented in the table by delta. These two together give a fuller picture of the model performance. As should be expected, the R-squared is lower in the differenced model because the linear trend that occurs across variables has been removed to avoid the problems caused by cointegration.

TABLE 5.5
R² values for models

Dependent variable	$R^2(Y,\hat{Y})$	$R^2 \Delta Y. \widehat{\Delta Y}$
Economic texts	.715	.121
Philosophical texts	.324	.074
Political texts	.527	.257

As one further check, I narrowed the number of publications included in the count to exclude those that were not primarily about trade and finance. Many of the texts included in the Making of the Modern World database combine different subject matter; thus, it is possible to refine the outcome of interest, the publication rate of economic texts, to focus more narrowly on those we might consider closer to the style of classical economic discourse. I did not use this approach for the main analysis, as I am of the opinion that an inclusive approach used by those who catalogued the original collection was more appropriate for two reasons. First, the larger literature created a context in which more focused interventions into trade theory would have a literate readership. Second, as we have seen, authors often disguised their economic intentions in political or moral language and subject matter. But reanalysis on a narrower set of works is a useful a robustness check.

This reanalysis involved coding all texts into different subject areas, which was done using titles and keywords when possible and through further reading when not. The same model was then run with a new dependent variable, an annual count of publications whose central subject matter was trade, finance, or a chartered company. Figure 5.13 presents the results. As can be seen, the effect of chartered companies is slightly larger and remains significant. *Merchants in Parliament* remains negative, but is no longer significant. The finding that increases in the prevalence of companies were related to the rise of this new economic literature is supported, while the impact of *Merchants in Parliament* seems to have been stronger mainly in the more political subsection of the larger field of economic literature, which is not entirely surprising.

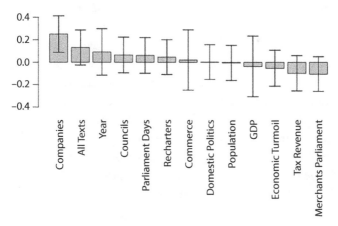

FIGURE 5.13. Coefficients with confidence intervals for trade and finance texts

CONCLUSION

This chapter provides a different kind of evidence than yet offered by looking at temporal change and specifically considering the relationship between changes in company founding rates, rates of merchant representation, and publication rates for economic texts. As shown in previous chapters, the seventeenth century saw increasing attention to the concerns of the merchants in the economic literature. Individual morality, just price, and usury declined in importance as merchants increasingly set an agenda that was framed within a new moral virtue: national prosperity. I have argued that merchants were prodded into publishing works within this new moral framework by their lack of political power and the controversy, resources, and high stakes introduced by chartered companies. The analysis supports that idea.

The advantage of the VAR model is to offer a statistical test of several competing hypothesis—including my own institutional explanation based on the rise of companies and low rates of merchant political representation. In a temporal test of the association between different time series, only the number of chartered companies, the number of merchants in Parliament, and publication rates for all texts—all lagged to the previous year—have a significant relationship. The coefficients for the companies and merchant representation are larger than for all texts. In additional tests for unobserved heterogeneity, I found that neither companies nor merchant representation had an association with the rates of publication for philosophical texts, and only merchant representation had an association with political texts. The coefficients representing economic growth, state growth, population growth, domestic unrest, and political turmoil were insignificant. Merchant-state relations—specifically, the decline of merchant political representation and the rise of chartered companies—appear to have been important drivers of the quantitative increase in economic publications.

While the findings in this chapter may not provide final, conclusive evidence, the analysis goes much further than any existing work in systematically assessing existing hypotheses. It very much suggests that continuing negotiation and mutual attempts at influence that took place between the state and merchants had a large and long-lasting impact on economic thought.

Chapter Six

WHY NOT THE DUTCH?

England was the epicenter of economic thought in the seventeenth century, but it was not at the center of global history. The epicenter of European history in the seventeenth century was the Netherlands. The seventeenth century was the *Gouden Eeuw*, the Dutch Golden Age. The splendor and cultural richness of Dutch society were renowned across Europe, as beautifully chronicled by Simon Schama in *The Embarrassment of Riches*.[1] Art, philosophy, trade, law, finance, and democracy all reached notable peaks in the wealthy and prosperous Dutch Republic.

One of the mysteries of Dutch history is that country's failure to produce any noteworthy contributions to political economy during this era of commercial and cultural ascendancy. If any nation seemed to have captured the secrets of economic success, it was the dynamic and financially sophisticated Dutch Republic of the seventeenth century—the envy of the early modern commercial world. Yet while England experienced a dramatic surge in the publication of economic texts, the Dutch Republic saw only a modest, incremental increase and a near absence of works of lasting influence.

A comparison between England and the Dutch Republic provides another angle of illumination for revealing the factors that drove the increase in economic writings in England. The two emerging nations were similar in

---

1. Simon Schama, *The Embarrassment of Riches: An Interpretation of Dutch Culture in the Golden Age* (New York: Vintage, 1997).

many regards. Both were northern European nations with strong civic traditions, heavily engaged in expanding their overseas markets. Indeed, they were close competitors. The Dutch, however, were well ahead in that competition throughout the seventeenth century. The Dutch Republic was the most vital economy in Europe at the time and had captured a significantly larger share of overseas trade than the English. The Dutch had a strong republican, humanist, and liberal tradition and served as a center of the European book trade, which was supported by a large and thriving urban population. They adopted complex financial institutions, such as public debt, well before the English and had transitioned to a representative mode of governance more than a century before the Glorious Revolution of 1688.

What the Dutch also had, which England did not, was a government dominated by merchants. This power dynamic made a crucial difference to the kind of context that would have driven Dutch merchants to publish in the public sphere. An important stimulus to debate was absent: the Dutch economy produced only a small number of companies and continued to be populated mainly by partnerships, guilds, and independent merchants. The adoption of the company form in England was related to the need of merchants for a legal guarantee of state support for their endeavors, as well as the state's desire to exert more control over market transactions previously dominated by largely autonomous guilds and associations. The English government thus granted special privileges to chartered companies to pursue their own private interests. In the United Provinces, merchants were already well incorporated into the state and had less need of such guarantees and privileges. Instead, widespread merchant representation led to significant opposition to the creation of Dutch chartered companies precisely because they were controversial and granted special privileges to only a small set of merchants. In a more general sense, Dutch merchants' dominant position in the States General and the provincial governments made public appeals largely unnecessary. They had a more direct path to policy making through the exercise of political power.

COMPARATIVE ANALYSIS

Comparative Methods

The last chapter provided a temporal test of the argument. This chapter provides a cross-sectional assessment. In an ideal case, this could be another multivariate analysis across a large number of emerging nations, of which roughly half experienced a significant transition in economic thought and half did not. These nations would also ideally have experienced completely independent lines of development, with economic and social influences stopping at national borders. Unfortunately, such conditions cannot be met. This transition in economic thought was a rare event. It emerged once in England, and thereafter the writings produced in England—by authors such as Petty, Mun, and Locke—influenced other European thinkers. Later developments, such as the rise of physiocratic thought in France, cannot be separated out from the influence of the discourse in England. These conditions make the construction of a large-n study of country-level characteristics and their relationship to economic thought very difficult. Even if later transitions were included and the need for independence waived, there simply are not enough European nations for a robust statistical test.

The method I use instead is a classic tool of comparative historical sociology: the matched sample. England and the Dutch Republic are a match because of the large number of similarities between the two regions. In a counterfactual model of causal analysis, the ideal sample is two replications of the same subject. If it were possible to apply a treatment to the same person at the same instant, though some process of doubling, then the effect of the treatment for that individual could be reliably measured by comparing the state of the two after treatment. If a treatment and a control subject are matched on all factors related to the outcome of interest with the exception of the treatment, then the difference between the two can provide a good estimate of the effect of the treatment itself.[2] In the seventeenth century, the Dutch Republic and England were both tolerant, commercially expansive, northern European counties with similar rates of overseas trade based in thriving urban centers and experiencing similar surges in their populations. Both nations suffered through significant political turmoil, but also enjoyed an unprecedented expansion of the civil sphere and increase in democratic representation.[3] In this chapter, I revert to the 1580–1720 time frame used throughout most of the book. It is a necessary step because the

2. Stephen L. Morgan and Christopher Winship, *Counterfactuals and Causal Inference: Methods and Principles for Social Research*, 2nd ed. (New York: Cambridge University Press, 2014), 5, 90.

3. David Ormrod, *The Rise of Commercial Empires: England and the Netherlands in the Age of Mercantilism, 1650–1770* (Cambridge: Cambridge University Press, 2003), 58; and E. A. Wrigley, "The Growth of Population in Eighteenth-Century England: A Conundrum Resolved," *Past & Present* 98 (February 1983): 121–50.

Dutch Republic did not emerge until well after 1550. It was not until 1568 that the Dutch revolted against the Spanish Empire. The negotiated union between Dutch provinces began formally in 1579 with the Treaty of Utrecht.

The Dutch Republic was therefore newer than England's monarchy. No two nations are entirely alike. However, even imperfectly matched small samples may be used to eliminate hypotheses and indicate necessary factors using Mills's method of agreement,[4] which is the goal of this comparative analysis. While no method is perfect, there is widespread agreement that the careful selection of cases based on existing theory and knowledge attenuates many of the issues that have been used to criticize comparative research[5]— particularly in combination with an identification and analysis of the micro-level processes through which national-level institutional change had its effect and other methods of analysis, provided in previous chapters.

Dutch Political Economy

The best-known work of political economy produced in the Netherlands during the seventeenth century is Pieter de la Court's *The True Interest and Political Maxims, of the Republic of Holland* (1662).[6] The book was widely read upon publication and was translated into several languages. Pieter de la Court (1618–1665) was a prosperous cloth merchant who formed a close alliance with the elite family of the De Witts. *The True Interest* was his second and most significant work of political economy. He had earlier circulated a manuscript titled *Het Welvaren der Stad Leyden* (1659), which can be loosely translated as "the welfare of Leiden."[7] His other writings were purely political in nature. *The True Interest* is also largely concerned with politics. De la Court lies firmly in the early modern tradition of commercial

4. James Mahoney, "Strategies of Causal Inference in Small-N Analysis," *Sociological Methods & Research* 28, no. 4 (May 2000): 393, https://doi.org/10.1177/0049124100028004001.

5. Alberto Abadie, Alexis Diamond, and Jens Hainmueller, "Comparative Politics and the Synthetic Control Method," *American Journal of Political Science* 59, no. 2 (April 2015): 495–510; and Bernhard Ebbinghaus, "When Less Is More: Selection Problems in Large-N and Small-N Cross-National Comparisons," *International Sociology* 20, no. 2 (June 2005): 133–52.

6. Pieter de la Court, *The True Interest and Political Maxims, of the Republic of Holland* (London: Printed for J. Nourse, 1746; first published 1662), Making of the Modern World.

7. See Hans-Jürgen Wagener, "Free Seas, Free Trade, Free People: Early Dutch Institutionalism," *History of Political Economy* 26, no. 3 (1994): 397; Pieter de la Court, *Proeve uit een onuitgegeven Staathuishoudkundig Geschrift, Het Welvaren der Stad Leyden* (Leyden: S. & J. Luchtmans, 1845; first published 1659), Making of the Modern World.

republicanism; his foremost concern was to establish the central importance of the republican government to Dutch prosperity. More than two-thirds of the text concerns foreign and domestic strategic issues not linked to trade, commerce, or manufacturing. The remaining third deals with the roots of economic prosperity in the Dutch Republic. De la Court argued in this section that the four pillars of Dutch prosperity were manufacturing, shipping, fishing, and commerce. He argued for an increase in taxes on foreign goods and selective taxation of domestic industries designed to foster trades he considered beneficial to the nation as a whole. And he advocated for several types of individual freedoms: religious freedom, occupational freedom (ending existing restrictions that limited individuals' choice of occupation), and commercial freedom (in this case, the prohibition of the exclusionary tactics and monopoly privileges of chartered companies).

De la Court's work was exceptional for Dutch economic thought at the time, but it was about forty years behind what was current in English thought. Unlike English authors in the same era, De la Court's reasoning does not treat the economy as a separate sphere. He shows little awareness of the problems of labor mobility, monetary flows, or the relationship between supply and demand. There is no sign of free trade leanings, found, for example, in William Petty's work published in the same year. While De la Court embraced commercial expansion as a public good, he conveyed reservations about the benefits of long-distance overseas trade. His lasting contributions were political, not economic. His influence on later Dutch economists was minimal.[8] He does appear as a figure of note, however, in work on the republican tradition.[9]

Other noted Dutch figures from this era who addressed economic topics are few and far between. Willem Usselincx (1567–1647), one of the founders of the Dutch West India Company, wrote several tracts in the early seventeenth century that gained notoriety. In these tracts, Usselincx promoted colonialism and argued that chartered companies were necessary to the expansion of the Dutch empire. In 1651, Dirk Graswinckel (1600–1666) wrote *Placcaten, Ordonnantien ende Reglementen*, which has been

8. J. R. Zuidema, "Economic Thought in the Netherlands Between 1750 and 1870: From Commercial Mercantilism Towards the True Principles of Political Economy," in *Economic Thought in the Netherlands, 1650–1950*, ed. Jan van Daal and Arnold Heertje (Aldershot, UK: Avebury, 1992), 31.

9. Arthur Weststeijn, *Commercial Republicanism in the Dutch Golden Age: The Political Thought of Johan & Pieter de la Court* (Leiden: Brill, 2012).

rendered in English as "Decrees, Regulations, etc. on the subject of Wheat and Corn."[10] This work dealt with the impact of laws on the market for food staples. The humanist philosopher Franciscus van den Enden (1602–1674)—made famous by his pupil Baruch Spinoza—touched briefly on economic topics and free trade as part of his larger vision of the benefits of a free society. And Caspar Barlaeus (1584–1648) delivered the address *Mercator sapiens* (1632), translated as the "wise merchant."[11] In it, he defended merchants and their profession by arguing that the management of trade is the one of the mainstays of good governance.[12] Although it has been argued that an early sort of institutional economics was being developed—a kind of intellectual precursor to Douglas North and the new institutional economics[13]—these works lack the innovative conceptual and empirical elements that were appearing in English economic texts.

Specialists in the area agree. Jan van Daal and Arnold Heertje have complained of "the comparative poverty of Dutch economic thought in the Golden Age."[14] Ida Nijenhuis, an historian of early modern Dutch political economy, has called the lack of Dutch economic works in the age of their commercial ascendancy "one of the always returning questions of Dutch political economy."[15] The curator of the Broekema Collection of early modern Dutch pamphlets, Marinus Bierens noted that "economics does not seem to be a major recognizable item" among the pamphlets.[16] Theo van Tijn simply states that "lively [economic] debates did not arise."[17] J. R. Zuidema notes that no Dutch economist of international reputation

10. Dirck Graswinckel, *Placcaten, Ordonnantien ende Reglementen, Op't Stuck vande Lijf-Tocht, Sulcx als de selve van Outs tot herwaerts toe op alle voorvallen van Hongers-noot en Dieren-tijdt beraemt zijn ende ghedaen publiceeren* (Leyden: Ter druckerije van de Elseviers, 1651), Making of the Modern World.

11. Caspar Barlaeus, *The Wise Merchant*, ed. Anna-Luna Post, trans. Corinna Vermeulen (Amsterdam: Amsterdam University Press, 2019, originally published as *Mercator sapiens* (Amsterdam: Willem Blaeu, 1632).

12. Jacob Soll, "Accounting for Government: Holland and the Rise of Political Economy in Seventeenth-Century Europe," *Journal of Interdisciplinary History* 40, no. 2 (Autumn 2009): 225–26.

13. Wagener, "Free Seas."

14. Jan van Daal and Arnold Heertje, eds., *Economic Thought in the Netherlands, 1650–1950* (Aldershot, UK: Avebury, 1992), 8.

15. Ida Nijenhuis, email message to author, October 8, 2015.

16. Marinus Bierens, email message to author, April 23, 2015.

17. Theo van Tijn, "Dutch Economic Thought in the Seventeenth Century," in *Economic Thought in the Netherlands, 1650–1950*, ed. Jan van Daal and Arnold Heertje (Aldershot, UK: Avebury, 1992), 9.

emerged until 1870; Paul Slack concurs.[18] One of the earliest experts in Dutch political economy, Otto van Rees, observed that "economics did not share in the flowering of sciences in this country."[19] And no departments of economics existed in the Netherlands until the twentieth century. As late as the mid-nineteenth century, fewer than 2 percent of Dutch publications were about topics related to political economy.[20] Even the famous chronicler of Dutch economic texts Étienne Laspeyres agreed that economics was not born in the Netherlands.[21]

Given this context, it would appear that if an innovative and systematic Dutch thinker "Adam Smit" had attempted to build a great work of political economy upon the foundation of Dutch work from in the seventeenth century—as Adam Smith built upon the foundation of English seventeenth-century political economy—he would have had much less to work with. And the chances are high that Smit's work would have been much less magisterial, less encompassing, less empirical, and less influential.

Publication Rates

Quantitative evidence confirms the impressions of archivists and authors that Dutch economic texts were not as plentiful as English texts. The data on annual publication rates for economic texts in England and the Dutch Republic combine materials used for the analysis in chapter 5 with additional data on the Dutch titles included in the catalogs of The Making of the Modern World, Part I, as well as additional titles combined from the Short-Title Catalogue, Netherlands; Dutch Pamphlets Online (formerly The Early Modern Pamphlets Online); the *Nederlandse Centrale Catalogus*; the Leiden University Catalog; the *Digital bibliotheek voor Nederlandse Letteren*; the University of Amsterdam Library Catalog; and Étienne Laspeyres's comprehensive bibliography of early Dutch economic works,

---

18. Zuidema, "Economic Thought," 31; and Paul Slack, *The Invention of Improvement: Information and Material Progress in Seventeenth-Century England* (Oxford: Oxford University Press, 2015), 251.

19. Wagener, "Free Seas," 395.

20. Zuidema, "Economic Thought," 35.

21. Erik Reinert, "Emulating Success: Contemporary Views of the Dutch Economy Before 1800," in *The Political Economy of the Dutch Republic*, ed. Oscar Gelderblom (Farnham, UK: Ashgate, 2009), 21.

Geschichte der volkswirtschaftlichen Anschauungen der Niederländer und ihrer Litteratur zur Zeit der Republik (1863).[22]

The Short-Title Catalogue, Netherlands includes 500,000 Dutch texts produced between 1540 and 1800. *Dutch Pamphlets Online* is a repository based on two collections: the Knuttel Collection at the Koninklijke Bibliotheek (the National Library of the Netherlands) and the Van Alphen Collection, from the Groningen University Library and the Short-Title Catalogue of the Netherlands. The Knuttel Collection includes 34,000 printed pamphlets from 1486 to 1853 on a variety of subjects. The Van Alphen Collection includes 2,800 pamphlets, not included in the Knuttel Collection, on diverse topics published from 1542 to 1853. The *Nederlandse Centrale Catalogus* is a centralized collection of the catalogs of all Dutch universities, the Dutch National Library, and a number of other regional Dutch libraries. Also included were works listed in the Leiden University Catalog, the *Digitale bibliotheek voor de Nederlandse Letteren*, and the University of Amsterdam Library. These libraries provide coverage of all major Dutch pamphlet collections (the Broekema, Tiele, Meulman, Thysius, Someren, Knuttel, Van Alphen, and Rogge collections).

Data from the Dutch sources were scraped from online catalogs using an exhaustive list of search terms including economics/economy (*economie*), trade/commerce (*handel*), company (*compagnie*), market (*markten*), business (*bedrijfskunde*), business administration, organizational sciences, home economics (*huishoudkunde*), West India Company (*West-indische compagnie*), East India Company (*Verenigde oost-indische compagnie*), and industry (*industrie*). English and Dutch translations of the terms were used for search. The result was merged and cleaned to remove duplicates on an annual basis.[23]

---

22. Short-Title Catalogue, Netherlands (KB: National Library of the Netherlands), https://www .kb.nl/en/organisation/research-expertise/for-libraries/short-title-catalogue-netherlands-stcn; Dutch Pamphlets Online (Brill), https://primarysources.brillonline.com/browse/dutch-pamphlets -online; Nederlandse Centrale Catalogus, http://picarta.pica.nl/; Leiden University Catalog, https:// www.library.universiteitleiden.nl/subject-guides/catalogue; Digitale Bibliotheek voor de Nederlandse Letteren, https://www.dbnl.org/; University of Amsterdam Library, https://uba.uva.nl/; and Étienne Laspeyres, *Geschichte der volkswirtschaftlichen Anschauungen der Niederländer und ihrer Litteratur zur Zeit der Republik* (Leipzig, 1863).

23. New editions of previously published works in later years were retained. Publications with the same year, author, and title (or very similar title) were removed from the data. Although some popular books with multiple editions may be undercounted, such instances cannot be reliably differentiated from occasions on which the same book was entered with slight variations in the same or different databases. Some of the Dutch texts did not provide exact years of publication.

The now familiar English publication rates are represented here in binned form so that the comparison is easier to see. In figure 6.1, white bins represent the count of English economic texts and black bins represent the count of Dutch economic texts. In total, there are 1,511 Dutch economic texts compared to 6,585 English economic texts. The difference holds for the ratio of economic texts to all published texts, presented in figure 6.2. The count of all texts used to construct the ratios is taken from the English Short Title Catalogue for

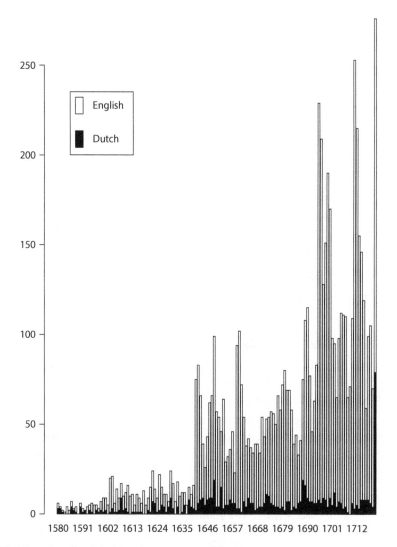

FIGURE 6.1. Frequency of English and Dutch economic texts

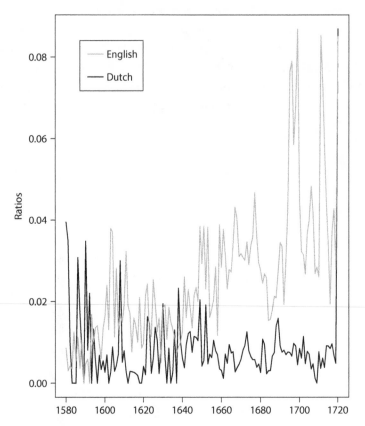

FIGURE 6.2. Ratio of economic texts to all texts

the English counts and the Short-Title Catalogue, Netherlands for the Dutch. The black line represents the Dutch Republic, which quickly falls behind the gray English line in the years leading up to the seventeenth century. In total, English economic texts represent 3.56 percent of all texts, compared with the Dutch rate of 1.76 percent. Even the per capita rate of publication favors England, despite its greater population. In 1600, the rate of publications per thousand persons was 0.0007 in the Netherlands and 0.0019 in England. In 1700, the two rates were 0.0047 in the Netherlands and 0.03 in England.[24]

24. Stephen Broadberry et al., *British Economic Growth, 1270–1870* (Cambridge: Cambridge University Press, 2015); and Richard Paping, "General Dutch Population Development, 1400–1850: Cities and Countryside" (paper presented at the First Conference of the European Society of Historical Demography [ESHD], Sassari/Alghero, Sardinia, Italy, September 25–27, 2014), 34, https://www.rug.nl/research/portal/files/15865622/articlesardinie21sep2014.pdf.

TABLE 6.1
Texts with keywords related to economics, 1580-1720

	Trade/commerce/*handel*	Economics/economy/*economie*	Price/*prijzen*
English	2,436	542	3,773
Dutch	570	3	10

TABLE 6.2
Texts with subjects related to economics, 1580-1720

	Trade/commerce/*handel*	Economics/economy/*economie*	Price/*prijzen*
English	1,276	61	92
Dutch	84	2	1

Because the Making of the Modern World collection is housed in an English-speaking nation, there may be some suspicion that English works are overrepresented in the data. It is, however, unlikely that selection bias at the level of the national catalogs is driving these differences. Consider, for example, the difference between rates of English-language and Dutch-language economic publications from this era within a Dutch library collection. Tables 6.1 and 6.2 present the volume of different types of economic texts drawn from the Dutch Central Catalogue (*Nederlandse Centrale Catalogus*). Table 6.1 compares the number of texts dating from 1580 to 1720 that are referenced by keywords related to economics and commerce, and table 6.2 compares the number of texts with subject headers related to economics, in both English and Dutch texts catalogued in the collection.

These counts are based on a broad interpretation of what constitutes an economic text, including, for example, any pamphlet that touches upon trade. A stricter approach to determining what counts as "economic" would have produced an even smaller number of Dutch texts. While Dutch intellectuals in other fields made significant contributions, Dutch works on political economy were few and far between.

POSSIBLE FACTORS

Civil Society and Cultural Influences

In the previous chapter, the relationship of company incorporation and merchants' political representation to publication rates for economic texts was assessed over time—i.e., I assessed whether increases or decreases in the first two factors in 1620 predict an uptick in the economic publications in 1621. In this chapter, I revisit the alternative explanations explored in chapter 5, but instead of asking how factors varied over time, I ask how conditions varied in two different cases at the same time. So for example, one of the explanations was that the efflorescence of economic thought was based in the growth of the civil sphere more generally. For this argument to hold cross-sectionally, it should follow that the civil sphere was more developed and larger in England than in the Netherlands in the seventeenth century, thus accounting for the different rates of the production of economic texts. Estimates of the literacy rate of the populations put England slightly ahead of the Netherlands in the seventeenth century, at 16 percent versus 12 percent.[25] Also, the raw production total of printed books was higher in Britain than in the Netherlands. England produced 32,912 books from 1600 to 1650 and 89,306 from 1650 to 1700; the Netherlands produced 15,009 in the first half of the seventeenth century and 30,149 in the second half.[26] However, given that England had nearly three times the population of the Netherlands, these rates favor the Netherlands. Per capita consumption of books in the Netherlands was nearly double that of England throughout the seventeenth century. Rates in England for 1600–1650, 1651–1700, and 1701–1750 were, respectively, 80, 191.8, and 168.3; in the Netherlands, the same rates were 139, 259.4, and 391.3.[27] There is little evidence that the Dutch population was at a disadvantage to the English in terms of the societal infrastructure required for producing or consuming economic texts.

With regard to the development of a civil society and educated public, it is worth considering the role of changes in education. The general rise in secular knowledge, of which economics was part, was assisted by the appearance of universities. However, economic texts in the seventeenth century did not emerge out of universities; they were produced by merchants, tradesmen, and statesmen. In the seventeenth century, the British Isles had seven universities and the Netherlands had five. These rates seem comparable or slightly in favor of the Netherlands once population size

25. Eltjo Buringh and Jan Luiten van Zanden, "Charting the 'Rise of the West': Manuscripts and Printed Books in Europe, A Long-Term Perspective from the Sixth through Eighteenth Centuries," *Journal of Economic History* 69, no. 2 (June 2009): 434, https://doi.org/10.1017/S0022050709000837.

26. Buringh and Van Zanden, "Charting the 'Rise of the West,'" 417.

27. Buringh and Van Zanden, "Charting the 'Rise of the West,'" 421.

is taken into account. It is also true that both England and the Nether-lands lagged significantly behind France and Germany in terms of univer-sity foundings. In the same century, France already had sixteen established campuses and Germany had twenty-two.[28] Neither France nor Germany saw large increases in economic texts until the eighteenth century.

Another way of considering this question is to ask whether there was some preexisting tendency for English intellectual discourse to take the particular turn evident in mercantilist economic thought. For example, the argument has been loosely made on several occasions that the English people had a special affinity for free trade. This argument does not hold up well under close scrutiny. The main problem is that "free trade" is a vague and abstract enough concept to have been embraced, rejected, and more generally to have served as an object of controversy and passionate discus-sion in many times and places prior to the seventeenth century and outside of England—and outside of Europe, for that matter. There was, for example, a clear appreciation of the potential benefits of low taxation and minimal government intervention in overseas trade in many Asian ports during and prior to this period.[29] The Dutch also proved to be a particularly bad coun-terexample on this point, as free trade was a more important governing principle for the Dutch than the English in this era.

Nor is it the case that the Dutch lacked an important intellectual tradi-tion or did not produce works of great and lasting value in this period. Gro-tius, or Hugo de Groot (1583–1645), pioneered the concept of natural law and the field of international law. He formulated a systematic defense of free trade in *Mare Liberum* (1609), taking a juridical rather than a commercial approach.[30] Indeed, Grotius was a particularly central and strong influence on Smith and the Scottish Enlightenment.[31] Istvan Hont and Michael Igna-tieff have outlined Smith's debt to Grotius, showing that Smith was work-ing within a general theoretical framework laid out by Grotius and later

---

28. Buringh and Van Zanden, "Charting the 'Rise of the West,'" 431.

29. Emily Erikson, *Between Monopoly and Free Trade: The English East India Company, 1600–1757* (Princeton, NJ: Princeton University Press, 2014).

30. Hugo Grotius, *Mare Liberum, sive De jure quod Batavis competit ad Indicana commercia Dissertatio* (Lugduni Batauorvm: Ex officinà Ludovici Elzevirij, 1609).

31. James Moore and Michael Silverthorne, "Gershom Carmichael and the Natural Jurispru-dence Tradition in Eighteenth-Century Scotland," in *Wealth and Virtue: The Shaping of Political Economy in the Scottish Enlightenment*, ed. Istvan Hont and Michael Ignatieff (Cambridge: Cam-bridge University Press, 1983), 73–87.

developed by Locke and Pufendorf, addressing the problem of the conflict between protecting the property of the wealthy and providing for the needs of the poor.[32] This side of Smith's work was closer to the moral perspective he was attempting to reinsert into the abstract, theoretical, and nationalist work of the mercantilists. Later in the seventeenth century, Spinoza (1632–1677) produced enduring works central to liberal philosophy and acted as a staunch defender of individual freedoms.[33] Both republicanism and liberalism flourished in the Netherlands before they took solid root in England.

There was no national shortage of humanistic moral philosophy within the Netherlands, but in truth this is somewhat beside the point, as intellectual discourse was not contained by national boundaries. Smith was influenced by Grotius, Pufendorf, Mandeville, and Cantillon. Hobbes was influenced by Galileo Galilei. Machiavelli was a profound influence on the civil republican tradition in England.[34] Writers in England, the Netherlands, France, Germany, Italy, and Spain had access to the works of other Europeans, and major works were available in translation. This intellectual pan-Europeanism was evident in both England and the Netherlands. A common ground in a tradition of European philosophy was available in the Netherlands and England. What is perhaps more interesting is that most contributions in England in the seventeenth century were made by people who stood outside of these global intellectual currents. Merchants were not members of the European intellectual community. Perhaps this is another reason why their writings had such a nationalist tone. Differences in the larger intellectual discourses of England and the Netherlands simply do not provide a solid foundation on which to understand the distinctive flourishing of English economic thought.

Economic Development

One of the most commonly articulated theories behind the development of economics is the increasing complexity of economic transactions. The

---

32. Istvan Hont and Michael Ignatieff, eds., *Wealth and Virtue: The Shaping of Political Economy in the Scottish Enlightenment* (Cambridge: Cambridge University Press, 1983), 2.

33. Stuart Hampshire, "Spinoza and the Idea of Freedom," in *Studies in Spinoza: Critical and Interpretive Essays*, ed. S. Paul Kashap (Berkeley: University of California Press, 1974), 330; and Gerald M. Mara, "Liberal Politics and Moral Excellence in Spinoza's Political Philosophy," *Journal of the History of Philosophy* 20, no. 2 (April 1982): 129–50.

34. John Greville Agard Pocock, *The Machiavellian Moment: Florentine Political Thought and the Atlantic Republican Tradition* (Princeton, NJ: Princeton University Press, 2009).

seventeenth century was a key phase in the commercial revolution. Global trade expanded significantly, and complex financial instruments were developed as stock markets emerged in Amsterdam and London. These processes, however, do little to explain the divergence between England and the Netherlands. Whereas the English and Dutch can be considered to have had civil spheres of at least roughly equal development, the Dutch held a clear advantage over England in terms of levels of economic development and improved state capacity.

Table 6.3 presents estimates of per capita GDP benchmarked by setting values relative to England in 1820, which is set at 100. As shown in the table, GDP per capita was higher in the Netherlands than in England through the sixteenth, seventeenth, and eighteenth centuries.[35] Urbanization rates were also consistently higher. In the Netherlands, the rates for the sixteenth, seventeenth, and eighteenth centuries were, respectively, 15.8, 24.3, and 33.6, compared with 3.1, 5.8, and 13.3 in England and Wales.[36] As of 1700, 60 percent of the Dutch population was employed in industry and service, compared with 44 percent of the English population; the remainder of both populations were engaged in agricultural labor or professional occupations.[37] The global trade to Asia was also more developed in the Dutch Republic. The Dutch East India Company (*Vereenigde Oostindische Compagnie*) sent 1,770 ships to Asia in the seventeenth century, while the English East India Company sent 811.[38] England only began to catch up with the impressive velocity of Dutch economic growth in the eighteenth century.[39]

TABLE 6.3
Estimates of per capita GDP

	c. 1500	c. 1570	c. 1650	c. 1700	c. 1750	1820
England	43	43–45	54	69	84	100
Netherlands	58	58	95	94	94	92

Source: Jan Luiten Van Zanden, *Long Road to the Industrial Revolution: The European Economy in a Global Perspective, 1000–1800* (Boston: Brill, 2009), 241. ProQuest Ebook Central.

35. Jan Luiten van Zanden, *Long Road to the Industrial Revolution: The European Economy in a Global Perspective, 1000–1800*, Global Economic History Series 1 (Boston: Brill, 2009), 241, ProQuest Ebook Central.

36. Jan de Vries, *European Urbanization, 1500–1800* (London: Methuen, 1984), 30, 36, 46; and Angus Maddison, *Contours of the World Economy, 1–2030 AD: Essays in Macro-Economic History* (Oxford: Oxford University Press, 2007), 43.

37. Maddison, *Contours*, 76.

38. Erikson, *Between Monopoly*; and Maddison, *Contours*, 112.

39. Van Zanden, *Long Road*, 95.

There is widespread agreement that the Netherlands was the first country to achieve sustained economic and technological development.[40] Market growth had begun in the Netherlands by the thirteenth and fourteenth centuries and there were developed factor markets there dating to the fourteenth century,[41] putting it well ahead of England in terms of development. England did not take the lead until the early nineteenth century—well after the emergence of a defined literature on economics in Britain. Indeed, Adam Smith held up the Dutch as a model for future prosperity in *The Wealth of Nations*, and contemporary authors have argued it was envy of the Dutch that spurred on the English mercantilists.[42]

State Capacity

In the time series analysis, there was no relationship between tax revenue or the number of days that Parliament was in session and economic text publication rates. A comparative approach allows for a more multidimensional assessment of state power. In this case, the alternative hypothesis that increasing state power led to the rise of the new economic literature would be upheld if the state with greater political and economic capacity and power also saw the publication of more economic theory.

Economic growth is related to state capacity, so it may not come as a surprise that the Dutch Republic held an advantage over the English state in this respect as well. After the Union of Utrecht (1579), the northern provinces of the Netherlands were joined together in revolt against King Philip II of Spain. This union became the Dutch Republic, a confederation of seven provinces that had a famously decentralized political structure in which each province retained significant autonomy. This decentralization has been identified as a barrier to the expansion of state power in the

40. Jan de Vries and Ad van der Woude, *The First Modern Economy: Success, Failure, and Perseverance of the Dutch Economy, 1500–1815* (Cambridge: Cambridge University Press, 1997); Angus Maddison, *Dynamic Forces in Capitalist Development: A Long-Run Comparative View* (New York: Oxford University Press, 1991), 30; Douglass C. North and Robert Paul Thomas, *The Rise of the Western World: A New Economic History* (Cambridge: Cambridge University Press, 1973), 145.

41. Bas van Bavel, *The Invisible Hand? How Market Economies Have Emerged and Declined Since AD 500* (Oxford: Oxford University Press, 2016); and Bas van Bavel, "Open Societies Before Market Economies: Historical Analysis," *Socio-Economic Review*, 2019, https://doi.org/10.1093/soceco/mwz007.

42. Sophus A. Reinert and Pernille Røge, eds., *The Political Economy of Empire in the Early Modern World* (Basingstoke, UK: Palgrave Macmillan, 2013).

Netherlands over the long term, but it did little to impede the progress of the nation-state's capacity in the seventeenth century, when the Dutch Republic was widely recognized as the leading power of Europe.

State capacity has been precisely defined as the ability to tax, raise troops, and create a national identity.[43] Unfortunately, the last is difficult to measure, and I will not attempt it here. Taxation was decentralized at the level of the Dutch Republic and centralized at the provincial level. Provincial centralization produced a high level of efficiency, enhancing tax yields in a "revolutionary way."[44] For most of the seventeenth century, per capita tax rates in the Netherlands were three to four times higher than in England. Not until the reforms implemented in the aftermath of England's Glorious Revolution, in the last decade of the seventeenth century, did the English state begin to close the gap with the Dutch.[45] The system of public finance that allowed governments to quickly raise money to cover military costs in times of war was pioneered by the Dutch in the early seventeenth century.[46] This system was implemented in England under the Dutch sovereign William of Orange, in power from 1689 to 1702.[47]

The Dutch had a comparatively advanced set of military institutions, including a system of courts, a teaching hospital, mobile surgery units, resident doctors for regiments, standardized weaponry, and instructional manuals.[48] Additionally, the Dutch navy was superior to the English until the late seventeenth century. Every indication was that the Dutch state, while fragmented, was also more powerful and had greater capacity than the English state.[49]

43. Hendrik Spruyt, "The Origins, Development, and Possible Decline of the Modern State," *Annual Review of Political Science* 5 (2002): 131, https://doi.org/10.1146/annurev.polisci.5.101501.145837.

44. Wantje Fritschy, "The Efficiency of Taxation in Holland," in *The Political Economy of the Dutch Republic*, ed. Oscar Gelderblom (Farnham, UK: Ashgate, 2009), 83.

45. Jan Luiten van Zanden and Maarten Prak, "Towards an Economic Interpretation of Citizenship: The Dutch Republic Between Medieval Communes and Modern Nation-States," *European Review of Economic History* 10, no. 2 (August 2006): 130, https://doi.org/10.1017/S1361491606001651.

46. James D. Tracy, *A Financial Revolution in the Habsburg Netherlands: Renten and Renteniers in the County of Holland, 1515–1565* (Berkeley: University of California Press, 1985).

47. Bruce G. Carruthers, *City of Capital: Politics and Markets in the English Financial Revolution* (Princeton, NJ: Princeton University Press, 1999); and Geoffrey Parker, "The 'Military Revolution,' 1560–1660—a Myth?," *Journal of Modern History* 48, no. 2 (June 1976): 212–13.

48. Geoffrey Parker, "The 'Military Revolution,'" 199, 202.

49. Marjolein 't Hart, "Freedom and Restrictions: State and Economy in the Dutch Republic, 1570–1670," in *The Dutch Economy in the Golden Age: Nine Studies*, ed. Karel Davids and Leo Noordegraaf (Amsterdam: Nederlandsch Economisch-Historisch Archief, 1993), 104; and Jonathan Israel, *Dutch Primacy in World Trade, 1585–1740* (Oxford: Oxford University Press, 1989), 411.

Political Upset

Even as state capacity increased, violent conflict erupted repeatedly in both contexts. To reprise briefly, the English state began the seventeenth century as a monarchy under the last of the Tudors, Queen Elizabeth I. In 1642, the English Civil War broke out, which led to the execution of King Charles I and the temporary creation of a republican form of government, the Commonwealth, declared in 1649. The Commonwealth was replaced by the Protectorate of Oliver Cromwell in 1653, and in 1660 the monarchy was reestablished. Significant discontent arose again in the late 1680s, culminating in widespread public demonstrations and violent eruptions.[50] Following the Glorious Revolution of 1688, a constitutional monarchy was installed.

Turmoil in the Netherlands began earlier and lasted longer. Philip II of Spain ruled the Netherlands in the mid-sixteenth century. After the Reformation, the spread of Puritanism throughout the Netherlands opened a rift between the newly converted Protestants and their still Catholic king. Additional tensions arose between Philip II and Dutch localities when he threatened their traditional urban privileges and attempted to exert greater political and fiscal control over the provinces.[51] In 1566, widespread violence broke out, which quickly escalated into an out-and-out revolution. In 1579, while still at war with the Spanish Empire, the Netherlands formally transitioned from a monarchy to a republic that united a mixed alliance of cities, counties, lordships, and duchies. In 1581, this confederation declared independence from King Philip II. This move did not end the hostilities with Spain, which lasted until formal recognition of the Dutch Republic at the Treaty of Westphalia in 1648.[52] During this time, the new republic was not spared internal struggles and popular unrest. From 1617 to 1621, conditions came very close to approximating civil war. Widespread discontent resulted in violent uprisings between 1652 and 1653, and again in

50. Steve Pincus, *1688: The First Modern Revolution* (New Haven, CT: Yale University Press, 2009).

51. Graham Darby, ed., *The Origins and Development of the Dutch Revolt* (London: Routledge, 2001); and Maarten Prak, *The Dutch Republic in the Seventeenth Century: The Golden Age*, trans. Diane Webb (Cambridge: Cambridge University Press, 2005), 16.

52. Marjolein 't Hart, *The Dutch Wars of Independence: Warfare and Commerce in the Netherlands, 1570–1680* (London: Routledge, 2014).

1672.[53] In 1672, the former *Raadpensionaris*, or Grand Pensionary of the States of Holland, the political leader of the Dutch Republic, Johan de Witt, was brutally lynched along with his brother by a mob of dissidents.[54] The shocking nature of this incident far surpassed the comparatively controlled circumstances of Charles I's beheading.

State-Merchant Relations and the Rise of the Chartered Company

While England and the Dutch Republic were similar on many other dimensions, the structure of state-merchant relations differed in crucial ways. Merchant representation in the offices of the government was one area of marked divergence.

The Dutch Republic had a different and more complex organizational structure than the Parliament and sovereign configuration of early modern Britain. During the active component of the Dutch Revolt (1566–1581), the Dutch commercial elite formed an enduring coalition with landed aristocrats, which resulted in a tight coupling between merchant capitalists and state elites. This coalition, in turn, led to the increasing economic and political power of Dutch merchants in the wake of the Dutch Revolt.[55] By the seventeenth century, the government was a confederation of several provinces that ruled together in the States General. There was also a *Stadtholder*, which evolved into a hereditary position held by the House of Orange. The *Stadtholder* was a largely titular position with significantly less power than either the provincial governments or the States General. Each of the seven provinces had one vote in the States General, but an unlimited number of delegates. Usually roughly twenty-five to thirty delegates were in attendance.[56] Delegates were chosen by the provincial governments. In theory, all binding votes of the States General had to be unanimous. In practice, this condition effectively

---

53. Rudolf M. Dekker, "Women in Revolt: Popular Protest and Its Social Basis in Holland in the Seventeenth and Eighteenth Centuries," *Theory and Society* 16, no. 3 (May 1987): 337–62.

54. Michel Reinders, *Printed Pandemonium: Popular Print and Politics in the Netherlands, 1650–72* (Leiden: Brill, 2013).

55. Julia Adams, *The Familial State: Ruling Families and Merchant Capitalism in Early Modern Europe* (Ithaca, NY: Cornell University Press, 2005), 41–42.

56. John H. Grever, "The Structure of Decision-Making in the States General of the Dutch Republic 1660–68," *Parliaments, Estates and Representation* 2, no. 2 (December 1982): 125–53.

ensured veto power for Holland, the most politically and economically powerful of the provinces.[57]

Holland was ruled by regents, wealthy individuals drawn from trade and manufacturing families. They held eighteen of the nineteen votes in the *Staten*, the provincial seat of formal political authority.[58] Over time, the regents drifted toward rent seeking, but the group retained its close relationship with the world of commerce and industry through the seventeenth century.[59] Zeeland was also firmly in the control of the towns, and therefore trade and manufacturing interests. The nobility and peasants had more control over Gelderland, Overjissel, Utrecht, Groningen, and Friesland, but even these agricultural provinces were ruled by a balance between the towns and the country. Trade and manufacturing had influence over the towns, and the nobility had more influence over the country. Groningen, for example, had a *Staten* with two votes, one from the town and one from the surrounding countryside. The latter was sometimes, but not always, held by the nobility.[60] Thus, merchants or manufacturing elites controlled the center of power, Holland, as well as Zeeland, and held partial control over the rest of the provinces. This system translated into a large and enduring dominant position for merchants within the state.[61]

Rates of merchant representation were lower in England than in the Dutch Republic in the sixteenth century and, as has already been shown, they decreased over most of the seventeenth century. In the Parliament of 1584, seventy-three elected officials, or 15.6 percent of the total, were merchants or businessmen. By 1614 to 1620, only twenty-six, or 5.5 percent, of the members were from the merchant class. Even as late as the 1715 Parliament, the numbers had not recovered. The same number of merchants

57. J. L. Price, *Holland and the Dutch Republic in the Seventeenth Century: The Politics of Particularism* (Oxford: Clarendon Press, 1994), 223.

58. Price, *Holland*, 11.

59. Price, *Holland*, 47.

60. Price, *Holland*, 226.

61. David Stasavage, *States of Credit: Size, Power, and the Development of European Polities* (Princeton, NJ: Princeton University Press, 2011), 110; Sheilagh Ogilvie and A. W. Carus, "Institutions and Economic Growth in Historical Perspective," in *Handbook of Economic Growth*, ed. Philippe Aghion and Steven N. Durlauf (Amsterdam: Elsevier, 2014), 2A:422, https://doi.org/10.1016/B978-0-444-53538-2.00008-3; and John Gilissen, "Les états généraux en Belgique et aux Pays-Bas sous l'ancien régime," in *Gouvernes et gouvernants*, vol. 11, 401–37 (Bruxelles: Ed. de la Librairie encyclopedique, 1965).

were serving as in 1584, but Parliament's size had increased, so their proportion of the total was only 9.8 percent.[62]

One outcome of the minority position of merchants in the English state was a level of distance and distrust between state elites—such as royal officials, parliamentary leaders, and nobles—and commercial actors. In 1624, the court of directors of the English East India Company refused membership to King James I.[63] Robert Ashton described the relationship between the commercial elite of London and the Crown in the 1630s as one of "intolerable strain."[64] Tensions increased in 1640 when the City of London, which represented the commercial and financial factions of the elite, began to side clearly with the Parliamentarians as the country moved toward civil war.[65]

A second and related divergence between England and the Netherlands was the state bias toward large-scale organizations in England. In the Elizabethan state, "the government showed a consistent preference for social and economic organizations that assigned men to masters and tied them to a particular occupation and place. It was far better to have a work force tidily organized under qualified masters in town guilds than straggling in the countryside."[66] The more empowered merchantry of the United Provinces chafed under similar attempts to control and organize commerce. In England, the developing state favored guilds and companies because it

---

62. David Hayton, Eveline Cruickshanks, and Stuart Handley, eds., *The House of Commons, 1690-1715*, 5 vols. (Cambridge: Published for the History of Parliament Trust by Cambridge University Press, 2002); P. W. Hasler, ed., *The House of Commons, 1558-1603*, 3 vols. (London: Published for the History of Parliament Trust by Her Majesty's Stationery Office, 1981); Basic Duke Henning, ed., *The House of Commons, 1660-1690* (London: Published for the History of Parliament Trust by Secker & Warburg, 1983); Romney Sedgwick, *The House of Commons, 1715-1754*, 2 vols. (London: Her Majesty's Stationery Office, 1970); and Andrew Thrush and John P. Ferris, eds., *The House of Commons, 1604-1629*, 6 vols. (Cambridge: Published for the History of Parliament Trust by Cambridge University Press, 2010). The number of merchants serving in the Long Parliament has not yet been compiled. All of these data, along with much other valuable information, are available online through the History of Parliament research project.

63. Jelle C. Riemersma, "Oceanic Expansion: Government Influence on Company Organization in Holland and England, 1550-1650," *Journal of Economic History* 10, supplement (1950): 38.

64. Robert Ashton, *The City and the Court, 1603-1643* (Cambridge: Cambridge University Press, 1979).

65. A detailed description of these shifting alignments may be found in Henning Hillmann, "Mediation in Multiple Networks: Elite Mobilization Before the English Civil War," *American Sociological Review* 73, no. 3 (June 2008): 426-54.

66. Peter Ramsey, "The Tudor State and Economic Problems," in *State and Trade: Government and the Economy in Britain and the Netherlands Since the Middle Ages*, ed. Simon Groenveld and Michael Joseph Wintle (Zutphen: Walburg Pers, 1992), 31.

was able to lean on these organizations for practical assistance, ranging from the consolidation of tax collection to the regulation of smuggling and illegal activity to capital loans.[67] In England, this tendency translated into an embrace of government-issued charters, and companies began to overtake the place of guilds in overseas trade.[68] Corporate bodies and state-sanctioned merchant organizations were much less common in the Netherlands. The bulk of trade there was conducted via partnerships and independent merchants.[69] The patrimonial structure of Dutch politics led to strong locally based regents with extensive ties to existing guilds, who were motivated by those ties to protect them.[70] As a result, guilds remained strongly entrenched in most Dutch cities throughout the seventeenth century.[71] More new guilds were formed in the seventeenth century in the Netherlands than ever before.[72]

Associations with a large number of partners, called *partenrederij*, did exist in the Netherlands, but these multiparty partnerships were rarely granted special privileges by the government.[73] Monopoly rights seem to have been granted only in cases where contemporaries believed open competition between Dutch merchants would produce commercial failure. For example, several regional trading associations in the 1590s were formed

---

67. Ramsey, "Tudor State."

68. Guilds remained an important part of the economic landscape until the eighteenth century even in England. Though chartered companies began to appear with greater frequency as early as the sixteenth century, it was not until the 1660s that the strength of guilds in England was significantly challenged—Michael Berlin would argue through the combined effects of the Civil War, the Interregnum, and the Great Fire of 1666. Michael Berlin, "Guilds in Decline? London Livery Companies and the Rise of a Liberal Economy, 1600–1800," in *Guilds, Innovation, and the European Economy, 1400–1800*, ed. S. R. Epstein and Maarten Prak (Cambridge: Cambridge University Press, 2008), 325.

69. Eli Heckscher, *Mercantilism* (London: George Allen & Unwin, 1935), 355–56; Abe de Jong, Joost Jonker, and Ailsa Röell, "Dutch Corporate Finance, 1602–1850," ERIM Report Series Reference No. ERS-2013-008-F&A, June 4, 2013, http://papers.ssrn.com/abstract=2274577; and Riemersma, "Oceanic Expansion," 35.

70. Julia Adams, "The Familial State: Elite Family Practices and State-Making in the Early Modern Netherlands," *Theory and Society* 23, no. 4 (August 1994): 521, https://doi.org/10.1007/BF00992826.

71. Ormrod, *Rise of Commercial Empires*, 19.

72. S. R. Epstein and Maartin Prak, eds., *Guilds, Innovation, and the European Economy, 1400–1800* (Cambridge: Cambridge University Press, 2008), 21.

73. Oscar Gelderblom and Joost Jonker, "Completing a Financial Revolution: The Finance of the Dutch East India Trade and the Rise of the Amsterdam Capital Market, 1595–1612," *Journal of Economic History* 64, no. 3 (September 2004): 645.

to pursue trade to the East Indies. These firms did not seek monopoly privileges from the government. Competition between them threatened to derail the trade. As they began to fail, the government stepped in to unify the concerns into the Dutch East India Company (*Vereenigde Oostindische Compagnie*), founded in 1602. A similar process occurred in whaling, where, after recurring difficulties, many competing firms were united into a chartered company with monopoly privileges. The resulting firm was the North Company (*Noordsche Compagnie*), founded in 1614. The same type of events also drove the formation of the New Netherlands Company (*Compagnie van Nieuw Nederland*), also formed in 1614, for trade to the Americas.[74] After the demise of the New Netherlands Company in 1618, part of its monopoly privileges were transferred to the Dutch West India Company (*Geoctroyeerde Westindische Compagnie*), founded in 1621.[75] At a later point, internal contestation within the West India Company led to the formation of the Society of Surinam (*Geoctroyeerde Sociëteit van Suriname*), which assumed the subset of existing monopoly privileges to the West Indies specific to Surinam in 1682.[76] These five constitute the whole of formally organized companies granted monopoly privileges by the States General up to 1720. Other overseas trades, such as to Russia, the Levant, and West Africa, were not conducted via chartered companies.[77]

State officials, who in any case were often of merchant origins, served on company boards. The largest of the companies, the Dutch East India Company, provides an example of the tight intertwining between state and commercial actors. The company was organized into six regional chambers, each managed by a group of directors (*bewindhebbers*). The town burgomaster served on the council of *bewindhebbers*, often alongside other state officials.[78] The state provided half of the starting capital for the Dutch West India Company, and the charter stipulated that the government had the right to nominate one of the directors of the company's ruling body.[79] The chartered companies that were created in the Netherlands were more closely bound to the state than their English counterparts.

74. De Vries and Van der Woude, *First Modern Economy*, 398.
75. Hart, "Freedom and Restrictions," 111.
76. De Vries and Van der Woude, *First Modern Economy*, 468.
77. Riemersma, "Oceanic Expansion," 36.
78. Heckscher, *Mercantilism*, 363, 366.
79. Heckscher, *Mercantilism*, 357, 367.

In fact, the few charters that were granted by the Dutch Republic were given to companies created expressly to serve public interests. The public dimension of state-granted charters persisted until 1720, when the process was reformed to emulate the English system.[80] In summary, the overall strength of the merchant community led to strong opposition to the granting of any new special privileges to some subset of the larger whole.[81] These conditions translated into far fewer chartered companies in the Netherlands.[82] The few that were incorporated differed from those in England in that they were formally granted privileges to serve *public* interests—not private interests, as in the English case.[83]

Figure 6.3 shows the frequency of the incorporation of chartered companies in the British Isles and the Netherlands from 1550 to 1720.[84] The bars represent the annual count of charterings; the line represents the cumulative number of company foundings up to that year. Black bars and lines are British; gray bars and lines are Dutch. The right vertical axis corresponds to the frequency and the left to the cumulative count. As is evident from the chart, there was a surge in chartered company foundings in 1690 and a peak (for the seventeenth and early eighteenth centuries) of eighteen incorporations in 1694.

80. Abe de Jong and Ailsa Röell, "Financing and Control in the Netherlands: A Historical Perspective," in *A History of Corporate Governance Around the World: Family Business Groups to Professional Managers*, ed. Randall K. Morck (Chicago: University of Chicago Press, 2003), 470.

81. Riemersma, "Oceanic Expansion," 36.

82. Riemersma, "Oceanic Expansion," 35.

83. Rik G. P. Frehen, William N. Goetzmann, and K. Geert Rouwenhorst, "New Evidence on the First Financial Bubble," *Journal of Financial Economics* 108, no. 3 (June 2013): 585–607; John F. Padgett, "Country as Global Market: Netherlands, Calvinism, and the Joint-Stock Company," in *The Emergence of Organizations and Markets*, ed. John F. Padgett and Walter W. Powell (Princeton, NJ: Princeton University Press, 2012), 226; and Lars van Vliet, "New Developments in Dutch Company Law: The 'Flexible' Close Corporation," *Journal of Civil Law Studies* 7, no. 1 (2014): 273–74.

84. As in chapter 5, data on organizational founding rates in England were drawn from George Cawston and Augustus Henry Keane, *The Early Chartered Companies (A.D. 1296–1858)* (London: Edward Arnold, 1896); and William Robert Scott, *The Constitution and Finance of English, Scottish and Irish Joint-Stock Companies to 1720*, 3 vols. (Cambridge: At the University Press, 1912). Because there were far fewer Dutch chartered companies, similar authoritative volumes on Dutch chartered companies do not exist. Data on Dutch chartered companies were drawn from a number of sources and exhaustively checked across secondary works on Dutch economic development, overseas trade, finance, entrepreneurialism, and merchant organization. De Vries and Van der Woude, *First Modern Economy*; Hart, "Freedom and Restrictions"; Israel, *Dutch Primacy*; De Jong and Röell, "Financing and Control," 470; De Jong, Jonker, and Röell, "Dutch Corporate Finance"; Ormrod, *Rise of Commercial Empires*; and Riemersma, "Oceanic Expansion."

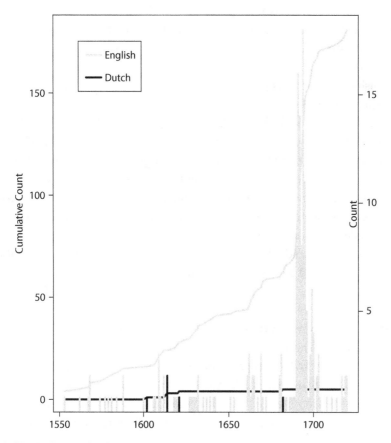

FIGURE 6.3. Company foundings

In the next sections, I revisit the two moments in the 1620s and the 1690s in which global trade patterns affected both the Dutch and the English but provoked different responses in terms of publications and the development of economic theory.

The Depression of the 1620s

In the 1620s, a widespread depression affected England and the Netherlands, as well as several other European nations. In the Netherlands, this episode was known as the *Kipper und Wipper* (1619–1623), meaning roughly "Clipper and Seesaw"; there was widespread price dislocation and inflation linked to coin debasement (or clipping). Paul Slack has credited this trade depression with stimulating the mercantilist revolution in economic thought.[85] In truth, the six-year period from 1620 to 1625 saw a peak in the number of English economic texts produced in any six-year period to date—a total of seventy-four. These texts include Thomas Mun's *A Discovrse of Trade*, *The maintenance of free trade* by Gerard de Malynes, and Edward Misselden's *Free Trade. Or, The Meanes to Make Trade Florish* and *The Circle of Commerce*. To briefly summarize what has been given lengthier treatment in chapter 2, the three texts were responding to the trade depression and a particular controversy surrounding the English East India Company's practice of exporting large amounts of bullion to Asia to finance its overseas trade. Contemporaries were concerned that the export of bullion was the cause of the trade depression (a common concern of early mercantilism). Malynes and Misselden came out against the export of bullion, while Mun, unsurprisingly, defended it. Mun was then a director of the East India Company. Misselden, later hired by the East India Company for contract negotiations, reversed his position after being hired and began to support the company.[86] The outcome of this debate was continued government support for the East India Company's business practice and the development of balance-of-trade theory, which pushed economic theory forward by deemphasizing the importance of bullion and focusing instead of multilateral international trade flows. This moment is widely recognized as significant in the development of economic theory,[87] and it is intimately related to the

85. Paul Slack, "The Politics of English Political Economy in the 1620s," in *Popular Culture and Political Agency in Early Modern England and Ireland: Essays in Honour of John Walter*, ed. Michael J. Braddick and Phil Withington (Woodbridge, UK: Boydell Press, 2017), 55–72.

86. E. A. J. Johnson, *Predecessors of Adam Smith: The Growth of British Economic Thought*. (New York: Prentice-Hall, 1937), 61.

87. Joyce Oldham Appleby, *Economic Thought and Ideology in Seventeenth-Century England* (Los Angeles: Figueroa Press, 1978); Douglas Irwin, *Against the Tide: An Intellectual History of Free Trade* (Princeton, NJ: Princeton University Press, 1996); E. A. J. Johnson, *Predecessors of Adam Smith*; Joseph A. Schumpeter, *A History of Economic Analysis: With a New Introduction*, Rev. ed. (New York: Oxford University Press, 1954); Barry E. Supple, "Currency and Commerce in the Early Seventeenth Century," *Economic History Review* 10, no. 2 (1957): 252, https://doi.org/10.2307/2590860; Parakunnel Joseph Thomas, *Mercantilism and the East India Trade: An Early Phase of the Protection v. Free Trade Controversy* (1926; reprint, Mansfield Center, CT: Martino Publishing, 2009); Jacob Viner, *Studies in the Theory of International Trade* (New York: Harper & Brothers, 1937); and Chi-Yuen Wu, *An Outline of International Price Theories* (London: Routledge, 1939).

public articulation of the material interests of a large, formally chartered organization and its relationship to the public good.

In contrast, there are records for nineteen Dutch publications on economics in the same six years. None were published by influential figures nor of lasting importance. The Dutch faced the same trade depression, and similar concerns arose over the practice of exporting bullion. Bullion export was essential to both the Dutch East India and the Dutch-Baltic trades. The Dutch East India Company retained monopoly rights to the Eastern trade, but the Baltic trade was pursued by many merchants in a competitive market with little government intervention and no formally granted monopoly privileges. Eventually, the Dutch East India Company found an alternative source of silver in Japan, and no public debate arose over the issue.

A different controversy arose regarding the Dutch East India Company at around the same time as the trade depression. Reacting to the infrequent administration of dividends and uncertainty regarding the company's performance, irate investors first complained to directors, then to the government, and finally made public appeals in the form of pamphlets. These pamphlets were focused on the company's internal organization, not the conduct of trade. The States General closed ranks with the company directors, and dissenting investors (the *doleanten*) made little progress until they threatened to withdraw funding from the West India Company. This threat was effective because both the government and the Dutch East India Company were heavily invested in the venture.[88]

Interestingly, two of most notable Dutch figures for economic history in the early seventeenth century were affiliated with two of the few Dutch chartered companies. Both published their significant contributions prior to the 1620s. Grotius has had a lasting influence, but his work lies primarily in the field of law rather than economics. Grotius was employed by the Dutch East India Company, and his defense of their rights to trade in the East Indies was central to his vision of international law. William Usselincx was a founding member of the Dutch West India Company (in 1621). His work was written largely to promote the company's creation.[89] Later, Pieter

---

88. Paul Frentrop, *A History of Corporate Governance, 1602–2002* (Amsterdam: Deminor, 2003), 81–98.

89. Wagener, "Free Seas."

de la Court produced works of note to economic historians in his battle against the monopoly privileges granted to the Dutch East India Company.

The existence of both companies (the English and the Dutch) created a space and an incentive for powerful figures to voice their opinions on economic matters related to company operations. The importance of the companies magnified the importance of their spokespersons. As theorized by Albert Hirschman, there are three possible ways discontent can express itself: action, voice, and exit.[90] In the Netherlands, the close intertwining of interests among the state, the Dutch East India Company, and the Dutch West India Company allowed merchants to act. In England, the weaker position of merchants led to fewer opportunities for action. Faced with potentially troubling government intervention, and without the opportunity to effectively exit, company officials chose voice. Public debate gained traction because of widespread dissatisfaction with the practice of state-sanctioned monopolies; many merchants were excluded from but wanted access to the profits being made in the Eastern trade. In the Dutch Republic, state-granted monopolies were infrequent exceptions to the general rule of private guilds and partnerships. They were constituted for public rather than private benefit and were thus less subject to contestation. The discord that did arise was effectively handled by the politically powerful merchants with a stake in the matter.

The Seeds of Comparative Advantage

As recounted in more detail in chapter 2, in the 1660s cotton imports from India began to take off in England's domestic market. Consumers switched from woolen goods to cotton goods, and the woolen industry shrank. Unemployment spiked, poverty and starvation increased, and riots erupted on the streets. The English East India Company was again a prime target in the public debate over the crisis. The company was already under pressure to provide increased investment opportunities,[91] and critics were able to attack it on the grounds that it was responsible for importing cotton goods

---

90. Albert O. Hirschman, *Exit, Voice, and Loyalty: Responses to Decline in Firms, Organizations, and States* (Cambridge, MA: Harvard University Press, 1970).

91. D. W. Jones, *War and Economy in the Age of William III and Marlborough* (Oxford: B. Blackwell, 1988).

to England. Defenders of the company were placed in the difficult position of arguing that the development of the cotton trade would ultimately be more beneficial to the British economy than the short-term damage it was doing to the woolen industry. Charles Davenant took on this task in his *An Essay on the East-India-Trade* (1696), as did Gardner in *Some Reflections on a Pamphlet, intituled, England and East-India Inconsistent in Their Manufactures* (1697) and Josiah Child in his less sophisticated and less original *A New Discourse of Trade* (1693).[92] Both Davenant and Gardner argued that British workers were better off employed in other industries and that British consumers would benefit from purchasing cheaper goods—seeding the soil for David Ricardo's formulation of comparative advantage.[93] Child was one of the most powerful directors of the English East India Company in its long history. Davenant was reportedly angling for a position within the company.[94] In the end, these merchants did not win the debate. Protectionist policies were implemented, but only after a prolonged public debate that produced many important economic insights.

In the late seventeenth century, Dutch manufacturers also confronted the incredible popularity of Indian textiles. Although slower to introduce cotton goods to the European market, the Dutch East India Company began to ship textiles back to Europe by the late 1600s. Textile manufactures in Leiden were particularly hard hit, although Leiden was experiencing difficulties even prior to the rise in Indian cotton imports.[95] In the Dutch case, there was a brief phase of protectionism, in which the import of Indian textiles was prohibited, but it was quickly reversed.[96] Unlike in the English case, no significant economic contributions emerged from this controversy or the rapid increase in foreign textile production.

It was in the discourse of the 1690s in Britain that the seeds of comparative advantage were first developed. These seminal texts were responding to

92. Charles Davenant, *An Essay on the East-India-Trade. By the Author of The Essay upon Wayes and Means* (London, 1696), Making of the Modern World; [Gardner], *Some Reflections on a Pamphlet, intituled, England and East-India Inconsistent in Their Manufactures* (London, 1696 [1967?]), Making of the Modern World; Josiah Child, *A New Discourse of Trade, Wherein is Recommended several weighty Points relating to Companies of Merchants* (London: John Everingham, 1693), Making of the Modern World.

93. Irwin, *Against the Tide*, 54–55.

94. David Waddell, "Charles Davenant (1656–1714): A Biographical Sketch," *Economic History Review* 11, no. 2 (December 1958): 279–88, http://doi.org/10.1111/j.1468-0289.1958.tb01641.x.

95. De Vries and Van der Woude, *First Modern Economy*, 285.

96. Thomas, *Mercantilism*, 86–87.

several issues, including trade depressions and the difficulties involved in providing adequate support to the military during the Nine Years' War, but company actors were key figures in the debate. Chartered companies supported central interlocutors with material resources and gave them significant incentive to participate in the debate. The balance of power between state and merchants, companies and private traders, and London and outport merchants were all unsettled, so the stakes for shaping new policies and commercial practices were high.[97] Company privileges were contested, and large parts of the commercial population felt excluded from profitable sections of trade. English companies could not count on unwavering government support and necessarily turned to public discourse in order to persuade the government and the public that their private commercial activities were to the long-term benefit of the public. The enfranchised merchants of the Dutch Republic had little need to take their battles public.

CONCLUSION

Existing explanations of the early rise of economic thought have been based around increasing state capacity, the rise of the public sphere, and economic growth. These theories are not well supported by cross-national comparison. The Netherlands was more commercially advanced and economically developed than England. The Dutch Republic was a representative government that had larger state capacity, a proportionately larger print culture, and a proportionately larger number of universities. Although the Dutch were better positioned to withstand economic disruptions, they weathered the same trade depressions and economic dislocations that affected the English. These events did not translate into sustained public discussion of commerce or trade and did not generate deep economic insights in the Netherlands. Britain lagged slightly behind the Dutch and therefore may have had reason to work hard to articulate a path by which to catch up. This situation, however, would apply to many other European countries that did not experience a sizable increase of public interest in economic topics. Economic dislocations, depressions, growth, and the rise of the nation-state

---

97. Robert Brenner, *Merchants and Revolution: Commercial Change, Political Conflict, and London's Overseas Traders, 1550–1653* (London: Verso, 2003); and Pincus, *1688: The First Modern Revolution.*

and civil sphere may have been necessary causes, but the case comparison I have employed here strongly suggests that they were not sufficient.

The important source of variation between the cases lies in the difference in state-merchant relations and the existence of large private ventures with state-granted monopoly privileges. Nearly all of the recognized contributions to economics produced in the seventeenth century—those singled out for attention by economic historians—were embroiled in debates over the rights, prerogatives, and benefits of these chartered companies. Even in the Dutch Republic, the most significant contributions were produced in relation to company trade. Such contributions, however, occurred at a much lower rate in the Netherlands.

Overall, the comparison supports the argument that state-merchant relations—particularly the prevalence of chartered companies and the lack of merchant representation—played a central role in the development of economic thought in England in the seventeenth century. Companies formed for private benefit gained legitimacy by arguing that they contributed to the public good. And the distance between state and commercial actors led to efforts to bridge that gulf through public debate. All of this suggests that changing patterns and increasing formalization of state-merchant relations generated a new discursive form: an empirical and abstract version of economics grounded in the values of national prosperity and economic growth.

CONCLUSION

Today, the discipline of economics is mainly concerned with economic growth. In one sense, equity is baked into current economics. Free exchange takes place only when the terms for each party are seen as equal—or at least mutually advantageous. But there is another sense in which the old medieval concerns for fair conduct, just price, and overt concern for the impoverished fell out of focus. They were picked up in large part, later in time, by sociology and its attention to the problems of inequality. But in the shorter term, the moral framework of just price and equity in exchange was taken over by an insistent emphasis on the importance of national growth and prosperity. Companies and politics had everything to do with that change.

In this book, I have argued that the roots of this change lay in the complexities of the relationship between the English state and its merchants in the early modern era. Courtship, dance, negotiation, or contest—no matter how it is characterized, the interaction between the state and merchants was central to the development of the new literature. The transformation and proliferation of economic thought arose from attempts to bridge the gap between the state and commercial spheres. It was Harrison White who showed me the importance of difference and distance in the creation of language.[1] Being different is the condition that creates the

1. Harrison C. White, *Identity and Control: A Structural Theory of Social Action* (Princeton, NJ: Princeton University Press, 1992).

need for communication. This process plays itself out differently at various scales of social existence and institutional contexts. It will not always result in published works, the advancement of scientific knowledge, and a public discourse, but it has been essential for my understanding of the causes behind this particular change in the culture of economic thought. Merchant political marginalization is an indispensable component of the explanation. The rise of the chartered companies plays a slightly different causal role: it is not clear that it was indispensable, but it does appear to have been a central catalyst.

This book has provided several types of empirical evidence in support of this explanation, first describing the change that took place and then showing how state-merchant relations were responsible. Chapter 1 portrays the corpus-wide shift in economic thought that was underway in the seventeenth century. Authors turned from the moral concerns of the scholastic toward the problems of trade, finance, and the nation-state. Just price, usury, poverty, sin, corruption, and equity were replaced as central issues by a new interest in debating corporate privileges, specie flow, and the import and export of manufactured goods.

Chapter 2 explores two significant debates in order to illuminate the microprocesses animating publication. Who are the authors? What is at stake for them? What are their strategies? A few themes emerge. Debates over company privileges or behavior were common. The authors often framed these debates in terms of national interest. They also began to draw upon techniques of empiricism, scientific explanation, and logic to shore up their arguments. The works took on an empirical cast; tables and statistics began to appear as central pillars of larger arguments. Authors began to see themselves as contributing to a larger, comprehensive body of knowledge about economic processes. Laws were formulated and debated. The literature was casting off its Christian trappings and taking on a new mantle of abstract, rational—even scientific—expertise.

Chapter 3 provides the institutional and organizational information necessary to piece together a historically specific theory behind the transformation of economic thought. The explanation is relational: it does not rest upon the intrinsic characteristics of either the state or the merchants, but instead on the way they interacted. The chapter focuses on the relational and organizational conditions that were unique aspects of England's state-merchant relations. Merchants in seventeenth-century England were not well represented in the state and did not have great power to set commercial policy. Merchants lacked the kind of voice they believed they should have in state affairs. As a recourse, they turned to the public sphere. They used publications to amplify their voice and persuade elites and their constituents. In trying to reach the state, the merchants wrapped their work in appeals to the security and prosperity of the nation and the Crown. The result was a new moral framework centered on national wealth.

One topic seemed to excite merchants like no other—the special rights and privileges granted to the chartered companies. The companies raised the stakes of debate and fractured the merchant class. Free trade became a central topic of debate—carried out throughout the century. The monopoly privileges bestowed upon corporations stimulated great angst and controversy. And the corporations themselves provided resources that encouraged public debate. At times, companies set up their own printing presses to publish pamphlets. Many hired authors to make public arguments. Others simply encouraged their own principals to write books defending their activities. The culture of debate and rhetoric internal to the companies fostered this type of self-expression as well.

These changes were directly related to the increasing number of merchant authors. Merchants and their surrogates had begun to participate in the economic discourse in a more significant way than ever before. Merchants brought their data-rich empirical mindset to the texts they wrote—along with their knowledge of how trade and exchange were actually conducted. They often wrote in abstract terms in order to hide the way their discursive positions dovetailed with their material interests. Sometimes this strategy must have been taken with corrupt intent, to convince the state to take a course of action that was good for them but bad for others. Other times, they may just have known that their arguments would never otherwise be taken seriously. Either way, the abstraction lent itself to a more systematic, formalistic view of economic processes.

Chapter 4 shows that merchants were increasingly authoring texts over the course of the seventeenth century and were directly responsible for the second largest proportion of texts written by any class or occupational group. It is very possible that they were indirectly responsible for even more. By the end of the century, they were authoring more than 40 percent of the texts on trade and finance, a rate much higher than any other group. And these figures, based on known authorship, almost certainly undercount merchant contributions because merchants were more likely to publish anonymously or to hire professional authors to carry on their public debates by proxy.

The second part of the chapter turns from the demographic to the structural, providing systematic network data in support of the relational aspects of the argument. The company and committee worlds stimulated authorship. Authors of economic texts tended to be more deeply embedded, with high or at least average connections in both these networks—more deeply connected particularly in the council network. Despite this, merchants occupied a marginal position in the state's trade policy apparatus. Network analysis of trade committee membership shows that merchants held less prominent positions than other groups serving on the councils and committees of trade. Central in the commercial world but consigned to the outskirts of state operations, merchants had to bridge the gap between arenas of action.

Chapters 5 and 6 test the structural and organizational theories temporally and comparatively. Chapter 5 uses time series analysis to analyze the effect of the increasing number of chartered companies and rates of merchant representation in Parliament on economic text publications. Controlling for a variety of other factors, the only significant associations are to companies and merchant representation: an increase in the number of companies is associated with an increase in publications one year later and a decrease in merchant representation is associated with an increase in publications one year later.

The time series analysis compares subsequent years to each other. Another, more common approach in historical sociology is to compare similar cases or events. For example, in order to understand the causes of regime change, nations that have experienced regime change may be compared with nations that have not. The outcome of interest—the abrupt increase in economic works coupled with a qualitative transition in their contents—has not taken place in many countries. Indeed, in the seventeenth century, it was a singularly English phenomenon. To provide an additional test of the hypotheses, in chapter 6 I compare England with its close competitor, the Dutch Republic, over the same time period. Existing theories about the roots of the development of economic thought have generally been formulated with England in mind. They do not do a good job of predicting why the Netherlands did not experience a similar intellectual blossoming. Indeed, they tend to suggest that the Netherlands should have had an earlier and larger boom in economic thought. Instead, the comparison strongly supports the hypothesis that merchant political marginalization and the fractures created by the companies were crucial to the process. Dutch merchants had much greater representation within the government and therefore little need to take their arguments to the public sphere. They also were much less exercised about chartered companies, because these exclusionary and highly privileged associations was much less common in the Dutch Republic.

In all, several layers of quantitative and qualitative evidence—textual, structural, temporal, cross-sectional, and historical—indicate that two components of the relationship between the state and merchants—the companies and marginal political representation—played central roles in the transition to the new mode of economic thought. The analysis does not suggest that other factors were not also important. The declining moral authority of the church, the expansion of overseas trade, the rise of parliamentary politics—all of these may have been necessary conditions. What the analysis indicates, however, is that those factors were not sufficient conditions.

WHAT IS NEW ABOUT THIS ARGUMENT

Formulating these ideas about what caused economic thought to flourish was the result of applying new methods to studying an old phenomenon. My approach differs from other existing work on the problem in that it is more systematic, uses comparative methods, and focuses on providing a causal—though neither simple nor monocausal—explanation for the outcome.

The topic model used not just the work of the few relatively famous authors picked out by Joseph Schumpeter or other economic historians; it used all the machine-readable works available from 1580 to 1720, a total of 2,353 texts. It is very difficult for the human brain to compare that many texts against each other in a systematic and consistent way. That is, after all, 5,534,256 paired comparisons. A computer has a much easier time with these kinds of large-scale comparisons, given expert guidance—where expertise in the texts themselves is the most important aspect of that guidance. The great advantage of the assistance provided by computational methods is a more comprehensive evaluation of a larger proportion of works, which shifts the analysis from a great-man theory to a more realistic assessment of scientific progress as the result of large-scale group processes.

This approach does more than shift the theoretical lens to something more sociological than a belief in individual genius. For one, it avoids the instability of interpretation caused by cherry-picking. There have been waves of history in which mercantilism goes in and out of favor. This ripple effect is due in large part to using the lens of contemporary economics to identify which texts of the past have made the largest contributions. Because contemporary economics changes over time, the contributions deemed most important from the past also change. Considering as many texts as possible, without picking out only exceptional works, leads to a more stable and reliable appraisal of what advances actually occurred, which leads to a second related advantage.

Corpus-wide assessment focuses inquiry on truly important cultural shifts, rather than on isolated and uncelebrated contributions. I have always been struck by the story of Antonio Serra. Serra was an Italian thinker who authored the text *Breva trattato delle cause che possono far abbondaree li regni d'oro e d'argento dove non sono miniere* (1613). This title has been recently translated by the eminent historian of economic thought Sophus Reinert as "A short treatise on the wealth and poverty of nations."[2] Others have translated it as "A short treatise on the causes that make kingdoms abound in gold and silver even in the absence of mines." These different translations clearly locate Serra in different positions in the history of economic thought, with the more recent one giving him greater weight and prescience. Either way, Serra has been widely credited as the first real economic thinker and appears to have developed a theory of the balance of trade and currency valuation prior to Thomas Mun's work on the topic. He was a brilliant and sophisticated man—more sophisticated than Mun— who made important conceptual advances for his time.

So, you might legitimately ask, why am I not considering the birth of modern economic thought in Italy through the lens of Serra's treatise? The answer is that Serra wrote his treatise in prison for treason, and his work lay unread and undiscovered until sometime in the mid-eighteenth century.[3] Even geniuses need an audience. It is possible to credit Serra's genius, but

2. Sophus A. Reinert, *Translating Empire: Emulation and the Origins of Political Economy* (Cambridge, MA: Harvard University Press, 2011), ProQuest Ebook Central.

3. Theodore A. Sumberg, "Antonio Serra: A Neglected Herald of the Acquisitive System," *American Journal of Economics and Sociology* 50, no. 3 (July 1991): 372.

it is impossible to credit him with the advances in economic thought that took place in the seventeenth century. Serra had no immediate followers. When he was alive—and even long after his death—no one debated the principles of his argument, and he did not contribute to a larger transformation of Italian economic thought in the early modern era.

Serra is an extreme case, but no matter how brilliant someone is, if their ideas are not picked up by others, they are not transformative thinkers. No one transforms thought without influencing other people. A focus on the corpus of economic thought is consistent with the fact that real advances in economic thought are not the result of a few great individuals in isolation. Rather, such advances are the sum total of the contributions of a large number of authors and readers creating a context in which a new, meaningful, and creative dialogue emerges involving many actors. One should consider not only the great, groundbreaking works of Mun, Petty, and Davenant but also the many other, less innovative, more mundane works that stimulated and contributed to the more profound insights of greater works. A systematic approach captures the larger ecology of research that is essential to the advancement of a discipline.

While a systematic approach sets me apart from authors like Schumpeter (who, I would argue, was very much a cherry-picker!), it is not a departure in spirit from other thinkers, such as Appleby, Finkelstein, Schabas, who undertook wide, though unassisted, reviews of the corpus. And the innovative work of Sophus Reinert, who did a systematic assessment of which economic tracts were translated and republished in other nations, should be noted.[4] Still, the potential benefits of using topic models to better understand the history of economic thought—and other topics in the evolution and transformation of thought and culture—are only beginning to be tapped.[5]

I combine this corpus-wide approach with comparative methods that have been even more essential to my understanding of the problem. I began this project with the idea that the growth of overseas trade, early

---

4. Sophus A. Reinert, "The Empire of Emulation: A Quantitative Analysis of Economic Translations in the European World, 1500–1849," in *The Political Economy of Empire in the Early Modern World*, ed. Sophus A. Reinert and Pernille Røge, 105–28 (Basingstoke, UK: Palgrave Macmillan, 2013).

5. One recent and exciting work in a later period is Cheryl Schonhardt-Bailey, *From the Corn Laws to Free Trade: Interests, Ideas, and Institutions in Historical Perspective* (Cambridge, MA: MIT Press, 2006).

modern globalization, and precolonial contact with Asia and the Americas had to be central to the efflorescence of economic thought. The moment I applied a comparative lens to the project, those ideas were fundamentally uprooted. In fact, once considered from a comparative perspective, most existing theories about why this moment occurred fell completely flat. Rapidly expanding global overseas trade was widespread across European, but the sudden increase in economic thought was confined to England. Precisely because the economic resurgence was ultimately an English phenomenon, most historians of economic thought focusing on this question have kept their inquiry to within England's borders. Those works that cover other areas operate more like calendars of economic thought in different nations or are meant to be purely descriptive, such as Schumpeter's *History of Economic Analysis*. Only Sophus Reinert's work has made analytical use of national difference—but in these cases it is actually the relationship between nations that is the object of his inquiry. Thus, because it has been so rarely used, the comparative framework was extremely revealing of what had been otherwise hidden.

Comparison is often motivated by an interest in causality. Since the second half of the twentieth century, sociology has become very interested in identifying causes. Causal identification has been a central area of methodological research that has greatly influenced all of the substantive areas of the field. History is much more descriptive. Most of the previous work on this early modern era has been done by historians. It follows that the mission of this book is fundamentally different from that of many similar existing works written by historians because, as a social scientist, I have the tendency to want to identify causes. Historians working on the era generally offer some brief explanation in passing as to why this transformation occurred, but the bulk of their inquiry is focused on describing what occurred—not assessing which factor was most important in bringing it about. Rigorously establishing causal claims in a historical context is difficult, and not something I can claim to have ultimately achieved given the current standards of causal estimation. Certainly, there is no possibility for a random trial. But concerns about causality have influenced my approach, and I believe adapting statistical, structural, and comparative methods to the historical context have provided significant new insight.

While other sociologists who might have employed similar methods have not addressed this same historical puzzle, I have very much been building upon a rich and insightful literature on economic thought, the development of the public sphere, and cultural and institutional transformation more generally. A large body of work within sociology has explored the links between institutional settings and the contents of economic thought.[6] Sociologists dealing with economic theory have identified recurring institutional and contextual features that stimulate or direct economic discourse—in both different nations and different time periods. Frank Dobbin has shown how political culture can drive industrial policy.[7] Marion Fourcade has shown that political culture and conceptions of political order shape the character of economics—also implying that economic thought varies across political cultures.[8] Somers and Block revealed the connection between trends in economic thought and larger cultural logics.[9] Sarah Babb linked global trade liberalization to the adoption of neoliberal economics in contexts with heavy dependencies on foreign trade.[10] And Monica Prasad found that that the neoliberal shift in the United States was due to political contention and disruption.[11] These scholars have convincingly shown that culture, politics, international trade, and political contention affect the trajectory of economic thought. I have added to this work by reaching earlier to an inflection point where economics diverged from moral philosophy and scholasticism. It is in a sense an origins story—the beginnings of a new discursive field.

6. See, for example, Sarah Babb, *Managing Mexico: Economists from Nationalism to Neoliberalism* (Princeton, NJ: Princeton University Press, 2004); Nitsan Chorev, "A Fluid Divide: Domestic and International Factors in US Trade Policy Formation," *Review of International Political Economy* 144, no. 4 (October 2007): 653–89, https://doi.org/10.1080/09692290701475395; Marion Fourcade-Gourinchas and Sarah L. Babb, "The Rebirth of the Liberal Creed: Paths to Neoliberalism in Four Countries," *American Journal of Sociology* 108, no. 3 (November 2002): 533–79, https://doi.org/10.1086/367922; Marion Fourcade, *Economists and Societies: Discipline and Profession in the United States, Britain, and France, 1890s to 1990s* (Princeton, NJ: Princeton University Press, 2009); Monica Prasad, *The Politics of Free Markets: The Rise of Neoliberal Economic Policies in Britain, France, Germany, and the United States* (Chicago: University of Chicago Press, 2006); and Margaret R. Somers, *Genealogies of Citizenship: Markets, Statelessness, and the Right to Have Rights* (Cambridge: Cambridge University Press, 2008). Frank Dobbin, *Forging Industrial Policy: The United States; Britain, and France in the Railway Age* (Cambridge: Cambridge University Press, 1994.

7. Dobbin, *Forging Industrial Policy*.

8. Fourcade, *Economists and Societies*.

9. Margaret R. Somers and Fred Block, "From Poverty to Perversity: Ideas, Markets, and Institutions Over 200 Years of Welfare Debate," *American Sociological Review* 70, no. 2 (April 2005): 260–87, https://doi.org/10.1177/000312240507000204.

10. Babb, *Managing Mexico*.

11. Prasad, *Politics of Free Markets*.

Economic historians and historians of economic thought have, of course, looked as far back as I and noticed the transformative nature of the period. And there is overlap between my arguments and their insights. Andrea Finkelstein, for one, attributes the sudden increase in economic texts to material conditions: the rapidly changing economic system and the particular role of Parliament in English government. We agree that the ability of merchants to appeal to Parliament was central to the rise of economic thought.[12] But Finkelstein locates the dynamic driving the development of economic thought in the internal constraints of the discourse. She argues that mercantilist economic discourse had internal inconsistencies that had to be resolved, driving new works, new logics, and new ideas. In her telling, William Petty, Josiah Child, and John Locke created new models of economic systems in an attempt to reconcile the materialist assumption that economic actors were self-interested with the idea of a harmonious universe. Their failure to completely resolve this question led to a new set of attempts by Dudley North, Nicholas Barbon, and Charles Davenant. It is a beautiful way to explore the literature but, for me, does not explain why this was an English phenomenon.

I also overlap with Perry Gauci, Max Beer, and William Letwin's class-based accounts. However, I ultimately find it impossible to explain what occurred without considering additional market and state institutions and the relationships between them. In his book *The Politics of Trade*, Gauci argued that the central underlying theme of political economy in the seventeenth century was the moral status of merchants and that the economic theory produced in that century was an outgrowth of the merchants' needs, or perhaps desires, to justify themselves in the public eye and raise the status of their profession. "Recognition of the important functions of merchants begged wider questions concerning the social and political role of the overseas trader. . . . Thus, increasing professionalism prompted a more searching debate about the state's response to the expansion of trade which went far beyond the realm of the didactic economic press."[13] William Letwin made the related argument that the origins of a scientific economic

12. Andrea Finkelstein, *Harmony and the Balance: An Intellectual History of Seventeenth-Century English Economic Thought* (Ann Arbor: University of Michigan Press, 2009), 4.

13. Perry Gauci, *The Politics of Trade: The Overseas Merchant in State and Society, 1660–1720* (Oxford: Oxford University Press, 2001), 174.

discourse lay in the status problems of the merchants who wrote economic texts.[14] The distinction between Letwin and Gauci is that Letwin emphasized the specific character of the discourse—its new overtones of rationality, abstraction, and empiricism. Suspicion haunted the efforts of merchants to influence economic policy because of their low social and moral status. Letwin argued that anonymity could not fully protect the legitimacy of the arguments they made, and in the end, the solution they found to defend their arguments was to incorporate a scientific method in which all arguments must be clearly and logically constructed out of evidently true beginning propositions. Letwin concluded that "in the search for a way of dispelling the problem of special pleading, a scientific method was hit on. The needs of rhetoric brought forth the method of economic theory."[15] Max Beer, writing much earlier, did not provide as detailed a theory, but he was consistent in sentiment, describing the texts as "one long campaign for the political control of trade and commerce by the merchant class."[16]

These three arguments (Gauci's, Letwin's, and Beer's) are clearly not inconsistent with my findings or interpretation. Where I differ is in arguing that the low status of merchants alone cannot provide a sufficient explanation. Merchants had long had low status. It was the particular institutional and organizational setting that triggered the very specific activity of publishing in the public sphere.

By offering a more detailed explanation of the institutional setting, I am following in the theoretical footsteps of Joyce Appleby. Appleby's *Economic Thought and Ideology in Seventeenth Century England* is a great classic of the history of economic thought.[17] The book is a beautifully written investigation of the contents of early modern economic works and their underlying conceptual foundations. While it is not her main focus, Appleby does allocate a small number of paragraphs to speculation about the possible causes of this efflorescence. Here she emphasizes the importance of economic development and growth. She makes the important conceptual

---

14. William Letwin, *The Origins of Scientific Economics: English Economic Thought, 1660–1776* (London: Methuen, 1963).

15. Letwin, *Origins of Scientific Economics*, 97.

16. Max Beer, *Early British Economics from the XIIIth to the Middle of the XVIIIth Century* (London: George Allen & Unwin, 1938), 186.

17. Joyce Oldham Appleby, *Economic Thought and Ideology in Seventeenth-Century England* (Los Angeles: Figueroa Press, 1978).

distinction, however, that the impact derived not from economic growth in itself, but rather from the way the expanding market was transforming social relations across England.[18] While I reject the idea that economic growth was a sufficient cause, I believe I am advancing her larger theoretical approach by thinking through the effect of the institutional structures of society. I just dig more deeply into the institutional components of market development that she emphasized. She was explicit in encouraging the further exploration of institutional and organizational settings and their dynamics on ideological transformation. I hope she would have enjoyed this book.

There is nothing in my account that suggests these past works of scholarship are wrong. I would argue, however, that that they had not yet offered a completely specified argument. Economic growth, self-interest, and the status anxiety of merchants did play a role in this development, but these factors were not restricted to England. The sudden rise of the chartered companies and the merchants' marginal political representation were aspects of their lived experience that created a situation in which publishing made sense. And the evidence bears out their impact.

IMPLICATIONS

The most direct consequence of this configuration of merchant-state relations was a vital and flourishing literature on economics, but other implications follow for how we might think about the expansion of the public sphere, the role (or non-role) of self-interest in economic theory, the importance of this era of economic thought, more general processes of cultural change, and the goals of economic inquiry.

The Expansion of the Public Sphere

First, the upsurge in economic texts also affected the public sphere more generally, expanding its territory and range. Habermas explained the rise of the public sphere through two phenomena and their relationship to each other: the privatization of the economic functions of the household and

18. Appleby, *Economic Thought and Ideology*, 35.

the increasing power of the state.[19] However, he neglected a critical component of this process: the rise of privately held companies. The structural transformation of nonstate organizations that existed outside of individual households had a major impact on the expansion of the public sphere. Whereas Habermas says the public sphere resulted from the privatization of economic life, at least one part of that emerging public sphere was more closely related to the corporatization of economic life.

The Role of Self-Interest

Second, what does this tell us about the role of self-interest in economic analysis? Because the bulk of the innovative new economic thought in the seventeenth century was driven by self-interested individuals, some might take this to mean that naked self-interest is really behind the development of economic theory and that, by extension, economics is somehow corrupt or not a "true science." This would be a very serious misinterpretation of what I am trying to express.

As I see it, even if self-interest had been the main deciding and sufficient factor behind the emergence of this literature, it would not follow that economic thought suffered because of it. The English mercantilists are criticized for being undisciplined—i.e., logically incoherent as a group—and most of all for being nakedly self-interested. But these characteristics are part of what made the English authors so innovative. Their contributions were unlike any existing discourse—and that is why they were an important turning point. It was the combination of the new, undisciplined, often petty, and frequently self-serving works on commerce with the older, more sober, and methodical philosophical tradition that made economics what is it today—a logically grounded, theoretically rich, empirical discipline about the satisfaction of material needs that provides invaluable tools for averting painful financial catastrophes and improving life quality for billions.

More to the point, however, self-interest figures into this story in the same way that rationality figures into the story—as a background assumption about what motivates people to act in different ways in different

19. Jürgen Habermas, *The Structural Transformation of the Public Sphere: An Inquiry Into a Category of Bourgeois Society*, trans. Thomas Burger with the assistance of Frederick Lawrence (Cambridge, MA: MIT Press, 1991); originally published as *Strukturwandel der Öffentlichkeit* (Darmstadt and Neuwied: Hermann Luchterhand Verlag, 1962).

historical, social, and institutional contexts. Self-interest alone does little to explain the transformation and expansion of the literature. To illustrate, consider the work of economists Robert Ekelund, Robert Hébert, and Robert Tollison on responses to usury in the medieval period.[20] A naive perspective might assume that the scholastic literature on usury was motivated by the otherworldly concerns of just price and virtuous conduct in the eyes of the Christian god. As Ekelund, Hébert, and Tollison pointed out however, the Catholic Church was both a religious organization and a complex monetary institution that borrowed and lent large sums of money. They argued that the church patrolled the practice of usury in order to selectively enforce regulations that worked in its financial favor—i.e., to improve the terms of its loans as both debtor and creditor.[21] The inference to be drawn is that the literature on just price, which wrestled with the technicalities of new financial instruments in order to determine whether an exchange was equitable, was in fact part of an effort on the part of church to obtain the most favorable terms for its own financial transactions. If their thesis is correct, the relationship between the self-interested motivations of actors and the financial literature was not unique to the seventeenth century.

The economic literature of the seventeenth century was unique, however, both quantitatively and qualitatively. It was the institutional environment in which actors operated that changed over time—not the existence of self-interested justifications. The larger point is that it is very hard to understand why people take any action without assuming some motivation that derives from self-interest. It is fairly safe to say that all people are motivated by some mixture of self-interest, family interest, concern for others, and other moral and religious beliefs. This truth is not restricted to the production of economic thought in the seventeenth century. Just as now, some of the authors were more public-minded and some were more duplicitous, but there was a range of motivations and behaviors—all of which had at least a small fragment of self-interest in there somewhere. In the end, changes in innate behavioral responses are just too rare to have much explanatory power for social and cultural change.

20. Robert B. Ekelund, Jr., Robert F. Hébert, and Robert D. Tollison, "An Economic Model of the Medieval Church: Usury as a Form of Rent Seeking," *Journal of Law, Economics, & Organization* 5, no. 2 (Autumn 1989): 307–31.

21. Ekelund, Hébert, and Tollison, "Economic Model."

Mercantilism Matters

One of the problems with the idea of self-interest is that it has too often been used to dismiss the work of the mercantilists. I hope to have convinced readers that mercantilist writings and authors should *not* be consigned to the dustbin of history. Most early work in the history of economic thought either ignored or sharply criticized this era. Jacob Viner and William Allen have been particularly dismissive.[22] Eli Heckscher began his two-volume work on the broader topic of mercantilism by claiming it never existed in the first place, and E. A. J. Johnson described the English works of this era as "a variegated fabric of economic ideas unsound and inartistic as an entity," though he conceded that it contained "much that was sound and worth preserving."[23] But even later authors such as Keith Tribe and Margaret Schabas have contested the value of mercantilist contributions to economic thought.[24]

On the other hand, there has been a twenty-first-century movement to appreciatively reevaluate mercantilism and seventeenth-century English economic thinkers. Perry Gauci has been an important figure in this movement, as are Lars Magnusson, Philip Stern, Carl Wennerlind, and Steven Pincus. I would like add additional support to their efforts. The seventeenth century was crucial to setting the moral agenda for economics for centuries to come and is worthy of further study.

Recognizing the importance of the seventeenth century also implies a reevaluation of the work of Adam Smith. Adam Smith is, of course, famously known as both the founder of classical economics and the original champion of free trade and laissez-faire capitalism. And if you dismiss all of the economic writings of the seventeenth and early eighteenth centuries as incoherent nonsense, then this is a fairly apt representation. But acknowledging the contributions of seventeenth-century economic thinkers also dramatically alters how Smith's contributions should be viewed.

22. Jacob Viner, "Mercantilist Thought," in *International Encyclopedia of the Social Sciences*, ed. David L. Sills, vol. 4, 435–42 (New York: Macmillan, 1968); and William R. Allen, "Modern Defenders of Mercantilist Theory," *History of Political Economy* 2, no. 2 (Fall 1970): 381–97, https://doi.org/10.1215/00182702-2-2-381.

23. Eli Heckscher, *Mercantilism* (London: George Allen & Unwin, 1935); and E. A. J. Johnson, *Predecessors of Adam Smith: The Growth of British Economic Thought* (New York: Prentice-Hall, 1937), 4.

24. Keith Tribe, *Land, Labour and Economic Discourse* (London: Routledge & Kegan Paul, 1978); and Margaret Schabas, *The Natural Origins of Economics* (Chicago: University of Chicago Press, 2009).

In the first place, Smith's work was not a complete break with existing work. As has already been noted, it was highly influenced by and somewhat derivative of these earlier authors. This fact has been acknowledged by several historians of economic thought.[25] Geoffrey Poitras went so far as to cast Smith as an unfortunate detour from the intellectual progress made by this earlier generation: "How much different would nineteenth century economic progress have been if Smith had spent considerable time musing about the applications of insurance techniques to topics such as social security and bank deposits, instead of pontificating on scholarly problems such as 'value in use' versus 'value in exchange'?"[26]

Poitras's point is an apt one because there was one very significant way in which Smith diverged from other mercantilist writers. As has been widely noted, Smith had a more nuanced approach to free trade than was widely acknowledged in the twentieth century. He was not against all state regulation of trade; he was against the state regulation of trade that benefited the rich to the disadvantage of the poor.[27] Smith agitated against state regulation

25. Gary M. Anderson and Robert D. Tollison, "Sir James Steuart as the Apotheosis of Mercantilism and His Relation to Adam Smith," *Southern Economic Journal* 51, no. 2 (October 1984): 456–68, https://doi.org/10.2307/1057824; Mark Blaug, *Economic Theory in Retrospect* (Cambridge: Cambridge University Press, 1962), 31; Raymond de Roover, "Monopoly Theory Prior to Adam Smith: A Revision," *Quarterly Journal of Economics* 65, no. 4 (November 1951): 492–524, https://doi.org/10.2307/1882577; William D. Grampp, "The Liberal Elements in English Mercantilism," *Quarterly Journal of Economics* 66, no. 4 (November 1952): 465–501, https://doi.org/10.2307/1882100, 499; Alexander Gray, *The Development of Economic Doctrine: An Introductory Survey* (London: Longmans, Green, 1933), https://mises.org/library/development-economic-doctrine-introductory-survey; Terence W. Hutchison, *Before Adam Smith: The Emergence of Political Economy, 1662–1776* (Oxford: B. Blackwell, 1988); John A. La Nauze, "The Substance of Adam Smith's Attack on Mercantilism," in *Adam Smith: Critical Assessments*, ed. John Cunningham Wood, vol. 4, *Specialised Topics* (London: Routledge, 2004), 55–57; Lars Magnusson, *Mercantilism: The Shaping of an Economic Language* (London: Routledge, 1994), 2; Salim Rashid, "Smith, Steuart, and Mercantilism: Comment," *Southern Economic Journal* 52, no. 3 (January 1986): 843–52, https://doi.org/10.2307/1059280; Salim Rashid, *The Myth of Adam Smith* (Cheltenham, UK: Edward Elgar, 1998); and Joseph A. Schumpeter, *History of Economic Analysis: With a New Introduction*, Rev. ed. (New York: Oxford University Press, 1954), 184.

26. Geoffrey Poitras, *The Early History of Financial Economics, 1478–1776: From Commercial Arithmetic to Life Annuities and Joint Stocks* (Cheltenham, UK: Edward Elgar, 2000), 3–4.

27. Craig Muldrew, "From Commonwealth to Public Opulence: The Redefinition of Wealth and Government in Early Modern Britain," in *Remaking English Society: Social Relations and Social Change in Early Modern England*, ed. Steve Hindle, Alexandra Shepard, and John Walter (Woodbridge, UK: Boydell Press, 2015), 317–40; Elizabeth Anderson, "Adam Smith on Equality," in *Adam Smith: His Life, Thought, and Legacy*, ed. Ryan Patrick Hanley (Princeton, NJ: Princeton University Press, 2016), 157–72; and Amartya Sen, "Adam Smith and Economic Development," in *Adam Smith: His Life, Thought, and Legacy*, ed. Ryan Patrick Hanley (Princeton, NJ: Princeton University Press, 2016), 281–302.

because it served the rich at the expense of the poor. He attacked monopolies, racketeering, tariffs and bounties that raised the price of consumer goods and criticized forced labor, sharecropping, slavery, and the system of imperialism that extracted so much at such great cost from colonized lands and peoples.[28] In Amartya Sen's words, *The Wealth of Nations* was "his attempt to marry the pursuit of the interests of the poor and the deprived with combined use of the market economy and well-chosen state intervention."[29]

For a reader familiar with the economic literature two centuries prior to the publication of *The Wealth of Nations*, what is most striking about Smith was his reincorporation of philosophical and moral concerns into a literature on trade that had largely left these matters by the wayside. Even the more advanced thinkers of the seventeenth century believed that low wages were necessary to induce labor participation and secure good terms of trade overseas.[30] Their greatest concerns regarding the poor were to find means by which to coerce them into performing cheaper labor. This project was entirely opposite to Smith's views, in which he repeatedly championed the rights of the poor and advocated for benevolence.[31] Looked at from a perspective that includes the seventeenth century, Smith was not advocating for unfettered growth. He was trying to reintroduce the moral framework of justice, equity, and benevolence that had dominated the literature in the medieval era but had been discarded by seventeenth-century merchant-authors. He wanted to bring moral concerns back into a conversation that had pivoted to national wealth and prosperity.

A long-standing and faulty interpretation of Smith as an advocate of unfettered capital accumulation is one of the costs of forgetting history. If we excise the mercantilists from the history of economic thought, this kind of interpretation of Smith becomes possible. The truth, however, is that he was pushing against a strong tide heading in that direction. Understanding how Smith fits into the larger history of economic thought offers a new perspective on his very significant accomplishments. A Smithian revision is underway.[32] Perhaps a reappreciation of his legacy will help us to deal

28. Elizabeth Anderson, "Adam Smith on Equality," 159.

29. Sen, "Smith and Economic Development."

30. Jacob Viner, *Studies in the Theory of International Trade* (New York: Harper & Brothers, 1937), 56–57.

31. Muldrew, "Commonwealth to Public Opulence," 338–39.

32. Ryan Patrick Hanley, ed., *Adam Smith: His Life, Thought, and Legacy* (Princeton, NJ: Princeton University Press, 2016).

with some of the more adverse consequences of our particular pattern of economic growth.

CULTURAL SHIFTS

Currently, the reappreciation of Smith is limited mainly to academics specializing in economic history and thought. Will there be a large-scale public shift in the way Smith is conceived? Could the words most often associated with Smith go from "free market" to "moral economy"?

This shift could be a major transformation involving a move from one value, freedom, to another, morality, where morality stands for something closer to ethical conduct toward others than any principled value system. If this shift took place, it would be similar to the one that occurred in the seventeenth century—a major change in moral frameworks—although it seems to be moving in the opposite direction in terms of specific values. If generalizable, the evidence and analysis I have presented should provide a useful tool for evaluating the likelihood of this or other major changes in literatures, or even the emergence of new styles of discourse.

Clearly the question cannot be whether marginal merchant representation in the state and a resurgence of chartered companies might change the path of economic discourse. The question instead could be whether a marginally represented population might be triggered into an outpouring of public sentiment by some change in their relationship with the state.

Many of the people interested in the legacy of Adam Smith are academics. Could universities play a similar role to that of the chartered companies in the earlier shift? Universities provide a platform to individuals that provides resources. They differ from the companies, however, in tending (I hope) to increase authors' legitimacy, rather than decrease it. They foster an internal community of debate and even serve—at least in the United States—as a focal point for controversy. And one thing that seventeenth-century merchants and twenty-first-century academics have largely in common is the feeling of being underrepresented in the state. Indeed, academics often publish books with the hope of influencing state policy. So, in some sense, there is a similar dynamic already at work.

But this contemporary dynamic does not seem similar enough to predict a contemporary shift in thought about Adam Smith and the path to national prosperity. Other differences make it less likely. The chartered companies were a new institutional development, and brought with them new habits of mind. Universities have been around since before the chartered companies, so there is no new population or organizational form shaking up established norms. There is instead a somewhat cyclical discourse that regularly issues challenges to many different established perspectives. Because of the institutionalized nature of the discourse, its impact on the public sphere may be diminished relative to that of the merchants of the early modern era.

In a sense, the conversation between academics and the state has been going on for long enough that other people tune it out. In the seventeenth century, the conversation between merchants and the state was much newer and more exciting. There were not yet clearly defined limits to the potential impact of the arguments. The audience, the interlocutors, the actors, all these positions and relationships were much less routinized and therefore less contained. To me this suggests that a larger public transformation of Adam Smith's legacy would have to involve a new set of actors—some destabilization of the existing dialogue that would allow for or demand new authors and audiences.[33]

When I first wrote this conclusion in 2019, the chance of this kind of transformation seemed remote. Now, as I revise it in the summer of 2020, big recalibrations seem much more likely.

The Idea of a Moral Economics

Considering only the generalized theoretical question of what drives cultural transformations begs the other question of whether such a transformation is desirable. Unpacking the historical contingencies involved in a major shift in moral frameworks challenges the inevitability of prioritizing national growth above all other concerns. Should that framework be challenged?

It should be acknowledged that there were real benefits to the transformation that occurred. Enduring scientific knowledge and the foundation of an empirical approach to economic processes have their roots in this

---

33. This condition is also suggested by John W. Mohr and Harrison C. White, "How to Model an Institution," *Theory and Society* 37, no. 5 (October 2008): 485–512, https://doi.org/10.1007/s11186 -008-9066-0.

era. The idea of growth and the shift to national prosperity preceded the real gains made in the Industrial Revolution. Perhaps these ideas even contributed to that prosperity. Economic growth itself is something I consider a good thing. Unlocking additional knowledge about how to achieve it by reframing the inquiry I would have to conclude is beneficial. I would also have large and lasting reservations about returning to a mode of economic inquiry dominated by a Christian ethos and institutionally supported by the concerns of the Catholic Church, as was the case in the medieval era.

Still, Adam Smith demonstrated that you can combine capitalism with a concern for equity and justice, and with the desire to alleviate poverty and suffering by eliminating corruption and exploitation, and place it all on a new institutional footing based in the idea of national prosperity. Given the increases in inequality that have been occurring since the late twentieth century, and the existential threat this inequality seems to pose for basic human rights and the principles of democracy, I think the answer is obvious.

BIBLIOGRAPHY

PRIMARY SOURCES

The Advantages of the Kingdome of England, both abroad and at home, by Manageing and Issuing the Drapery, and Woollen Manufactures of this Kingdom, under the Ancient Government of the Fellowship of Merchants-Adventurers of England. N.p., [1662?]. Making of the Modern World.

Advertisement. Whereas divers people are at great expence in printing, publishing and dispersing of Bills of Advertisement: Observing how practical and Advantagious to Trade and Business, &c. this Method is in parts beyond the Seas [. . .]. London: Printed by Andrew Clark in Aldersgatestreet, 1675. Early English Books Online.

Aquinas, Thomas. *The "De Malo" of Thomas Aquinas.* Edited by Brian Davies. Translated by Richard Regan. Oxford: Oxford University Press, 2001. Written ca. 1269–70.

——. *Summa theologicae tertia pars.* Venetiis: B. Stagninus, 1486. Making of the Modern World.

Bacon, Francis. *Sylva Sylvarum: or, A Naturall Historie.* London: Printed by J. H. for William Lee, 1626. Making of the Modern World.

Barbon, Nicholas. *A Discourse Concerning Coining the New Money Lighter. In Answer to Mr. Lock's Considerations about raising the Value of Money.* London: Printed for Richard Chiswell, 1696. Making of the Modern World.

——. *A Discourse of Trade.* London: Printed by Tho. Milbourn for the Author, 1690. Making of the Modern World.

Barlaeus, Caspar. *The Wise Merchant.* Edited by Anna-Luna Post. Translated by Corinna Vermeulen. Amsterdam: Amsterdam University Press, 2019. Originally published as *Mercator sapiens* (Amsterdam: Willem Blaeu, 1632).

Bedel, Henry. *A Sermon exhortyng to pitie the poore.* London: Iohn Awdely, [1572?]. Making of the Modern World.

Bethel, Slingsby. *The Present Interest of England Stated. By a Lover of his King and Countrey.* London: Printed for D. B., 1671. Making of the Modern World.

Bieston, Robert. *The bayte & snare of fortune*. London: John Wayland, [1554?]. Making of the Modern World.

Bland, John. *Trade Revived, Or a Way Proposed To Restore, Increase, Inrich, Strengthen and Preserve the Decayed and even Dying Trade of this our English Nation, in its Manufactories, Coin, Shiping and Revenue*. London: Printed for Thomas Holmwood for the use of the People of England, 1659. Making of the Modern World.

Cary, John. *An Essay, on the Coyn and Credit of England: As they stand with Respect to its Trade*. Bristol: Will. Bonny, 1696. Making of the Modern World.

——. *An Essay on the State of England, In Relation to its Trade, Its Poor, and Its Taxes, For carrying on the present War against France*. Bristol: Printed by W. Bonny, for the Author, 1695. Making of the Modern World.

Chamberlayne, Edward. *Englands Wants: Or Several Proposals Probably beneficial for England, Humbly offered to the Consideration of all Good Patriots in Both Houses of Parliament*. London: Printed for Jo. Martyn, 1667. Making of the Modern World.

Child, Josiah. *Brief Observations Concerning Trade, and Interest of Money*. London: Printed for Elizabeth Calvert, 1668. Making of the Modern World.

——. *A Discourse About Trade, Wherein the Reduction of Interest of Money to 4 l. per Centum, is Recommended*. London: A. Sowle, 1690. Making of the Modern World.

——. *A Discourse Concerning Trade, And that in particular of The East-Indies, Wherein several weighty Propositions are fully discussed, and the State of the East-India Company is faithfully stated*. [London: Andrew Sowle, 1689?]. Making of the Modern World.

——. *A New Discourse of Trade, Wherein is Recommended several weighty Points relating to Companies of Merchants*. London: John Everingham, 1693. Making of the Modern World.

——. *A Short Addition to the Observations Concerning Trade and Interest of Money*. London: Printed for Henry Mortlock, 1668. Making of the Modern World.

——. *A Treatise Wherein is Demonstrated I. That the East-India Trade is the most National of all Foreign Trades [. . .]*. London: Printed by J. R. for the Honourable the East-India Company, 1681. Making of the Modern World.

Clayton, David. *A Short System of Trade: Or, An Account of What in Trade must necessarily be Advantageous to the Nation, and What must of Consequence be Detrimental*. London: Printed by R. Tookey for the Author, 1719. Making of the Modern World.

Cockburn, John. *A Short History of the Revolution in Scotland. In a Letter from a Scotch Gentleman in Amsterdam to his Friend in London*. London: Printed by the Booksellers of London and Westminster, 1712. Making of the Modern World.

Coke, Roger. *England's Improvements. In Two Parts*. London: Printed by J. C. for Henry Brome, 1675. Making of the Modern World.

Collins, John. *A Plea For the bringing in of Irish cattel, And keeping out of Fish Caught by Foreigners*. London: A. Godbid and J. Playford, 1680. Making of the Modern World.

——. *Salt and Fishery, A Discourse thereof Insisting on the following Heads*. London: A. Godbid and J. Playford, 1682. Making of the Modern World.

Culpeper, Thomas. *A Tract Against Vsvrie*. London: Printed by W. I. for Walter Burre, 1621. Making of the Modern World.

Davenant, Charles. *Discourses on the Publick Revenues, and on the Trade of England. In Two Parts*. London: Printed for James Knapton, 1698. Making of the Modern World.

——. *An Essay on the East-India-Trade. By the Author of The Essay upon Wayes and Means*. London, 1696. Making of the Modern World.

The Death of Vsvry, or, the Disgrace of Vsvrers. Cambridge: John Legatt, Printer to the University of Cambridge, 1594. Making of the Modern World.

Defoe, Daniel. *Taxes no Charge: in A Letter from a Gentleman, to A Person of Quality. Shewing The Nature, Use, and Benefit of Taxes in this Kingdom; and compared with the Impositions of Foreign States. Together with their Improvement of Trade in Time of War*. London: Printed for R. Chiswell, 1690. Making of the Modern World.

De la Court, Pieter. *Proeve uit een onuitgegeven Staathuishoudkundig Geschrift, Het Welvaren der Stad Leyden*. Leyden: S. & J. Luchtmans, 1845. First published 1659. Making of the Modern World.

——. *The True Interest and Political Maxims, of the Republic of Holland*. London: Printed for J. Nourse, 1746. First published 1662. Making of the Modern World.

Digges, Dudley. *The Defence of Trade. In a Letter To Sir Thomas Smith Knight, Gouernour of the East-India Companie, &c*. London: Printed by William Stansby for Iohn Barnes, 1615. Making of the Modern World.

Ercker, Lazarus, and John Pettus. *Fleta Minor, Or, The Laws of Art and Nature, in Knowing, Judging, Assaying, Fining, Refining and Inlarging the Bodies of confin'd Metals*. London: Printed for the Author, by Thomas Dawks, 1683. Making of the Modern World.

Farthing, John. *The Excise Rectify'd: Or, a Plain Demonstration, That The Revenue now raised thereby, is capable of being Improved at least Four or Five Hundred Thousand Pounds per Annum, which is now paid by the Subject, but diverted from its proper Chanel into private Hands*. London, 1695/6. Making of the Modern World.

[Ferguson, Robert]. *The East-India-Trade a most Profitable Trade to the Kingdom. And Best Secured and Improved in a Company, and a Joint-Stock*. London, 1677. Making of the Modern World.

Fills, Robert, trans. *The Lawes and Statutes of Geneua, as well concerning ecclesiastical discipline, as ciuill regiment, with certeine proclamations duly executed, whereby Gods religion is most purelie mainteined, and their common wealth quieth gouerned*. London: Rouland Hall, 1562. Making of the Modern World.

Finley, Moses I. *The Ancient Economy*. Berkeley: University of California Press, 1973.

Fitzroy, A. W., W. L. Grant, J. Munro, and Great Britain. *Acts of the Privy Council of England*, vol. 33, *1613–1614*. Burlington, ON: TannerRitchie, 2010. First published 1921 by His Majesty's Stationery Office. http://sources.tannerritchie.com/browser. php?bookid=936.

Fortrey, Samuel. *Englands Interest and Improvement. Consisting in the increase of the store, and trade of this Kingdom*. Cambridge: John Field, Printer to the University, 1663. Making of the Modern World.

[Gardner]. *Some Reflections on a Pamphlet, intituled, England and East-India Inconsistent in Their Manufactures*. London, 1696 [1967?]. Making of the Modern World.

Gentleman, Tobias. *Englands Way To Win Wealth, and to employ Ships and Marriners: Or, A plaine description what great profite, it will bring vnto the Common-wealth of England, by the Erecting, Building, and aduenturing of Busses, to Sea, a fishing [. . .]*. London: Printed for Nathaniel Butter, 1614. Making of the Modern World.

Gervaise, Isaac. *The System or Theory of the Trade of the World [. . .]*. London: H. Woodfall, 1720. Making of the Modern World.

The Grand Concernments of England Ensured: Viz. Liberty of Conscience, Extirpation of Popery, Defence of Property, [. . .], With a Sad Expostulation, and some smart Rebukes to the Army. London, 1659. Making of the Modern World.

Graswinckel, Dirck. *Placcaten, Ordonnantien ende Reglementen, Op't Stuck vande Lijf-Tocht, Sulcx als de selve van Outs tot herwaerts toe op alle voorvallen van Hongers-noot en Dieren-tijdt beraemt zijn ende ghedaen publiceeren.* Leyden: Ter druckerije van de Elseviers, 1651. Making of the Modern World.

Grotius, Hugo. *Mare Liberum, sive De jure quod Batavis competit ad Indicana commercia Dissertatio.* Lugduni Batauorvm: Ex officinà Ludovici Elzevirij, 1609.

Heresbach, Conrad. *The Whole Art and Trade of Hvsbandry, contained In foure Bookes.* London: Printed by T. S. for Richard More, 1614. Making of the Modern World (Gale Document Number U0100089077).

Hodges, John. *The true and only Causes of the want of Money in these Kingdoms; And the Remedies. Mentioned in these General Assertions, in order to more particular Demonstrations, how these Kingdomes may yet be made the Richest, and most Powerful, Kingdoms in the World.* London, 1666. Making of the Modern World.

Holles, Denzil. *Mr. Hollis, His Speech in Parliament: On Munday the 31th of January, Vpon the delivery of a Message from the House of Commons, concerning the poore Tradesmens Petition.* London: J. Hammond, 1642. Making of the Modern World (Gale Document Number U0109132611).

In This Volvme Are Conteyned the Statutes, made and established from the time of Kinge Henrye the thirde, vnto the firste yeare of the reygne of our moste gracious and victorious soveraigne Lord, King Henry the viii. N.p., 1577. Making of the Modern World.

Jeffreys, George. *The Argument of the Lord Chief Justice of the Court of King's Bench concerning The Great Case of Monopolies, between The East-India Company, Plaintiff, and Thomas Sandys, Defendant. Wherein their Patent for Trading to the East-Indies, Exclusive of all others, is adjudged good.* London: Randal Taylor, 1689. Making of the Modern World.

[Johnson, Thomas]. *A Discourse Consisting of Motives for The Enlargement and Freedome of Trade. Especially That of Cloth, and other Woollen Manufactures, [. . .].* London: Printed by Richard Bishop for Stephen Rowtell, 1645. Making of the Modern World.

Johnson, Thomas. *A Plea for Free-Mens Liberties: or The Monopoly of the Eastland Marchants anatomized by divers arguments (wch will also serve to set forth the unjustnesse of the Marchant-Adventurers Monopoly,) [. . .].* N.p., 1646. Making of the Modern World (Gale Document Number U0100144924).

Kayll, Robert. *The Trades Increase.* London: Nicholas Okes, 1615. Making of the Modern World.

Keymor, John. *England's Interest Asserted, in the Improvement of its Native Commodities; And more especially the Manufacture of Wool: Plainly shewing its Exportation Unmanufactured, amounting unto Millions of Loss to His Majesty, and Kingdom [. . .].* London: Printed for Francis Smith, 1669. Making of the Modern World.

Lambarde, William. *A Perambulation of Kent: conteining the Description, Hystorie, and Customes of That Shire.* Chatham: W. Burrill; London: Baldwin, Cradock, and Joy, 1826. Originally written 1570; first published 1576. Making of the Modern World.

Locke, John. *Some Considerations of the Consequences of the Lowering of Interest, and Raising the Value of Money.* London: Printed for Awnsham and John Churchill, 1692. Making of the Modern World.

Lodge, Thomas. *An Alarum against Usurers*. London: Imprinted by T. Este for Sampson Clarke, 1584. Making of the Modern World.

A Lover of his Countrey, and Well-Wisher to the Prosperity both of the King and Kingdoms [pseud.]. *The Grand Concern of England Explained; in Several Proposals Offered to the Consideration of the Parliament*. London, 1673. Making of the Modern World.

Mackworth, Humphrey. *England's Glory; or, the Great Improvement Of Trade in General, by a Royal Bank, or Office of Credit, to be Erected in London; Wherein many Great Advantages that will hereby accrue to the Nation, to the Crown, and to the People, are mentioned; with Answers to the Objections that may be made against this Bank*. London: Printed by T. W. for Tho. Bever, 1694. Making of the Modern World.

Malynes, Gerard [de]. *The Center of The Circle of Commerce. Or, A Refutation of a Treatise, Intituled The Circle of Commerce, or The Ballance of Trade, lately published by E.M*. London: William Jones, 1623. Making of the Modern World.

——. *Consuetudo, Vel, Lex Mercatoria, or The Ancient Law-Merchant*. London: Printed by William Hunt, for Nicolas Bourne, 1656. First published 1622 by Adam Islip (London). Making of the Modern World.

——. *The Maintenance of Free Trade, According to the Three Essentiall Parts of Traffique; Namely, Commodities, Moneys, and Exchange of Moneys, by Bills of Exchanges for other Countries. Or, An answer to a Treatise of Free Trade, or the meanes to make Trade flourish, lately Published*. London: Printed by I. K. for William Sheffard, 1622. Making of the Modern World.

——. *Saint George For England, Allegorically described*. London: Imprinted by Richard Field for William Tymme Stationer, 1601. Making of the Modern World.

——. *A Treatise of the Canker of Englands Common wealth*. London: Imprinted by Richard Field for William Iohnes printer, 1601. Making of the Modern World.

Manley, Thomas. *The Sollicitor. Exactly and plainly declaring, Both as to Knowledge and Practice, how such an Undertaker ought to be qualified. [. . .]*. London: J. Streater, 1663. Early English Books Online.

Markham, Gervase. *Country Contentments: Or, The Husbandmans Recreations*. 4th ed. London: Printed by Nicholas Okes for Iohn Harison, 1631. Making of the Modern World.

——. *Covntry Contentments, or The English Huswife*. London: Printed by I. B. for R. Jackson, 1623. Originally published as the second book of the two-volume *Covntrey Contentments* (London: Printed by I. B. for R. Jackson, 1615). Early English Books Online.

——. *Markhams farewell to Hvsbandry or, The enriching of all sorts of Barren and Sterile grounds in our Kingdome, to be as fruitfull in all manner of Graine, Pulse, and Grasse, as the best grounds whatsoeuer [. . .]*. 3rd ed. London: Printed by Nicholas Okes for Iohn Harison, 1631. Making of the Modern World.

Martyn, Henry. *Considerations on the East-India Trade*. London: Printed for J. Roberts, 1701. https://EconPapers.repec.org/RePEc:hay:hetboo:martyn1701.

May, John. *A Declaration of the Estate of Clothing Now Vsed Within This Realme Of England*. London: Adam Islip, 1613. Making of the Modern World.

Milburn, William. *Oriental Commerce; containing A Geographical Description of the principal places in The East Indies, China, and Japan, [. . .]; also, The Rise and Progress of the Trade of the various European nations with the Eastern world*. London: Printed for the Author, and published by Black, Parry, 1813. Making of the Modern World.

Miller, Charles. *Three Sermons, Or Homilies, to move compassion towards The Poor and Needy, set forth by authority, A.D. 1596.* New ed. London: Printed for J. G. F. & J. Rivington, 1842. Originally published 1596. Making of the Modern World.

Milles, Thomas. *The Cvstvmers Apology. That is to say, A general Asnwere to Informers of all sortes, and their iniurouis complaints, against the honest reputation of the Collectors of her Maiesties Cvstvmes, specially in the Ovt-Portes of this Realme. [. . .].* [London?], 1599. Making of the Modern World.

Misselden, Edward. *The Circle of Commerce. Or The Ballance of Trade, in defence of free Trade: Opposed To Malynes Little Fish and his Great Whale, poized against them in the Scale. [. . .].* London: Printed by Iohn Dawson, for Nicholas Bourne, 1623. Making of the Modern World.

——. *Free Trade. Or, The Meanes to Make Trade Florish. Wherein, The Causes of the Decay of Trade in this Kingdome, are discouered: And the Remedies also to remooue the same, are represented.* 2nd ed. London: Printed by Iohn Legatt, for Simon Waterson, 1622. Making of the Modern World.

Mun, Thomas. *A Discovrse of Trade, From England vnto the East-Indies: Answering to diuerse Obiections which are vsvally made against the same.* London: Printed by Nicholas Okes for John Pyper, 1621. Making of the Modern World.

——. *England's Treasure by Forraign Trade. Or, The Ballance of our Forraign Trade is The Rule of our Treasure.* London: Printed by J. G. for Thomas Clark, 1664. Making of the Modern World.

North, Dudley. *Discourses upon Trade; Principally Directed to the Cases of the Interest, Coynage, Clipping, Increase of Money.* London: Printed for Tho. Basset, 1691. Making of the Modern World.

Papillon, Thomas. *The East-India-Trade a most Profitable Trade to the Kingdom. And Best Secured and Improved in a Company, and a Joint-Stock. Represented In a Letter written upon the Occasion of two Letters lately published, insinuating the Contrary.* London, 1677. Making of the Modern World.

Parker, Henry. *Of a Free Trade. A Discourse Seriously Recommending to our Nation the wonderfull benefits of Trade, especially of a rightly Governed, and Ordered Trade. [. . .].* London: Printed by Fr: Neile for Robert Bostock, 1648. Making of the Modern World.

Petty, William. *Political Arithmetick, or A Discourse Concerning, The Extent and Value of Lands, People, Buildings; Husbandry, Manufacture, Commerce, Fishery, Artizans, Seamen, Soldiers; [. . .].* London: Printed for Robert Clavel, 1690. Making of the Modern World (Gale Document Number U0100311687).

——. *A Treatise of Taxes & Contributions. Shewing the Nature and Measures of [. . .]. The same being frequently applied to the present State and Affairs of Ireland.* London: Printed for N. Brooke, 1662. Making of the Modern World.

Petyt, William. *Britannia Languens, or a Discourse of Trade: Shewing The Grounds and Reasons of the Increase and Decay of Land-Rents, National Wealth and Strength. With Application to the late and present State and Condition of England, France, and the United Provinces.* London: Printed for Tho. Dring and Sam. Crouch, 1680. Making of the Modern World.

Plat, Hugh. *The Jewel House of Art and Nature. Containing diuers rare and profitable Inventions, together with sundry new experimentes in the Art of Husbandry, Distillation, and Moulding.* London: Peter Short, 1594. Early English Books Online.

Pollexfen, Henry. *A Discourse of Trade, Coyn, and Paper Credit: And of Ways and Means to Gain, and Retain Riches. To which is added the Argument of a Learned Counsel, upon an Action of the Case brought by the East-India-Company against Mr. Sands and Interloper.* London: Printed for Brabazon Aylmer, 1697. Making of the Modern World.

Potter, William. *The Key of Wealth: Or, A new Way, for Improving of Trade: Lawfull, Easie, Safe and Effectuall: Shewing how A few Tradesmen agreeing together, may (borrow wherewith to) double their Stocks, and the increase thereof, [. . .].* London: R. A., 1650. Making of the Modern World.

——. *The Trades-Man's Jewel: or A safe, easie, speedy and effectual Means, for the incredible advancement of Trade, And Multiplication of Riches; shewing How men of Indifferent Estates, may abundantly increase [. . .].* London: Edward Husband and John Field, Printers to the Parliament of England, 1650. Making of the Modern World.

Rastell, William, ed. *A colleccion of all the Statutes (from the begynning of Magna Carta vnto the yere of our Lorde, 1557) whiche were before that yere imprinted. [. . .].* London, 1559. Making of the Modern World.

Reasons for Preserving the Publick Market of Blackwell-Hall, and restraining the Levant Company of Merchants from deferring their Shipping as long as they please. Humbly Offer'd to the Parliament. [London, 1696?]. Making of the Modern World.

A Remonstrance of the Shee-Citizens of London. [London?], 1647. Early English Books Online.

Roberts, Lewes. *The Marchants Mappe of Commerce, wherein The Universall Manner and Matter of Trade is compendiously handled. [. . .].* [London, 1638?]. Making of the Modern World.

——. *The Treasure of Traffike, or A Discourse of Forraigne Trade.* London: Printed by E. P. for Nicholas Bourne, 1641. Making of the Modern World.

Robinson, Henry. *Briefe Considerations, Concerning the advancement of Trade and Navigation, Humbly tendred unto all ingenious Patriots; Purposely to incite them to endeavour the felicitie of this Nation, [. . .].* London: Matthew Simmons, 1649. Making of the Modern World.

——. *Englands Safety, in Trades Encrease. Most humbly presented to the High Court of Parliament.* London: Printed by E. P. for Nicholas Bourne, 1641. Making of the Modern World.

Roe, Thomas. *Sir Thomas Roe his Speech in Parliament. Wherein He sheweth the cause of the decay of Coyne and Trade in this Land, especially of Merchants Trade. [. . .].* N.p., 1641. Making of the Modern World.

Sandys, Thomas, and England and Wales, Court of King's Bench. East India Company v. Thomas Sandys, 1683–1685. HLS MS 1268, Harvard Law School Library.

Serra, Antonio. *A Short Treatise on the Wealth and Poverty of Nations (1613).* Edited by Sophus A. Reinert. Translated by Jonathan Hunt. London: Anthem Press, 2011. Cambridge Core. Originally published as *Breva trattato delle cause che possono far abbondaree li regni d'oro e d'argento dove non sono miniere* (1613).

Smith, Adam. *The Wealth of Nations.* New York: Bantam Classics, 2003. First published 1776.

Smith, John. *England's Improvement Reviv'd: Digested into Six Books.* London: Printed by Tho. Newcomb for the Author, 1670. Making of the Modern World.

Smith, Thomas. *A Compendious or briefe examination of certayne ordinary complaints of diuers of our country men in these our days: which although they are in some part vniust & frivolous, [. . .].* London: Thomas Marshe, 1581. Early English Books Online.

——, comp. *De Republica Anglorum. The maner of Gouernement or policie of the Realme of England.* London: Printed by Henrie Midleton for Gregorie Seton, 1583. Early English Books Online.

Tavernier, John Baptista. *The Six Voyages of John Baptista Tavernier, Baron of Aubonne; Through Turky, into Persia and the East-Indies, For the space of Forty Years. [. . .] To which is added, A new Description of the Seraglio.* Translated by J. P. London: Printed by William Godbid, for Robert Littlebury, 1677. Early English Books Online.

Trevers, Joseph. *An Essay To the Restoring of our Decayed Trade. Wherein is Described, the Smuglers, Lawyers, and Officers Frauds, &c.* London: Printed for Gilew Widdowes, 1675. Making of the Modern World.

Tusser, Thomas. *Fiue hundreth pointes of good husbandry vnited to as many of good huswiferie [. . .].* London: Richard Tottill, 1573. Early English Books Online.

——. *A hundreth good pointes of husbandrie.* London: Richard Tottel, 1557. Early English Books Online.

Usselincx, Willem. *Grondich Discours over desen aen-staenden Vrede-handel.* [Amsterdam, 1608?]. Making of the Modern World.

——. *Naerder Bedenckingen, Over de zee-vaerdt, Coophandel ende Neeringhe, als mede de versekeringhe vanden Staet deser vereenichde Landen, inde teghenwoordighe Vrede-handelinghe met den Coninck van Spangnien ende de Aerts-hertoghen.* N.p., 1608. Making of the Modern World.

——. *Vertoogh, hoe nootwendich, nut ende profijtelick het sy voor de vereenighde Nederlanden te behouden de Vryheyt van te handelen op West-Indien, Inden vrede metten Coninck van Spaignen.* N.p., [1608?]. Making of the Modern World.

Van den Enden, Franciscus. *Kort Verhael Van Nieuw-Nederlants Gelegenheit, Deughden, Natuerlijcke Voorrechten, en byzondere bequaemheidt ter bevolkingh: Mitsgaders eenige Requesten, Vertoogen, Deductien, enz. [. . .].* [Amsterdam?], 1662. Sabin Americana.

Verstegan, Richard. *The Post of the World: Wherein is contayned the antiquities and originall of the most famous Cities in Europe.* London: Thomas East, [1576?]. Making of the Modern World.

Violet, Thomas. *The Advancement of Merchandize: or, Certain Propositions For the Improvment of the Trade of this Common-wealth, humbly presented to the Right Honorable the Council of State.* London: W. DuGard, Printer to the Council of State, 1651. Making of the Modern World.

——. *To the Kings most Excellent Majesty, And to the Lords Spiritual and Temporal; with the Commons Assembled in Parliament. A true Discovery of the great Damage His late Majesty King Charles the First received, [. . .].* N.p., [1662?]. Making of the Modern World.

Wheeler, John. *A Treatise of Commerce, Wherein Are Shewed the Commodies Arising by a Wel Ordered, and Rvled Trade, Such as that of the Socieitie of Merchantes Adventurers is proved to bee, [. . .].* Middleburgh: Richard Schilders, Printer to the States of Zeland, 1601. Early English Books Online.

Whitelocke, Bulstrode. *Memorials of the English Affairs: or, an Historical Account of What passed from the beginning of the Reign of King Charles the First, to King Charles the Second His Happy Restauration.* London: Printed for Nathaniel Ponder, 1682. Making of the Modern World.

Wilson, Thomas. *A Discovrse vpon vsurie, by waie of Dialogue and oracions, for the better varietie, and more delight of all those, that shall read this treatise.* London: Roger Warde, 1584. Making of the Modern World.

DATABASES AND SOURCES

Bonney, R. European State Finance Database: English Revenues, 1485–1816. UK Data Service (SN 3118), October 13, 1993. http://doi.org/10.5255/UKDA-SN-3118-1.

Digitale Bibliotheek voor de Nederlandse Letteren (DBNL). https://www.dbnl.org/.

Dutch Pamphlets Online (database). Brill. https://primarysources.brillonline.com/browse/dutch-pamphlets-online.

Early English Books Online Text Creation Partnership (EEBO-TCP). https://quod.lib.umich.edu/e/eebogroup/.

Early English Books Online (EEBO). ProQuest. https://eebo.chadwyck.com/home.

English Short Title Catalogue (database). British Library. http://estc.bl.uk/.

The History of Parliament: British Political, Social & Local History. The History of Parliament Trust. https://www.historyofparliamentonline.org/.

Laspeyres, Étienne. *Geschichte der volkswirtschaftlichen Anschauungen der Niederländer und ihrer Litteratur zur Zeit der Republik.* Leipzig, 1863.

Leiden University Catalog. https://www.library.universiteitleiden.nl/subject-guides/catalogue.

The Making of the Modern World (database). Gale. https://www.gale.com/primary-sources/the-making-of-the-modern-world.

Nederlandse Centrale Catalogus (NCC). http://picarta.pica.nl/.

Oxford Dictionary of National Biography. Oxford: Oxford University Press, 2004; online ed., 2008. https://www.oxforddnb.com/.

Palgrave, Robert Harry Inglis. *Palgrave's Dictionary of Political Economy.* New ed. London: Macmillan, 1925.

Sainty, John Christopher. *Office-Holders in Modern Britain: III, Officials of the Boards of Trade, 1660–1870.* London: Athlone Press, 1974.

Short-Title Catalogue, Netherlands (STCN). KB: National Library of the Netherlands. https://www.kb.nl/en/organisation/research-expertise/for-libraries/short-title-catalogue-netherlands-stcn.

University of Amsterdam Library. https://uba.uva.nl/.

Visualizing English Print (VEP). http://graphics.cs.wisc.edu/WP/vep/.

Wikipedia. https://www.wikipedia.org.

SOFTWARE PACKAGES

Hamilton, Mark. mhamilton723/tseries: Version 0.2.1 (filename: "mhamilton723/tseries-0.2.1.zip"). Zenodo, September 20, 2017. https://doi.org/10.5281/zenodo.897193.

Hamilton, Mark, and Emily Erikson. mhamilton723/sociology: Version 0.1 (filename: "mhamilton723/sociology-0.1.zip"). Zenodo, September 24, 2017. https://doi.org/10.5281/zenodo.995677.

Pfaff, Bernhard, and Matthieu Stigler. *Package 'urca'* (Version 1.2-8). CRAN Repository, June 6, 2013. https://cran.r-project.org/src/contrib/Archive/urca/.

Roberts, Molly, Brandon Stewart, and Dustin Tingley. *stm: An R Package for the Structural Topic Model.* https://www.structuraltopicmodel.com/.

SECONDARY TEXTS

Abadie, Alberto, Alexis Diamond, and Jens Hainmueller. "Comparative Politics and the Synthetic Control Method." *American Journal of Political Science* 59, no. 2 (April 2015): 495–510.

Adams, Julia. "The Familial State: Elite Family Practices and State-Making in the Early Modern Netherlands." *Theory and Society* 23, no. 4 (August 1994): 505–39. https://doi.org/10.1007/BF00992826.

——. *The Familial State: Ruling Families and Merchant Capitalism in Early Modern Europe.* Ithaca, NY: Cornell University Press, 2005.

Agnew, Jean-Christophe. *Worlds Apart: The Market and the Theater in Anglo-American Thought, 1550–1750.* Cambridge: Cambridge University Press, 1986.

Alexander, Jeffrey C. "The Societalization of Social Problems: Church Pedophilia, Phone Hacking, and the Financial Crisis." *American Sociological Review* 83, no. 6 (December 2018): 1049–78. https://doi.org/10.1177/0003122418803376.

Allen, William R. "Modern Defenders of Mercantilist Theory." *History of Political Economy* 2, no. 2 (Fall 1970): 381–97. https://doi.org/10.1215/00182702-2-2-381.

Anderson, Elizabeth. "Adam Smith on Equality." In *Adam Smith: His Life, Thought, and Legacy,* ed. Ryan Patrick Hanley, 157–72. Princeton, NJ: Princeton University Press, 2016.

Anderson, Gary M., and Robert D. Tollison. "Sir James Steuart as the Apotheosis of Mercantilism and His Relation to Adam Smith." *Southern Economic Journal* 51, no. 2 (October 1984): 456–68. https://doi.org/10.2307/1057824.

Andrews, Charles M. *British Committees, Commissions, and Councils of Trade and Plantations, 1622–1675.* Baltimore: Johns Hopkins Press, 1908. http://archive.org/details/britishcommittee00andrgoog.

Appleby, Joyce Oldham. *Economic Thought and Ideology in Seventeenth-Century England.* Los Angeles: Figueroa Press, 1978.

Archer, Ian. "The London Lobbies in the Later Sixteenth Century." *Historical Journal* 31, no. 1 (March 1988): 17–44.

Aristotle. *Nicomachean Ethics.* Translated by H. Rackham. 2nd ed. Loeb Classical Library 73. Cambridge, MA: Harvard University Press, 1934.

Aristotle. *Oeconomica.* Oxford: Clarendon Press, 1920.

Ashley, W[illiam] J. *An Introduction to English Economic History and Theory.* New York: Kelley, 1966.

Ashton, Robert. *The City and the Court, 1603–1643.* Cambridge: Cambridge University Press, 1979.

——. "The Parliamentary Agitation for Free Trade in the Opening Years of the Reign of James I." *Past & Present,* no. 38 (December 1967): 40–55.

Babb, Sarah. *Managing Mexico: Economists from Nationalism to Neoliberalism.* Princeton, NJ: Princeton University Press, 2004.

Barber, William J. *British Economic Thought and India, 1600–1858: A Study in the History of Development Economics*. Oxford: Clarendon Press, 1975.

——. *A History of Economic Thought*. Middletown, CT: Wesleyan University Press, 2010.

Barrat, A., M. Barthélemy, R. Pastor-Satorras, and A. Vespignani. "The Architecture of Complex Weighted Networks." *Proceedings of the National Academy of Sciences of the United States of America* 101, no. 11 (March 16, 2004): 3747–52. https://doi.org/10.1073/pnas.0400087101.

Bearman, Peter S. *Relations Into Rhetorics: Local Elite Social Structure in Norfolk, England, 1540–1640*. Arnold and Caroline Rose Monograph Series of the American Sociological Association. New Brunswick, NJ: Rutgers University Press, 1993.

Beer, Max. *Early British Economics from the XIIIth to the Middle of the XVIIIth Century*. London: George Allen & Unwin, 1938.

Berlin, Michael. "Guilds in Decline? London Livery Companies and the Rise of a Liberal Economy, 1600–1800." In *Guilds, Innovation, and the European Economy, 1400–1800*, ed. S. R. Epstein and Maarten Prak. Cambridge: Cambridge University Press, 2008.

Blaug, Mark. *The Early Mercantilists: Thomas Mun (1571–1641), Edward Misselden (1608–1634), Gerard de Malynes (1586–1623)*. Aldershot, UK: Elgar, 1991.

——. *Economic Theory in Retrospect*. Cambridge: Cambridge University Press, 1962.

Bohun, James. "Protecting Prerogative: William III and the East India Trade Debate, 1689–1698." *Past Imperfect* 2 (1993): 63–68. https://doi.org/10.21971/P74S3M.

Braddick, Michael. "The Early Modern English State and the Question of Differentiation, from 1550 to 1700." *Comparative Studies in Society and History* 38, no. 1 (January 1996): 92–111.

Brenner, Robert. *Merchants and Revolution: Commercial Change, Political Conflict, and London's Overseas Traders, 1550–1653*. London: Verso, 2003.

Broadberry, Stephen, Bruce Campbell, Alexander Klein, Mark Overton, and Bas van Leeuwen. *British Economic Growth, 1270–1870*. Cambridge: Cambridge University Press, 2015.

Brunton, Douglas, and Donald H. Pennington. *Members of the Long Parliament*. London: Allen & Unwin, 1954.

Buringh, Eltjo, and Jan Luiten van Zanden. "Charting the 'Rise of the West': Manuscripts and Printed Books in Europe, A Long-Term Perspective from the Sixth through Eighteenth Centuries." *Journal of Economic History* 69, no. 2 (June 2009): 409–45. https://doi.org/10.1017/S0022050709000837.

Burt, Ronald S. *Structural Holes*. Cambridge, MA: Harvard University Press, 1995.

——. "Structural Holes and Good Ideas." *American Journal of Sociology* 110, no. 2 (September 2004): 349–99. https://doi.org/10.1086/421787.

Canterbery, E. Ray. *A Brief History of Economics: Artful Approaches to the Dismal Science*. Singapore: World Scientific, 2011.

Carlos, Ann M., and Stephen Nicholas. "Agency Problems in Early Chartered Companies: The Case of the Hudson's Bay Company." *Journal of Economic History* 50, no. 4 (December 1990): 853–75. https://doi.org/10.1017/S0022050700037852.

——. "Managing the Manager: An Application of the Principal Agent Model to the Hudson's Bay Company." *Oxford Economic Papers* 45, no. 2 (April 1993): 243–56.

——. "Theory and History: Seventeenth-Century Joint-Stock Chartered Trading Companies." *Journal of Economic History* 56, no. 4 (December 1996): 916–24.

Carruthers, Bruce G. *City of Capital: Politics and Markets in the English Financial Revolution.* Princeton, NJ: Princeton University Press, 1999.

Carus-Wilson, E. M. "The Origins and Early Development of the Merchant Adventurers' Organization in London as Shown in Their Own Mediaeval Records." *Economic History Review* 4, no. 2 (April 1933): 147–76.

Cawston, George, and Augustus Henry Keane. *The Early Chartered Companies (A.D. 1296–1858).* London: Edward Arnold, 1896.

Centola, Damon. "The Social Origins of Networks and Diffusion." *American Journal of Sociology* 120, no. 5 (March 2015): 1295–1338. https://doi.org/10.1086/681275.

Chorev, Nitsan. "A Fluid Divide: Domestic and International Factors in US Trade Policy Formation." *Review of International Political Economy* 144, no. 4 (October 2007): 653–89. https://doi.org/10.1080/09692290701475395.

Collins, Randall. *Interaction Ritual Chains.* Princeton, NJ: Princeton University Press, 2005.

Crawford, Anne. *A History of the Vintners' Company.* London: Constable, 1977.

Cunningham, William. *The Growth of English Industry and Commerce.* Cambridge: At the University Press, 1882.

Darby, Graham, ed. *The Origins and Development of the Dutch Revolt.* London: Routledge, 2001.

De Jong, Abe, and Ailsa Röell. "Financing and Control in the Netherlands: A Historical Perspective." In *A History of Corporate Governance Around the World: Family Business Groups to Professional Managers,* ed. Randall K. Morck, 467–515. Chicago: University of Chicago Press, 2003.

De Jong, Abe, Joost Jonker, and Ailsa Röell. "Dutch Corporate Finance, 1602–1850." ERIM Report Series Reference No. ERS-2013-008-F&A, June 4, 2013. http://papers .ssrn.com/abstract=2274577.

De Roover, Raymond. "Monopoly Theory Prior to Adam Smith: A Revision." *Quarterly Journal of Economics* 65, no. 4 (November 1951): 492–524. https://doi .org/10.2307/1882577.

De Vries, Jan. *European Urbanization, 1500–1800.* London: Methuen, 1984.

De Vries, Jan, and Ad van der Woude. *The First Modern Economy: Success, Failure, and Perseverance of the Dutch Economy, 1500–1815.* Cambridge: Cambridge University Press, 1997.

Dekker, Rudolf M. "Women in Revolt: Popular Protest and Its Social Basis in Holland in the Seventeenth and Eighteenth Centuries." *Theory and Society* 16, no. 3 (May 1987): 337–62.

Deringer, William. *Calculated Values: Finance, Politics, and the Quantitative Age.* Cambridge, MA: Harvard University Press, 2018.

Dewar, Mary. "The Authorship of the 'Discourse of the Common Weal.'" *Economic History Review* 19, no. 2 (1966): 388–400.

Dobb, Maurice. *Theories of Value and Distribution Since Adam Smith: Ideology and Economic Theory.* Cambridge: Cambridge University Press, 1975.

Dobbin, Frank. *Forging Industrial Policy: The United States; Britain, and France in the Railway Age.* Cambridge: Cambridge University Press, 1994.

Durlauf, Steven N., and Lawrence Blume, eds. *The New Palgrave Dictionary of Economics.* Basingstoke, UK: Palgrave Macmillan, 2008.

Eagly, Robert. *Events, Ideology, and Economic Theory: The Determinants of Progress in the Development of Economic Analysis.* Detroit, MI: Wayne State University Press, 1968.

Ebbinghaus, Bernhard. "When Less Is More: Selection Problems in Large-*N* and Small-*N* Cross-National Comparisons." *International Sociology* 20, no. 2 (June 2005): 133–52.

Ekelund, Robert B., Jr., Robert F. Hébert, and Robert D. Tollison. "An Economic Model of the Medieval Church: Usury as a Form of Rent Seeking." *Journal of Law, Economics, & Organization* 5, no. 2 (Autumn 1989): 307–31.

Ekelund, Robert B., Jr., and Robert D. Tollison. *Mercantilism as a Rent-Seeking Society: Economic Regulation in Historical Perspective*. College Station: Texas A&M University Press, 1981.

Epstein, S. R., and Maarten Prak, eds. *Guilds, Innovation, and the European Economy, 1400–1800*. Cambridge: Cambridge University Press, 2008.

Erikson, Emily. *Between Monopoly and Free Trade: The English East India Company, 1600–1757*. Princeton, NJ: Princeton University Press, 2014.

——, ed. *Chartering Capitalism: Organizing Markets, States, and Publics*. Bingley, UK: Emerald Group, 2015.

——. "The Influence of Trade with Asia on British Economic Theory and Practice." In *Global Historical Sociology*, ed. Julian Go and George Lawson, 182–98. Cambridge: Cambridge University Press, 2017.

Finkelstein, Andrea. *Harmony and the Balance: An Intellectual History of Seventeenth-Century English Economic Thought*. Ann Arbor: University of Michigan Press, 2009.

Fourcade, Marion. *Economists and Societies: Discipline and Profession in the United States, Britain, and France, 1890s to 1990s*. Princeton, NJ: Princeton University Press, 2009.

Fourcade-Gourinchas, Marion, and Sarah L. Babb. "The Rebirth of the Liberal Creed: Paths to Neoliberalism in Four Countries." *American Journal of Sociology* 108, no. 3 (November 2002): 533–79. https://doi.org/10.1086/367922.

Franks, Julian, Colin Mayer, and Hannes F. Wagner. "The Origins of the German Corporation—Finance, Ownership and Control." *Review of Finance* 10, no. 4 (2006): 537–85.

Fratianni, Michele. "Government Debt, Reputation and Creditors' Protections: The Tale of San Giorgio." *Review of Finance* 10, no. 4 (2006): 487–506. https://doi.org/10.1007/s10679-006-9006-7.

Frehen, Rik G. P., William N. Goetzmann, and K. Geert Rouwenhorst. "New Evidence on the First Financial Bubble." *Journal of Financial Economics* 108, no. 3 (June 2013): 585–607.

Frentrop, Paul. *A History of Corporate Governance, 1602–2002*. Amsterdam: Deminor, 2003.

Friedland, Roger. "The Endless Fields of Pierre Bourdieu." *Organization* 16, no. 6 (November 2009): 887–917. https://doi.org/10.1177/1350508409341115.

Fritschy, Wantje. "The Efficiency of Taxation in Holland." In *The Political Economy of the Dutch Republic*, ed. Oscar Gelderblom, 55–85. Farnham, UK: Ashgate, 2009.

Furner, Mary O., and Barry Supple, eds. *The State and Economic Knowledge: The American and British Experiences*. Cambridge: Cambridge University Press, 2002.

Gadd, Ian Anders, and Patrick Wallis. "Reaching Beyond the City Wall: London Guilds and National Regulation, 1500–1700." In *Guilds, Innovation, and the European Economy, 1400–1800*, ed. S. R. Epstein and Maarten Prak, 288–316. Cambridge: Cambridge University Press, 2008.

Galbraith, John Kenneth. *Economics in Perspective: A Critical History.* Boston: Houghton Mifflin, 1988.

Gauci, Perry. *The Politics of Trade: The Overseas Merchant in State and Society, 1660–1720.* Oxford: Oxford University Press, 2001.

Gelderblom, Oscar, and Joost Jonker. "Completing a Financial Revolution: The Finance of the Dutch East India Trade and the Rise of the Amsterdam Capital Market, 1595–1612." *Journal of Economic History* 64, no. 3 (September 2004): 641–72.

Gilissen, John. "Les états généraux en Belgique et aux Pays-Bas sous l'ancien régime." In *Gouvernes et gouvernants*, vol. 11, 401–37. Recueils de la Société Jean Bodin pour l'histoire comparative des institutions 24. Bruxelles: Ed. de la Librairie encyclopedique, 1965.

Gordon, Alexander. "Cockburn, John." In *Dictionary of National Biography, 1885–1900*, ed. Leslie Stephen, vol. 11. London: Smith, Elder, 1887. http://www.archive.org/details/dictionaryofnati11stepuoft.

Gordon, Barry. *Economic Analysis Before Adam Smith: Hesiod to Lessius.* London: Macmillan, 1975.

Gould, J. D. "The Trade Crisis of the Early 1620's and English Economic Thought." *Journal of Economic History* 15, no. 2 (June 1955): 121–33.

Grampp, William D. "The Liberal Elements in English Mercantilism." *Quarterly Journal of Economics* 66, no. 4 (November 1952): 465–501. https://doi.org/10.2307/1882100.

Granovetter, Mark S. "The Strength of Weak Ties." *American Journal of Sociology* 78, no. 6 (May 1973): 1360–80.

Grassby, Richard. *The Business Community of Seventeenth-Century England.* Cambridge: Cambridge University Press, 2002.

Grassby, Richard. "North, Sir Dudley (1641–1691)." In *Oxford Dictionary of National Biography.* Oxford: Oxford University Press, 2004; online ed., 2008. https://doi.org/10.1093/ref:odnb/20297.

Gray, Alexander. *The Development of Economic Doctrine: An Introductory Survey.* London: Longmans, Green, 1933. https://mises.org/library/development-economic-doctrine-introductory-survey.

Grever, John H. "The Structure of Decision-Making in the States General of the Dutch Republic 1660–68." *Parliaments, Estates and Representation* 2, no. 2 (December 1982): 125–53.

Grice-Hutchinson, Marjorie. *Economic Thought in Spain: Selected Essays of Marjorie Grice-Hutchinson.* Edited by Laurence S. Moss and Christopher K. Ryan. Aldershot, UK: E. Elgar, 1993.

——. *The School of Salamanca: Readings in Spanish Monetary Theory, 1544–1605.* Oxford: Clarendon Press, 1952.

Habermas, Jürgen. *The Structural Transformation of the Public Sphere: An Inquiry Into a Category of Bourgeois Society.* Translated by Thomas Burger with the assistance of Frederick Lawrence. Cambridge, MA: MIT Press, 1991. Originally published as *Strukturwandel der Öffentlicheit* (Darmstadt and Neuwied: Hermann Luchterhand Verlag, 1962).

Halliday, Paul D. *Dismembering the Body Politic: Partisan Politics in England's Towns, 1650–1730.* Cambridge: Cambridge University Press, 2003.

Hampshire, Stuart. "Spinoza and the Idea of Freedom." In *Studies in Spinoza: Critical and Interpretive Essays*, ed. S. Paul Kashap, 310–31. Berkeley: University of California Press, 1974.

Hanley, Ryan Patrick, ed. *Adam Smith: His Life, Thought, and Legacy.* Princeton, NJ: Princeton University Press, 2016.

Harpham, Edward J. "Class, Commerce, and the State: Economic Discourse and Lockean Liberalism in the Seventeenth Century." *Western Political Quarterly* 38, no. 4 (December 1985): 565–82. https://doi.org/10.2307/448613.

Harris, Ron. "The Bubble Act: Its Passage and Its Effects on Business Organization." *Journal of Economic History* 54, no. 3 (September 1994): 610–27.

——. *Going the Distance: Eurasian Trade and the Rise of the Business Corporation, 1400–1700.* Princeton, NJ: Princeton University Press, 2020.

Hart, Marjolein 't. *The Dutch Wars of Independence: Warfare and Commerce in the Netherlands, 1570–1680.* London: Routledge, 2014.

——. "Freedom and Restrictions: State and Economy in the Dutch Republic, 1570–1670." In *The Dutch Economy in the Golden Age: Nine Studies,* ed. Karel Davids and Leo Noordegraaf, 105–30. Amsterdam: Nederlandsch Economisch-Historisch Archief, 1993.

Hasler, P. W., ed. *The House of Commons, 1558–1603.* 3 vols. London: Published for the History of Parliament Trust by Her Majesty's Stationery Office, 1981.

Hayton, David, Eveline Cruickshanks, and Stuart Handley, eds. *The House of Commons, 1690–1715.* 5 vols. Cambridge: Published for the History of Parliament Trust by Cambridge University Press, 2002.

Heckscher, Eli. *Mercantilism.* London: George Allen & Unwin, 1935.

Henning, Basil Duke, ed. *The House of Commons, 1660–1690.* London: Published for the History of Parliament Trust by Secker & Warburg, 1983.

Hill, Christopher. *The Century of Revolution, 1603–1714.* 2nd ed. New York: W. W. Norton, 1961.

Hillmann, Henning. "Mediation in Multiple Networks: Elite Mobilization Before the English Civil War." *American Sociological Review* 73, no. 3 (June 2008): 426–54.

Hinton, R. W. K. *The Eastland Trade and the Common Weal in the Seventeenth Century.* Cambridge: At the University Press, 1959.

Hirschman, Albert O. *Exit, Voice, and Loyalty: Responses to Decline in Firms, Organizations, and States.* Cambridge, MA: Harvard University Press, 1970.

Hodacs, Hanna. "Chartered Companies." In *The Encyclopedia of Empire,* ed. John M. MacKenzie. New York: John Wiley & Sons, 2016.

Hoffman, Mark Anthony. "The Materiality of Ideology: Cultural Consumption and Political Thought After the American Revolution." *American Journal of Sociology* 125, no. 1 (July 2019): 1–62. https://doi.org/10.1086/704370.

Hont, Istvan, and Michael Ignatieff, eds. *Wealth and Virtue: The Shaping of Political Economy in the Scottish Enlightenment.* Cambridge: Cambridge University Press, 1983.

Hoppit, Julian. "The Contexts and Contours of British Economic Literature, 1660–1760." *Historical Journal* 49, no. 1 (March 2006): 79–110. https://doi.org/10.1017/S0018246X05005066.

Horvath, Steve. *Weighted Network Analysis: Applications in Genomics and Systems Biology.* New York: Springer, 2011.

Hotchkiss, George Burton. Introduction to *A Treatise of Commerce,* by John Wheeler, 3–120. Clark, NJ: Lawbook Exchange, 2004.

Hussey, Roland D. "Antecedents of the Spanish Monopolistic Overseas Trading Companies (1624–1728)." *Hispanic American Historical Review* 9, no. 1 (February 1929): 1–30. https://doi.org/10.2307/2506638.

Hutchison, Terence W. *Before Adam Smith: The Emergence of Political Economy, 1662–1776.* Oxford: B. Blackwell, 1988.

Ikegami, Eiko. "A Sociological Theory of Publics: Identity and Culture as Emergent Properties in Networks." *Social Research* 67, no. 4 (Winter 2000): 989–1029.

Irwin, Douglas. *Against the Tide: An Intellectual History of Free Trade.* Princeton, NJ: Princeton University Press, 1996.

Israel, Jonathan. *Dutch Primacy in World Trade, 1585–1740.* Oxford: Oxford University Press, 1989.

——. "England's Mercantilist Response to Dutch World Trade Primacy, 1647–1674." In *State and Trade: Government and the Economy in Britain and the Netherlands Since the Middle Ages,* ed. Simon Groenveld and Michael Joseph Wintle, 50–61. Zutphen: Walburg Pers, 1992.

Johnson, E. A. J. "Gerard De Malynes and the Theory of the Foreign Exchanges." *American Economic Review* 23, no. 3 (September 1933): 441–55.

——. *Predecessors of Adam Smith: The Growth of British Economic Thought.* New York: Prentice-Hall, 1937.

Jones, D. W. *War and Economy in the Age of William III and Marlborough.* Oxford: B. Blackwell, 1988.

Jones, S. R. H., and Simon P. Ville. "Efficient Transactors or Rent-Seeking Monopolists? The Rationale for Early Chartered Trading Companies." *Journal of Economic History* 56, no. 4 (December 1996): 898–915.

——. "Theory and Evidence: Understanding Chartered Trading Companies." *Journal of Economic History* 56, no. 4 (December 1996): 925–26.

Kaye, Joel. *A History of Balance, 1250–1375: The Emergence of a New Model of Equilibrium and Its Impact on Thought.* New York: Cambridge University Press, 2014.

Kearney, H. F. "The Political Background to English Mercantilism, 1695–1700." *Economic History Review* 11, no. 3 (1959): 484–96.

Kelly, Patrick. "The Irish Woollen Export Prohibition Act of 1699: Kearney Re-visited." *Irish Economic and Social History* 7, no. 1 (June 1980): 22–44. https://doi.org/10.1177/033248938000700103.

Keynes, John Maynard. *The General Theory of Employment, Interest and Money.* 1936. Reprint, New Delhi: Atlantic, 2008.

Kuran, Timur. "The Absence of the Corporation in Islamic Law: Origins and Persistence." *American Journal of Comparative Law* 53, no. 4 (Fall 2005): 785–834.

Kyle, Chris R. "Parliament and the Politics of Carting in Early Stuart London." *London Journal* 27, no. 2 (2002): 1–11.

Lake, Peter, and Steve Pincus. "Rethinking the Public Sphere in Early Modern England." *Journal of British Studies* 45, no. 2 (April 2006): 270–92.

Lamond, Elizabeth, and William Cunningham, eds. *A Discourse of the Common Weal of This Realm of England.* Cambridge: At the University Press, 1893.

La Nauze, John A. "The Substance of Adam Smith's Attack on Mercantilism." In *Adam Smith: Critical Assessments,* ed. John Cunningham Wood, vol. 4, *Specialised Topics,* 55–57. London: Routledge, 2004.

Larraz, José. *La época del mercantilismo en Castilla (1500–1700).* Madrid: Ediciones Atlas, 1945.

Lena, Jennifer C., and Mark C. Pachucki. "The Sincerest Form of Flattery: Innovation, Repetition, and Status in an Art Movement." *Poetics* 41, no. 3 (June 2013): 236–64. https://doi.org/10.1016/j.poetic.2013.02.002.

Leng, Thomas. "Epistemology: Expertise and Knowledge in the World of Commerce." In *Mercantilism Reimagined: Political Economy in Early Modern Britain and Its Empire*, ed. Philip J. Stern and Carl Wennerlind, 97–116. New York: Oxford University Press, 2013.

——. "Interlopers and Disorderly Brethren at the Stade Mart: Commercial Regulations and Practices Amongst the Merchant Adventurers of England in the Late Elizabethan Period." *Economic History Review* 69, no. 3 (August 2016): 823–43.

Letiche, J. M. "Isaac Gervaise on the International Mechanism of Adjustment." *Journal of Political Economy* 60, no. 1 (February 1952): 34–43.

Letwin, William. *The Origins of Scientific Economics: English Economic Thought, 1660–1776.* London: Methuen, 1963.

——. *Sir Josiah Child: Merchant Economist.* Kress Library of Business and Economics 14. Boston: Baker Library; Harvard Graduate School of Business Administration, 1959.

Li, Ai, and Steve Horvath. "Network Module Detection: Affinity Search Technique with the Multi-Node Topological Overlap Measure." *BMC Research Notes* 2, no. 1 (July 2009): 142. https://doi.org/10.1186/1756-0500-2-142.

Maddison, Angus. *Contours of the World Economy, 1–2030 AD: Essays in Macro-Economic History.* Oxford: Oxford University Press, 2007.

——. *Dynamic Forces in Capitalist Development: A Long-Run Comparative View.* New York: Oxford University Press, 1991.

Magnusson, Lars, ed. *Free Trade, 1793–1886.* Vol. 2, *The National System Builders.* Routledge, 1997.

——. *Mercantilism: The Shaping of an Economic Language.* London: Routledge, 1994.

——, ed. *Mercantilist Economics.* New York: Springer, 2012.

Mahoney, James. "Strategies of Causal Inference in Small-N Analysis." *Sociological Methods & Research* 28, no. 4 (May 2000): 387–424. https://doi.org/10.1177/0049124100028004001.

Mahoney, James, and Dietrich Rueschemeyer, eds. *Comparative Historical Analysis in the Social Sciences.* Cambridge: Cambridge University Press, 2003.

Mara, Gerald M. "Liberal Politics and Moral Excellence in Spinoza's Political Philosophy." *Journal of the History of Philosophy* 20, no. 2 (April 1982): 129–50.

Marx, Karl. *Capital: A Critique of Political Economy.* Vol. 1, Book One: *The Process of Production of Capital.* Edited by Frederick Engels. Translated by Samuel Moore and Edward Aveling. Moscow: Progress Publishers, 1887. First German edition published 1867. https://www.marxists.org/archive/marx/works/1867-c1/.

——. *Theories of Surplus-Value [Volume IV of Capital].* Written 1862–63. Originally part of the *Economic Manuscripts of 1861–1863.* https://www.marxists.org/archive/marx/works/1863/theories-surplus-value/.

McLynn, Frank. *Crime and Punishment in Eighteenth-Century England.* Abingdon, UK: Routledge, 2013.

McNulty, Paul J. *The Origins and Development of Labor Economics: A Chapter in the History of Social Thought.* Cambridge, MA: MIT Press, 1980.

Meek, Ronald. *Economics and Ideology and Other Essays: Studies in the Development of Economic Thought*. London: Chapman and Hall, 1967.

Mini, Piero V. *Philosophy and Economics: The Origins and Development of Economic Theory*. Gainesville: University Presses of Florida, 1974.

Mische, Ann, and Harrison White. "Between Conversation and Situation: Public Switching Dynamics Across Network Domains." *Social Research* 65, no. 3 (Fall 1998): 695–724.

Mohr, John W., and Harrison C. White. "How to Model an Institution." *Theory and Society* 37, no. 5 (October 2008): 485–512. https://doi.org/10.1007/s11186-008-9066-0.

Moody, James, and Douglas R. White. "Structural Cohesion and Embeddedness: A Hierarchical Concept of Social Groups." *American Sociological Review* 68, no. 1 (February 2003): 103–27. https://doi.org/10.2307/3088904.

Moore, James, and Michael Silverthorne. "Gershom Carmichael and the Natural Jurisprudence Tradition in Eighteenth-Century Scotland." In *Wealth and Virtue: The Shaping of Political Economy in the Scottish Enlightenment*, ed. Istvan Hont and Michael Ignatieff, 73–87. Cambridge: Cambridge University Press, 1983.

Morgan, Stephen L., and Christopher Winship. *Counterfactuals and Causal Inference: Methods and Principles for Social Research*. 2nd ed. New York: Cambridge University Press, 2014.

Muchmore, Lynn. "A Note on Thomas Mun's 'England's Treasure by Forraign Trade.'" *Economic History Review* 23, no. 3 (December 1970): 498–503. https://doi.org/10.2307/2594618.

Muldrew, Craig. "From Commonwealth to Public Opulence: The Redefinition of Wealth and Government in Early Modern Britain." In *Remaking English Society: Social Relations and Social Change in Early Modern England*, ed. Steve Hindle, Alexandra Shepard, and John Walter, 317–40. Woodbridge, UK: Boydell Press, 2015.

Murphy, Anne L. *The Origins of English Financial Markets: Investment and Speculation Before the South Sea Bubble*. Cambridge: Cambridge University Press, 2009.

Neal, Zachary. "The Backbone of Bipartite Projections: Inferring Relationships from Co-Authorship, Co-Sponsorship, Co-Attendance and Other Co-Behaviors." *Social Networks* 39 (October 1, 2014): 84–97. https://doi.org/10.1016/j.socnet.2014.06.001.

Newman, M. E. J. "Scientific Collaboration Networks: I. Network Construction and Fundamental Results." *Physical Review E* 64, no. 1 (July 2001): 016131. https://doi.org/10.1103/PhysRevE.64.016131.

North, Douglass C., and Robert Paul Thomas. *The Rise of the Western World: A New Economic History*. Cambridge: Cambridge University Press, 1973.

O'Brien, D. P., and A. C. Darnell. *Authorship Puzzles in the History of Economics: A Statistical Approach*. London: Macmillan, 1982. https://doi.org/10.1007/978-1-349-05697-2.

O'Brien, Patrick, Trevor Griffiths, and Philip Hunt. "Political Components of the Industrial Revolution: Parliament and the English Cotton Textile Industry, 1660–1774." *Economic History Review* 44, no. 3 (August 1991): 395–423. https://doi.org/10.2307/2597536.

Ogilvie, Sheilagh. *Institutions and European Trade: Merchant Guilds, 1000–1800*. Cambridge: Cambridge University Press, 2011.

Ogilvie, Sheilagh, and A. W. Carus. "Institutions and Economic Growth in Historical Perspective." In *Handbook of Economic Growth*, ed. Philippe Aghion and Steven N. Durlauf, vol. 2A, 403–513. Amsterdam: Elsevier, 2014. https://doi.org/10.1016/B978-0-444-53538-2.00008-3.

Ormrod, David. *The Rise of Commercial Empires: England and the Netherlands in the Age of Mercantilism, 1650–1770*. Cambridge: Cambridge University Press, 2003.

Pachucki, Mark A., and Ronald L. Breiger. "Cultural Holes: Beyond Relationality in Social Networks and Culture." *Annual Review of Sociology* 36 (2010): 205–24. https://doi.org/10.1146/annurev.soc.012809.102615.

Padgett, John F. "Country as Global Market: Netherlands, Calvinism, and the Joint-Stock Company." In *The Emergence of Organizations and Markets*, by John F. Padgett and Walter W. Powell, 168–207. Princeton, NJ: Princeton University Press, 2012.

Padgett, John F., and Walter W. Powell. *The Emergence of Organizations and Markets*. Princeton, NJ: Princeton University Press, 2012.

Paping, Richard. "General Dutch Population Development, 1400–1850: Cities and Countryside." Paper presented at the First Conference of the European Society of Historical Demography (ESHD), Sassari/Alghero, Sardinia, Italy, September 25–27, 2014. https://www.rug.nl/research/portal/files/15865622/articlesardinie21sep2014.pdf.

Parker, Geoffrey. "The 'Military Revolution,' 1560–1660—a Myth?" *Journal of Modern History* 48, no. 2 (June 1976): 196–214.

Patterson, Margaret, and David Reiffen. "The Effect of the Bubble Act on the Market for Joint Stock Shares." *Journal of Economic History* 50, no. 1 (March 1990): 163–71.

Peirce, Charles Sanders. "How to Make Our Ideas Clear." *Popular Science Monthly* 12 (1878): 286–302.

Pennington, David. "Beyond the Moral Economy: Economic Change, Ideology and the 1621 House of Commons." *Parliamentary History* 25, pt. 2 (2006): 214–31.

Pettigrew, William A. *Freedom's Debt: The Royal African Company and the Politics of the Atlantic Slave Trade, 1672–1752*. Williamsburg, VA: Omohundro Institute of Early American History and Culture; Chapel Hill: University of North Carolina Press, 2013.

Pfaff, Bernhard, Eric Zivot, and Matthieu Stigler. Reference manual for Package 'urca' (Version 1.3-0): Unit Root and Cointegration Tests for Time Series Data. CRAN Repository, September 6, 2016. https://cran.r-project.org/web/packages/urca/urca.pdf.

Phillips, Damon J. *Shaping Jazz: Cities, Labels, and the Global Emergence of an Art Form*. Princeton, NJ: Princeton University Press, 2013.

Piepenbrink, Anke, and Ajai S. Gaur. "Methodological Advances in the Analysis of Bipartite Networks: An Illustration Using Board Interlocks in Indian Firms." *Organizational Research Methods* 16, no. 3 (July 2013): 474–96. https://doi.org/10.1177/1094428113478838.

Pincus, Steve. *1688: The First Modern Revolution*. New Haven, CT: Yale University Press, 2009.

——. "'Coffee Politicians Does Create': Coffeehouses and Restoration Political Culture." *Journal of Modern History* 67, no. 4 (December 1995): 807–34.

——. "Rethinking Mercantilism: Political Economy, the British Empire, and the Atlantic World in the Seventeenth and Eighteenth Centuries." *William and Mary Quarterly* 69, no. 1 (January 2012): 3–34. https://doi.org/10.5309/willmaryquar.69.1.0003.

Pocock, John Greville Agard. *The Machiavellian Moment: Florentine Political Thought and the Atlantic Republican Tradition*. Princeton, NJ: Princeton University Press, 2009.

Poitras, Geoffrey. *The Early History of Financial Economics, 1478–1776: From Commercial Arithmetic to Life Annuities and Joint Stocks.* Cheltenham, UK: Edward Elgar, 2000.

Poitras, Geoffrey, and Frederick Willeboordse. "The *Societas Publicanorum* and Corporate Personality in Roman Private Law." *Business History*, 2019, https://doi.org/10.10 80/00076791.2019.1656719.

Prak, Maarten. *The Dutch Republic in the Seventeenth Century: The Golden Age.* Translated by Diane Webb. Cambridge: Cambridge University Press, 2005.

Prasad, Monica. *The Politics of Free Markets: The Rise of Neoliberal Economic Policies in Britain, France, Germany, and the United States.* Chicago: University of Chicago Press, 2006.

Přibram, Karl. *A History of Economic Reasoning.* Baltimore: Johns Hopkins University Press, 1983.

Price, J. L. *Holland and the Dutch Republic in the Seventeenth Century: The Politics of Particularism.* Oxford: Clarendon Press, 1994.

Rabb, Theodore K. "Free Trade and the Gentry in the Parliament of 1604." *Past & Present*, no. 40 (July 1968): 165–73.

Ramsey, Peter. "The Tudor State and Economic Problems." In *State and Trade: Government and the Economy in Britain and the Netherlands Since the Middle Ages*, ed. Simon Groenveld and Michael Joseph Wintle, 28–38. Zutphen: Walburg Pers, 1992.

Rashid, Salim. *The Myth of Adam Smith.* Cheltenham, UK: Edward Elgar, 1998.

——. "Smith, Steuart, and Mercantilism: Comment." *Southern Economic Journal* 52, no. 3 (January 1986): 843–52. https://doi.org/10.2307/1059280.

Reinders, Michel. *Printed Pandemonium: Popular Print and Politics in the Netherlands, 1650–72.* Leiden: Brill, 2013.

Reinert, Erik S. "Emulating Success: Contemporary Views of the Dutch Economy Before 1800." In *The Political Economy of the Dutch Republic*, ed. Oscar Gelderblom, 19–40. Farnham, UK: Ashgate, 2009.

Reinert, Erik S., and Sophus A. Reinert. "Mercantilism and Economic Development: Schumpeterian Dynamics, Institution-Building and International Benchmarking." In *The Origins of Development Economics: How Schools of Economics Thought Have Addressed Development*, ed. Jomo K. S. and Erik S. Reinert, 1–23. New Delhi: Tulika Books; London: Zed Books, 2005.

Reinert, Sophus A. "The Empire of Emulation: A Quantitative Analysis of Economic Translations in the European World, 1500–1849." In *The Political Economy of Empire in the Early Modern World*, ed. Sophus A. Reinert and Pernille Røge, 105–28. Basingstoke, UK: Palgrave Macmillan, 2013.

——. *Translating Empire: Emulation and the Origins of Political Economy.* Cambridge, MA: Harvard University Press, 2011. ProQuest Ebook Central.

Reinert, Sophus A., and Pernille Røge, eds. *The Political Economy of Empire in the Early Modern World.* Basingstoke, UK: Palgrave Macmillan, 2013.

Riemersma, Jelle C. "Oceanic Expansion: Government Influence on Company Organization in Holland and England, 1550–1650." *Journal of Economic History* 10, supplement (1950): 31–39.

Rogers, Ruth R. "The Kress Library of Business and Economics." *Business History Review* 60, no. 2 (Summer 1986): 281–88. https://doi.org/10.2307/3115310.

Roll, Eric. *A History of Economic Thought.* London: Faber and Faber, 1992.

Roscher, Wilhelm. *Principles of Political Economy: With Additional Chapters Furnished by the Author [. . .] on Paper Money, International Trade, and the Protective System.* Translated by John J. Lalor. New York: Henry Holt, 1878.

Routh, Guy. *The Origin of Economic Ideas.* Basingstoke, UK: Macmillan, 1975.

Schabas, Margaret. *The Natural Origins of Economics.* Chicago: University of Chicago Press, 2009.

Schama, Simon. *The Embarrassment of Riches: An Interpretation of Dutch Culture in the Golden Age.* New York: Vintage, 1997.

Schattschneider, Elmer. *The Semi-Sovereign People: A Realist's View of Democracy in America.* Boston: Wadsworth, 1975.

Schmoller, Gustav von. *The Mercantile System and Its Historical Significance: Illustrated Chiefly from Prussian History; Being a Chapter from the Studien ueber die wirthschaftliche politik Friedrichs des Grossen.* Edited and translated by William James Ashley. New York: Macmillan, 1897. Making of the Modern World.

Schonhardt-Bailey, Cheryl. *From the Corn Laws to Free Trade: Interests, Ideas, and Institutions in Historical Perspective.* Cambridge, MA: MIT Press, 2006.

Schumpeter, Joseph A. *Economic Doctrine and Method: An Historical Sketch.* New York: Oxford University Press, 1954.

——. *History of Economic Analysis: With a New Introduction.* Rev. ed. New York: Oxford University Press, 1954.

Scott, James C. *Seeing Like a State: How Certain Schemes to Improve the Human Condition Have Failed.* New Haven, CT: Yale University Press, 1999.

Scott, William Robert. *The Constitution and Finance of English, Scottish and Irish Joint-Stock Companies to 1720.* 3 vols. Cambridge: At the University Press, 1912.

Sedgwick, Romney. *The House of Commons, 1715–1754.* 2 vols. London: Her Majesty's Stationery Office, 1970.

Sen, Amartya. "Adam Smith and Economic Development." In *Adam Smith: His Life, Thought, and Legacy,* ed. Ryan Patrick Hanley, 281–302. Princeton, NJ: Princeton University Press, 2016.

Shahani, Gitanjali. "'A Foreigner by Birth': The Life of Indian Cloth in the Early Modern English Marketplace." In *Global Traffic: Discourses and Practices of Trade in English Literature and Culture from 1550 to 1700,* ed. Barbara Sebek and Stephen Deng, 179–98. New York: Palgrave Macmillan, 2008. SpringerLink.

Sherman, Arnold A. "Pressure from Leadenhall: The East India Company Lobby, 1660–1678." *Business History Review* 50, no. 3 (Autumn 1976): 329–55. https://doi .org/10.2307/3112999.

Slack, Paul. *The Invention of Improvement: Information and Material Progress in Seventeenth-Century England.* Oxford: Oxford University Press, 2015.

——. "The Politics of English Political Economy in the 1620s." In *Popular Culture and Political Agency in Early Modern England and Ireland: Essays in Honour of John Walter,* ed. Michael J. Braddick and Phil Withington, 55–72. Woodbridge, UK: Boydell Press, 2017.

Soll, Jacob. "Accounting for Government: Holland and the Rise of Political Economy in Seventeenth-Century Europe." *Journal of Interdisciplinary History* 40, no. 2 (Autumn 2009): 215–38.

Somers, Margaret R. "Citizenship and the Place of the Public Sphere: Law, Community, and Political Culture in the Transition to Democracy." *American Sociological Review* 58, no. 5 (October 1993): 587–620. https://doi.org/10.2307/2096277.

——. *Genealogies of Citizenship: Markets, Statelessness, and the Right to Have Rights.* Cambridge: Cambridge University Press, 2008.

Somers, Margaret R., and Fred Block. "From Poverty to Perversity: Ideas, Markets, and Institutions Over 200 Years of Welfare Debate." *American Sociological Review* 70, no. 2 (April 2005): 260–87. https://doi.org/10.1177/000312240507000204.

Spengler, Joseph. "Exogenous and Endogenous Influences in the Formation of Post-1870 Economic Thought." In *Events, Ideology and Economic Theory: The Determinants of Progress in the Development of Economic Analysis,* ed. Robert V. Eagly, 159–205. Detroit, MI: Wayne State University Press, 1968.

Spruyt, Hendrik. "The Origins, Development, and Possible Decline of the Modern State." *Annual Review of Political Science* 5 (2002): 127–49. https://doi.org/10.1146/annurev.polisci.5.101501.145837.

Stasavage, David. *States of Credit: Size, Power, and the Development of European Polities.* Princeton, NJ: Princeton University Press, 2011.

Stern, Philip J. "Companies: Monopoly, Sovereignty, and the East Indies." In *Mercantilism Reimagined: Political Economy in Early Modern Britain and Its Empire,* ed. Philip J. Stern and Carl Wennerlind, 177–95. New York: Oxford University Press, 2013.

Stern, Philip J., and Carl Wennerlind. *Mercantilism Reimagined: Political Economy in Early Modern Britain and Its Empire.* New York: Oxford University Press, 2013.

Strohm, Reinhard. "Iphigenia's Curious *Ménage à Trois* in Myth, Drama, and Opera." In *(Dis)embodying Myths in Ancien Régime Opera: Multidisciplinary Perspectives,* ed. Bruno Forment, 117–38. Leuven, Belgium: Leuven University Press, 2012.

Stump, W. Darrell. "An Economic Consequence of 1688." *Albion: A Quarterly Journal Concerned with British Studies* 6, no. 1 (Spring 1974): 26–35. https://doi.org/10.2307/4048209.

Sumberg, Theodore A. "Antonio Serra: A Neglected Herald of the Acquisitive System." *American Journal of Economics and Sociology* 50, no. 3 (July 1991): 365–73.

Supple, Barry E. *Commercial Crisis and Change in England, 1600–1642: A Study in the Instability of a Mercantile Economy.* Cambridge: Cambridge University Press, 1959.

——. "Currency and Commerce in the Early Seventeenth Century." *Economic History Review* 10, no. 2 (1957): 239–55. https://doi.org/10.2307/2590860.

——. "Thomas Mun and the Commercial Crisis, 1623." *Bulletin of the Institute of Historical Research* 27, no. 75 (May 1954): 91–94. https://doi.org/10.1111/j.1468-2281.1954.tb01014.x.

Suprinyak, Carlos Eduardo. "Trade, Money, and the Grievances of the Commonwealth: Economic Debates in the English Public Sphere During the Commercial Crisis of the Early 1620's." Texto para discussão 427, Centro de Desenvolvimento e Planejamento Regional (CEDEPLAR) da UFMG, Belo Horizonte, Brazil, June 2011. http://www.cedeplar.ufmg.br/pesquisas/td/TD%20427.pdf.

Taviani, Carlo. "An Ancient Scheme: The Mississippi Company, Machiavelli, and the Casa Di San Giorgio (1407–1720)." In *Chartering Capitalism: Organizing Markets, States, and Publics,* ed. Emily Erikson, 239–56. Bingley, UK: Emerald Group, 2015.

Thomas, Parakunnel Joseph. *Mercantilism and the East India Trade: An Early Phase of the Protection v. Free Trade Controversy.* 1926. Reprint, Mansfield Center, CT: Martino Publishing, 2009.

Thrush, Andrew, and John P. Ferris, eds. *The House of Commons, 1604–1629*. 6 vols. Cambridge: Published for the History of Parliament Trust by Cambridge University Press, 2010.

Tracy, James D. *A Financial Revolution in the Habsburg Netherlands: Renten and Renteniers in the County of Holland, 1515–1565*. Berkeley: University of California Press, 1985.

Tribe, Keith. *Governing Economy: The Reformation of German Economic Discourse, 1750–1840*. Cambridge: Cambridge University Press, 1988.

——. *Land, Labour and Economic Discourse*. London: Routledge & Kegan Paul, 1978.

——. *Strategies of Economic Order: German Economic Discourse, 1750–1950*. Cambridge: Cambridge University Press, 2007.

Unwin, George. "The Merchant Adventurers' Company in the Reign of Elizabeth." *Economic History Review* 1, no. 1 (January 1927): 35–64.

Van Bavel, Bas. *The Invisible Hand? How Market Economies Have Emerged and Declined Since AD 500*. Oxford: Oxford University Press, 2016.

——. "Open Societies Before Market Economies: Historical Analysis." *Socio-Economic Review*, 2019. https://doi.org/10.1093/soceco/mwz007.

Van Daal, Jan, and Arnold Heertje, eds. *Economic Thought in the Netherlands, 1650–1950*. Aldershot, UK: Avebury, 1992.

Van Tijn, Theo. "Dutch Economic Thought in the Seventeenth Century." In *Economic Thought in the Netherlands, 1650–1950*, ed. Jan van Daal and Arnold Heertje, 7–28. Aldershot, UK: Avebury, 1992.

Van Vliet, Lars. "New Developments in Dutch Company Law: The 'Flexible' Close Corporation." *Journal of Civil Law Studies* 7, no. 1 (2014): 271–86.

Van Zanden, Jan Luiten. "Common Workmen, Philosophers, and the Birth of the European Knowledge Economy: About the Price and the Production of Useful Knowledge in Europe, 1350–1800." Paper presented at the GEHN conference on Useful Knowledge, Leiden, Belgium, September 2004; revised October 12, 2004. https://www.researchgate.net/publication/254428476_Common_workmen_philosophers _and_the_birth_of_the_European_knowledge_economy.

——. *Long Road to the Industrial Revolution: The European Economy in a Global Perspective, 1000–1800*. Global Economic History Series 1. Boston: Brill, 2009. ProQuest Ebook Central.

Van Zanden, Jan Luiten, and Maarten Prak. "Towards an Economic Interpretation of Citizenship: The Dutch Republic Between Medieval Communes and Modern Nation-States." *European Review of Economic History*, 10, no. 2 (August 2006): 111–45. https://doi.org/10.1017/S1361491606001651.

Vaughn, Karen Iversen. *John Locke, Economist and Social Scientist*. Chicago: University of Chicago Press, 1980.

Viner, Jacob. *Essays on the Intellectual History of Economics*. Princeton, NJ: Princeton University Press, 1991.

——. "Foreword." In *The System or Theory of the Trade of the World*, by Isaac Gervaise. Baltimore: Johns Hopkins Press, 1954.

——. "Mercantilist Thought." In *International Encyclopedia of the Social Sciences*, ed. David L. Sills, vol. 4, 435–42. New York: Macmillan, 1968.

——. *Studies in the Theory of International Trade*. New York: Harper & Brothers, 1937.

Waddell, David. "Charles Davenant (1656–1714): A Biographical Sketch." *Economic History Review* 11, no. 2 (December 1958): 279–88. http://doi.org/10.1111/j.1468-0289.1958.tb01641.x.

——. "The Writings of Charles Davenant (1656–1714)." *The Library* s5-XI, no. 3 (September 1956): 206–12.

Wagener, Hans-Jürgen. "Cupiditate et Potentia: The Political Economy of Spinoza." *European Journal of the History of Economic Thought* 1, no. 3 (1994): 475–93.

——. "Free Seas, Free Trade, Free People: Early Dutch Institutionalism." *History of Political Economy* 26, no. 3 (1994): 395–422.

Watts, Duncan J., and Steven H. Strogatz. "Collective Dynamics of 'Small-World' Networks." *Nature* 393 (June 4, 1998): 440–42.

Weber, Max. "Bureaucracy." In *From Max Weber: Essays in Sociology*, eds. Hans Gerth and C. Wright Mills (New York: Oxford University Press), 196–240.

Wennerlind, Carl. *Casualties of Credit: The English Financial Revolution, 1620–1720*. Cambridge, MA: Harvard University Press, 2011.

——. "Money: Hartlibian Political Economy and the New Culture of Credit." In *Mercantilism Reimagined: Political Economy in Early Modern Britain and Its Empire*, ed. Philip J. Stern and Carl Wennerlind, 74–96. New York: Oxford University Press, 2013.

Weststeijn, Arthur. *Commercial Republicanism in the Dutch Golden Age: The Political Thought of Johan & Pieter de la Court*. Leiden: Brill, 2012.

White, Harrison C. *Identity and Control: A Structural Theory of Social Action*. Princeton, NJ: Princeton University Press, 1992.

——. "Network Switchings and Bayesian Forks: Reconstructing the Social and Behavioral Sciences." *Social Research* 62, no. 4 (Winter 1995): 1035–63.

White, Harrison C., and Frédéric Godart. "Stories from Identity and Control." *Sociologica* 1, no. 3 (November–December 2007): 1–17. https://www.rivisteweb.it/doi/10.2383/25960.

Withington, Phil. "Intoxicants and Society in Early Modern England." *Historical Journal* 54, no. 3 (September 2011): 631–57. https://doi.org/10.1017/S0018246X11000197.

——. *The Politics of Commonwealth: Citizens and Freemen in Early Modern England*. Cambridge: Cambridge University Press, 2005.

——. "Public Discourse, Corporate Citizenship, and State Formation in Early Modern England." *American Historical Review* 112, no. 4 (October 2006): 1016–38.

Wrigley, E. A. "The Growth of Population in Eighteenth-Century England: A Conundrum Resolved." *Past & Present* 98 (February 1983): 121–50.

Wu, Chi-Yuen. *An Outline of International Price Theories*. London: Routledge, 1939.

Xenophon. *The Oeconomicus of Xenophon*. With explanatory notes and supplementary indexes by Hubert A. Holden. 4th ed. London: Macmillan, 1889.

Zastoupil, Lynn. *John Stuart Mill and India*. Stanford, CA: Stanford University Press, 1994.

Zuidema, J. R. "Economic Thought in the Netherlands Between 1750 and 1870: From Commercial Mercantilism Towards the True Principles of Political Economy." In *Economic Thought in the Netherlands, 1650–1950*, ed. Jan van Daal and Arnold Heertje, 29–74. Aldershot, UK: Avebury, 1992.

INDEX

Page numbers in *italics* indicate figures or tables.